AT HOME IN NINETEENTH-CENTURY AMERICA

At Home in Nineteenth-Century America

A Documentary History

Amy G. Richter

NEW YORK UNIVERSITY PRESS

New York and London

NEW YORK UNIVERSITY PRESS
New York and London
www.nyupress.org

© 2015 by New York University
All rights reserved

References to Internet websites (URLs) were accurate at the time of writing. Neither the author nor New York University Press is responsible for URLs that may have expired or changed since the manuscript was prepared.

ISBN: 978-0-8147-6914-0 (paperback)
ISBN: 978-0-8147-6913-3 (hardback)

For Library of Congress Cataloging-in-Publication data, please contact the Library of Congress.

New York University Press books are printed on acid-free paper, and their binding materials are chosen for strength and durability. We strive to use environmentally responsible suppliers and materials to the greatest extent possible in publishing our books.

Manufactured in the United States of America

10 9 8 7 6 5 4 3 2 1

Also available as an ebook

For Jim and Simon

CONTENTS

ILLUSTRATIONS

ACKNOWLEDGMENTS

At Clark University, I am grateful to the History Department and Higgins School of Humanities for funding my research and supporting the purchase of images and permissions. In addition to material support, my colleagues in the History Department consistently offer me multiple examples of how to be a dedicated teacher-scholar; I am truly thankful for this gentle and invaluable encouragement. I feel particularly fortunate that I got to know Jack Larkin through his affiliation with our department. What a treat to swap sources and stories of home with him! Outside of the History Department, I thank my friends and Clark colleagues Sarah Buie, Kristen Williams, and Kristina Wilson for their interest in my work and their willingness to share ideas, insights, and enthusiasm.

I owe a considerable debt to the students enrolled in my first-year seminar in Fall 2008. That course was the first iteration of this volume, and I have thought of you and our work as I have put the pieces together. Several graduate students have also taken time to think through documents and consider the themes of nineteenth-century American domesticity with me. Special thanks to Lindsay Allen, Diane Boucher, Madeline DeDe-Panken, and Melinda Marchand. Finally, there would be no book without the dedication and support of Diane Fenner in the History Department and Lisa Gillingham, Jennifer McGugan, and Sara Raffo at the Higgins School of Humanities. Thank you for being so good at what you do and for giving me time to write and revise when I needed it.

I have benefited from the hard work, skill, and patience of librarians, archivists, and staff at the following institutions: the American Antiquarian Society, the Library of Congress, the Minnesota Historical Society, the Nebraska State Historical Society, and the New York Public Library. Special thanks to Mary Hartman, Holly Howes, Rachael Shea, and Irene Walch at Clark University's Goddard Library. Elizabeth Watts Pope and Jaclyn Donovan Penny at the American Antiquarian Society made all the difference with their knowledge of the AAS's holdings and eagerness to share its rich collections.

I feel fortunate that this book found its home at NYU Press. I am grateful to Debbie Gershenowitz for saying yes and shaping the volume in its early stages. She and Gabrielle Begue offered encouragement and kept me on track. Clara Platter saw me through the final rounds of revision, and Constance Grady patiently helped tend to the details. I am especially grateful to the three anonymous reviewers. It is remarkable to have strangers pay such attention to one's work and to provide insightful and careful comment. The shape of the book changed in response to the readings by the first two reviewers, one of whom commented on the penultimate draft as well. A third reader came in late in the game, helped me see the volume afresh, and pushed for a few more documents. Next Andrew Katz did a heroic job copyediting the manuscript with such care for the primary documents and their original linguistic quirks. And just when I thought the work was done, Dorothea Halliday, Edith Alston, and Charles B. Hames made sure the final steps went smoothly. Thank you all!

The last thank-yous are for my family. Thank you to my mother, Adele Richter, and my in-laws, Janet and Jerry Eber, for your tireless and loving interest in what I do. Finally, Jim and Simon, every day you remind me of the richness of home life as we negotiate work and play, public and private, family ties and the marketplace together. I am grateful for the joy of it all.

Introduction

At Home in Nineteenth-Century America

According to the historian Elsa Barkley Brown, "History is everybody talking at once, multiple rhythms being played simultaneously. . . . In fact, at any given moment millions of people are talking all at once."[1] Throughout the nineteenth century, many Americans were talking all at once about home; they were speaking to and past one another and often meant very different things. *At Home in Nineteenth-Century America* focuses on the home as a physical site and cultural ideal in order to help re-create some of this unwieldy conversation. Using primary documents, it revisits the variety of places that Americans called home—middle-class suburban houses, slave cabins, working-class tenements, frontier dugouts, urban settlement houses—and explores the shifting interpretations and experiences of these spaces from within and without.

Rather than offering a history of material culture or architectural styles, this volume uses the home as a synthetic tool to pull together stories of nineteenth-century America. The result is less a tidy account of shared domestic values or a straightforward chronology of change over time than an opportunity to eavesdrop on a wide-ranging conversation that included a diverse group of historical actors: a domestic servant and Herman Melville, a newlywed housewife and W. E. B. Du Bois, an interior designer and Theodore Roosevelt, all of whom contemplated the power and boundaries of the American home. When brought together, these voices offer an intimate yet broad view of nineteenth-century American history.

And no wonder: few institutions were as central to nineteenth-century American culture. Beginning in the 1820s, the home emerged as a sentimental and celebrated space apart from the public world of commerce and politics, competition and corruption. Indeed the emergence of the new domestic ideal was itself inseparable from changing economic relations and the rise of the urban middle class.[2] Despite the initial association of the Victorian domestic ideal with the private lives of the white, native-born bourgeoisie, it crossed lines of race, ethnicity, class, and region, reshaping personal, political, and economic landscapes over the course of the century. Likewise, the boundary between home and public was itself moveable.[3] On the one hand, market concerns, consumer goods, and paid employment found their way into the most private reaches of respectable homes.[4] On the other hand, the values and spatial conventions of the single-family home crossed the threshold into public life, giving rise to public parlors, domesticated department stores, "homes" for female workers, settlement houses, and even public baths.[5] An imperfect description of reality, the domestic ideal was powerful nonetheless. Those excluded from it sought to claim respectable domesticity as their own, and those constrained by it stretched its boundaries to encompass an array of public concerns and institutions. In sum, "the Victorian home" literally embodied the power and tested the limits of nineteenth-century American values to shape everyday spaces and experiences.

As depicted in many documents, nineteenth-century homes and notions of domesticity seem simultaneously distant and familiar. This sense of surprise and recognition is ideal for the study of history, preparing us to view the past with curiosity and empathy. Exploring the spatial manifestations of American Victorianism inspires comparisons to the spaces we inhabit today—malls, movie theaters, college campuses, our own homes—and encourages us to see the lingering imprint of past ideals. The concreteness of studying houses, parks, and city streets helps frame sophisticated questions. For example: If women of all classes entered into public spaces in order to keep house, why was middle-class white femininity rooted so deeply in the home? How did men inhabit homes and interpret domesticity in both private and public life? How did class and racial differences shape domestic ideals, and in turn, how did ideals of domesticity both uphold and undermine these social divisions? Were domesticated public spaces ever truly public? How did differing interpretations of home create or circumscribe cultural or political power for various social actors? Through such questions, we move from the literal spaces to the ideals that shaped them—from homes to domesticity, from domesticity to politics and culture.[6]

This freedom of movement is essential to good history. Over the last several decades, it has become increasingly difficult to develop cohesive yet inclusive narratives of the American past—to wrap our arms around social, cultural, economic and political developments while simultaneously appreciating the variations of race, class, and gender.[7] The sheer variety of primary sources about domestic spaces and life—advice manuals and architectural designs, personal accounts and material culture, popular periodicals and fiction, advertising images and reform literature—makes it possible to integrate and explore the themes of nineteenth-century American social and cultural history. Recounting the ways in which a variety of women and men created, conformed to, critiqued, and transformed the ideal of home over the course of the nineteenth century, these sources sketch a narrative of both inclusion and difference. To this end, *At Home in Nineteenth-Century America* traces the popular celebration of home as a moral force, notes the movement of domesticity into the public worlds of politics and reform, and considers home's relationship with and penetration by and of the marketplace. In short, it charts the connections between spatial arrangements, cultural values, public policies, and lived experiences—connections at the heart of American Victorianism and history writ large.

Like today, American homes in the past served a variety of functions and accommodated a number of activities. Most commonly they were places for cooking and eating, for labor and leisure, for entertaining and sleeping. Of course, the spaces and goods devoted to these activities varied over time, by region, and according to economic and social distinctions of their inhabitants. Prior to 1800, for example, the bed might be the finest piece of furniture a family owned and stand in a place of honor in its parlor. By 1820, houses had grown in size and the parlor was a more formal room, the public face of the house; the bed was now removed to a private room. Such changes reflect more than growing wealth, a desire for comfort, or advances in home construction. For many Americans, setting aside a room (or part of a room) for formal entertaining meant sacrificing valuable living space. It served as a mark of respectability and reflected the growing separation of private and public life. The importance of this spatial and social divide is also evidenced in the emergence after 1800 of the entry hall to delineate the passage between private and public realms. Previously, one simply walked through the front door and right into a family's domestic life.[8]

Today entry halls, parlors, and bedrooms may seem like mundane domestic spaces, but their adoption reflects a considerable and growing commitment to privacy and domestic leisure over the first decades of the nineteenth century.[9] As these rooms took shape, houses often contained a great many people; not only a nuclear family but also extended kin, domestic servants, apprentices, and even boarders commonly filled out a household. Simply put, personal privacy was not easy to come by, and these spatial innovations required considerable cultural commitment. Houses were sites of family life and also of labor. When a New England farm family connected its barn and home and placed the parlor away from the barnyard, it balanced the needs and rhythms of labor against social aspirations and cultural ideals.[10] The same was true for middle-class families who mastered new cultural norms and invested in domestic goods and furnishings to define and support increasingly specialized domestic spaces.[11] Over the course of the nineteenth century, the cultural primacy of the single-family home was reinforced by the growing popularity of balloon-frame construction, the easy availability of house plans, and the production of ready-made houses, all of which could accommodate more modest budgets. Likewise, many Americans sought to re-create or approximate the ideals of refined and respectable domesticity in new settings—the frontier, overseas, or in a small flat.

There was, of course, considerable variation among the places Americans called home. Well into the nineteenth century, many Americans continued to inhabit small houses of only two rooms, while urban tradesmen might have lived in a house of two stories and wealthy businessmen in even finer dwellings with as many as four stories. Domestic inequality was even more clearly pronounced in the slaveholding South, where the large homes of great planters stood over the slave quarters and apart from the small houses of nonslaveholding white farmers.[12] And despite the American fascination with single-family homes, the nineteenth century saw the proliferation of multioccupancy housing types: boarding houses, residential hotels, tenements, and apartment houses. All of these confounded celebratory notions about domestic privacy and highlighted troubling connections between home and marketplace. Even though a third to a half of urban dwellers boarded or took in boarders, this is not what most nineteenth-century Americans envisioned when they spoke of home.[13]

At Home in Nineteenth-Century America uses the selection and juxtaposition of primary sources to compress the insights of several historical fields and approaches. The historian Thomas Schlereth has broken the field of house history into three stages. The first dates back to the nineteenth century itself and focuses on "collecting and authenticating." This stage of identification and preservation was followed in the first half of the twentieth century by the efforts of art historians interested in "describing and classifying" houses by style and structure. In the 1970s and 1980s, social historians turned their attention homeward and began "analyzing and explaining." This work tells us more about home life than about houses and privileges activities over artifacts.[14] Since Schlereth developed his schema, a fourth approach has emerged that reflects history's broader "cultural turn." Concerned with the cultural construction of home, this scholarship considers domesticity as a way of making meaning and has studied home's influence in public life.

The content of this volume benefits from each of these approaches, but its structure and analyses are informed most strongly by the last two. It also draws heavily from the work of women's historians, particularly scholarship exploring the "separate spheres" ideal. Dating back to the 1960s, the concept of separate spheres has been used both to define an oppressive set of cultural norms confining women to the home and to describe the private sphere as a site of female identity grounded in notions of respectability and nurturance. Scholars have tracked the movement of public policy into private life and of private values into the public. We have asked about the women excluded from this construct and documented the multiplicity of coexisting public and private spheres. We have blurred the lines between home and public to the point that speaking of separation seems like an exercise in futility at best and obfuscation at worst.[15] Yet the dichotomy between private and public, albeit flawed, had tremendous meaning in the nineteenth century. We can deconstruct it but not ignore it. Again and again, women and men used home and the language and values of domesticity to interpret and change their lives.[16]

Together, the documents in *At Home in Nineteenth-Century America* capture the most important scholarly arguments about the nineteenth-century home and domesticity and give voice to a variety of historical actors. Some are by famous people and others by ordinary men and women. Excerpts are drawn from advice manuals, architectural and design literature, personal accounts, popular periodicals and fiction, reform literature, newspaper articles, and speeches. In addition to texts, each chapter includes images from house plans, catalogs, advertisements, games, and sheet music as well as lithographs, photographs, and drawings. The images not only help document the physical meaning of home but also serve as examples of the material culture that people lived with as they gave meaning to their domestic spaces.

The six thematic chapters are also broadly chronological, moving from the early to the late nineteenth century. Chapter 1 explores the relationship between home and the emergence of a new middle-class moral order, highlighting the ways in which that morality was transmitted and embodied in house design and goods. Several documents in this chapter focus on home's separation from the world of work and the marketplace, with an eye to new gendered dynamics within the home. The chapter also introduces Victorian Americans' complex understanding of domestic goods as something more than markers of wealth. Homes and their contents reflected and shaped character, and at least in principle, good homes and morals were not exclusively tied to any one class or race.

Chapter 2 looks beyond the ideal home to explore the ongoing significance of paid and unpaid domestic labor and reveals the variety of work (economic and cultural) done at home. The sources document the ways in which commercial and domestic ideals undermined and reinforced one another, as men and women sought to balance business interests and moral concerns both within and outside the home. Together the documents belie notions of a universal moral home and instead show how domestic labor and paid employment in the home served as signs of class and racial difference. In short, domesticity served to define and mark social differences. The tension between domestic work, social status, and morality connects this chapter to the previous one while underscoring inconsistencies between ideals and experience.

The next two chapters explore the ways in which various Americans interpreted, manipulated, and challenged the ideals of domesticity. Chapter 3 documents how politically marginalized groups used domestic norms, goods, and labor to lay claim to "civilization" to make demands for equal status and new rights. While the goals of racial and gender equality, an inclusive citizenry, and control over one's own labor challenged the status quo, the reliance on a single domestic ideal gives these documents a conservative cast worth noting. Chapter 4 builds on the connections between home and civilization by focusing on the use of domestic goods and values to create feelings of stability and progress in the face of geographic mobility and the United States' global expansion. Taking up the two meanings of "domestic," these documents consider the give-and-take between home and nation and consider the use of domesticity in the creation and assertion of American identity at the end of the nineteenth century.

The final two chapters turn to the breakdown and rethinking of the nineteenth-century domestic ideal. Chapter 5 explores the ways in which city living challenged Victorian notions of domestic privacy and considers the range of cultural and spatial responses to this challenge. Many of the documents highlight the loss of privacy, respectability, family feeling, and morality at home, while others depict new public spaces designed to serve previously domestic functions. Chapter 6 hints at the changing importance of home as a cultural ideal at the turn of the century and considers the challenges posed by feminism, suburbanization, technology, and a growing focus on personality and privacy.

In the twenty-first century, home may no longer be the signature institution of American life, yet it remains a complex site of experience and meaning. A setting for private life, personal expression, leisure, and social intimacy, it is permeated by paid and unpaid labor, consumer values, technological networks, and public policy. Public and private blur in ways that that we seldom fully appreciate, and like our Victorian counterparts, contemporary Americans live with and simultaneously ignore these contradictions. Banks sell off home mortgages as investments, while federal tax policy incentivizes homeownership as an individual and public good. First-time homeowners dream of idealized domestic lives but often face destabilizing debt in pursuit of the goods that support that dream. The middle class sets aside personal space for home offices and shuts out the world in minivans that replicate living-room comforts. Domestic workers are treated "like family" but are too often denied benefits and protections associated with paid employment. In sum, by listening closely to the nineteenth century's sweeping conversation about home in its various guises, we may better hear our own.

Notes

1. Elsa Barkley Brown, "Polyrhythm and Improvization: Lessons for Women's History," *History Workshop* 31 (1991): 85.
2. See, for example, Nancy F. Cott, *The Bonds of Womanhood: "Woman's Sphere" in New England, 1780–1835* (New Haven: Yale University Press, 1977); Mary P. Ryan, *Cradle of the Middle Class: The Family in Oneida County, New York, 1790–1865* (New York: Cambridge University Press, 1981); and Clifford Edward Clark, Jr., *The American Family Home, 1800–1960* (Chapel Hill: University of North Carolina Press, 1986).
3. For different treatments of the moveable line between public and private, see Christine Stansell, *City of Women: Sex and Class in New York, 1789–1860* (Urbana: University of Illinois Press, 1987); Mary P. Ryan, *Women in Public: Between Banners and Ballots, 1825–1880* (Baltimore: Johns Hopkins University Press, 1990); Angel Kwolek-Folland, *Engendering Business: Men and Women in the Corporate Office, 1870–1930* (Baltimore: Johns Hopkins University Press, 1994); and Amy G. Richter, *Home on the Rails: Women, the Railroad, and the Rise of Public Domesticity* (Chapel Hill: University of North Carolina Press, 2005).
4. Jeanne Boydston's *Home and Work: Housework, Wages, and the Ideology of Labor in the Early Republic* (New York: Oxford University Press, 1990) underscores the ways in which the home was permeated by labor—both paid and unpaid—of tremendous economic value, while her notion of "pastoralization of housework" explains how this work became culturally invisible. For a different take on the market's place within the home, see Kristin L. Hoganson, *Consumers' Imperium: The Global Production of American Domesticity, 1865–1920* (Chapel Hill: University of North Carolina Press, 2007).
5. On public parlors, see Katherine Grier, *Culture and Comfort: People, Parlors, and Upholstery* (Rochester, NY: Strong Museum, 1988); and Louise L. Stevenson, *The Victorian Homefront: American Thought and Culture, 1860–1880* (Ithaca: Cornell University Press, 2001). On department stores as domesticated spaces, see Elaine Abelson, *When Ladies Go A-Thieving: Middle-Class Shoplifters in the Victorian Department Store* (New York: Oxford University Press, 1989); and William Leach, "Transformations in a Culture of Consumption: Women and Department Stores, 1890–1925," *Journal of American History* 71, no. 2 (September 1984): 319–342. On women's creation of domesticated urban spaces including homes for female workers and public baths, see Daphne Spain, *How Women Saved the City* (Minneapolis: University of Minnesota Press, 2001).
6. This line of analysis is indebted to Paula Baker's "The Domestication of American Politics: Women and American Political Society, 1780–1920," *American Historical*

Review 89, no. 3 (1984): 620–647. Other works have linked domesticity and politics through the cultural work of imperialism and conquest. See, for example, Vicente L. Rafael, "Colonial Domesticity: White Women and United States Rule in the Philippines," *American Literature* 67, no. 4 (December 1995): 639–666; Amy Kaplan, "Manifest Domesticity," *American Literature* 70, no. 3 (September 1998): 581–605; Laura Wexler, *Tender Violence: Domestic Visions in an Age of U.S. Imperialism* (Chapel Hill: University of North Carolina Press, 2000).

7. See Thomas Bender, "Wholes and Parts: The Need for Synthesis in American History," *Journal of American History* 73 (1986): 120–136; and Nell Irvin Painter's response, "Bias and Synthesis in History," *Journal of American History* 74 (1987): 109–112.

8. On the parlor and entry hall, see Jack Larkin, *Where We Lived: Discovering the Places We Once Called Home; The American Home from 1775–1840* (Newtown, CT: Taunton, 2006), 22–25. Also see Richard Bushman, *The Refinement of America: Persons, Houses, Cities* (New York: Vintage, 1992); and Grier, *Culture and Comfort*. For a gendered analysis of specialized domestic spaces, see Daphne Spain, *Gendered Spaces* (Chapel Hill: University of North Carolina Press, 1992).

9. For room histories, see part 1 of Jessica H. Foy and Thomas J. Schlereth, eds., *American Home Life, 1880–1930: A Social History of Spaces and Services* (Knoxville: University of Tennessee Press, 1992).

10. Thomas Hubka, *Big House, Little House, Back House, Barn: The Connected Farm Buildings of New England* (1984; repr., Lebanon, NH: University Press of New England, 2004), 121.

11. Bushman, *Refinement of America*, xiii. For a rich cataloging and analysis of the goods and furnishings of the American Victorian home, see Kenneth L. Ames, *Death in the Dining Room and Other Tales of Victorian Culture* (Philadelphia: Temple University Press, 1995).

12. For an excellent introduction to and analysis of American housing over time, see Gwendolyn Wright, *Building the Dream: A Social History of Housing in America* (Cambridge: MIT Press, 1983). On regional variation and housing, see Larkin, *Where We Lived*. On slave cabins, see John Michael Vlach, "'Snug Li'l House with Flue and Oven': Nineteenth-Century Reforms in Plantation Slave Housing," in *Gender, Class, and Shelter*, ed. Elizabeth C. Cromley and Carter L. Hudgins, 118–129 (Knoxville: University of Tennessee Press, 1995); and Clifton Ellis and Rebecca Ginsburg, eds., *Cabin, Quarter, Plantation: Architecture and Landscapes of North American Slavery* (New Haven: Yale University Press, 2010).

13. Wendy Gamber, *The Boarding House in Nineteenth-Century America* (Baltimore: Johns Hopkins University Press, 2007), 2–3. See also Wright, *Building the Dream*; as well as Catherine Cocks, *Doing the Town: The Rise of Urban Tourism in the United States* (Berkeley: University of California Press, 2001); Andrew Sandoval-Strausz, *Hotel: An American History* (New Haven: Yale University Press, 2007); Elizabeth Blackmar, *Manhattan for Rent, 1785–1850* (Ithaca: Cornell University Press, 1989); and Elizabeth Collins Cromley, *Alone Together: A History of New*

York's Early Apartments (Ithaca: Cornell University Press, 1990). In addition, Betsy Klimasmith's *At Home in the City: Urban Domesticity in American Literature and Culture, 1850–1930* (Lebanon: University of New Hampshire Press, 2005) offers insight into the variety of urban homes, with chapters on tenements, apartments, and hotels.

14. Thomas J. Schlereth, "Introduction: American Homes and American Scholars," in Foy and Schlereth, *American Home Life*, 1–5.

15. For a wonderful historiography of women's historians' use of separate spheres, see Linda Kerber, "Separate Spheres, Female Worlds, Woman's Place: The Rhetoric of Women's History," *Journal of American History* 75, no. 1 (June 1988): 9–39. On multiple publics, see Nancy Fraser, "Rethinking the Public Sphere: A Contribution to the Critique of Actually Existing Democracy," in *Habermas and the Public Sphere*, ed. Craig Calhoun (Cambridge: MIT Press, 1992), 109–142. On scholarly frustrations with the separate spheres ideal, see the special issue "No More Separate Spheres!," *American Literature* 70, no. 3 (September 1998).

16. Richter, *Home on the Rails*, 1–8.

1

The Emergence of the Nineteenth-Century Domestic Ideal

The documents in this chapter explore the relationship between home and a new middle-class moral order emerging in the early decades of the nineteenth century. As men's labor increasingly moved outside the home, domestic spaces came to be associated with women, who were expected to maintain them as bulwarks against the morally suspect, public world of business competition. Women's domestic work was recast in these terms—less and less depicted as productive labor with economic value and instead described as an extension of women's inherent nature and a form of feminine love and nurturance. The historian Jeanne Boydston has called this reframing "the pastoralization of housework."

The gradual erasure of women's domestic work as labor and the growing separation of the home from the world beyond are reflected in the letters of Mary Lee as well as in the advice offered by Catharine Beecher and the idealized image of "the sphere of woman" in *Godey's Lady's Book*. By contrast, Lydia Maria Child underscores the material significance and considerable training involved in women's home labor and makes a case for domestic education. Susan Warner's popular novel and its depiction of Ellen Montgomery suggest the cultural triumph of Beecher's moral comforter over Child's skilled housewife.

Proper morality was transmitted and embodied not only through women's domestic role but also in house design and goods. The separation of public and private was itself imprinted on domestic space through the proliferation of rooms with specialized uses—entrance hall, parlor, library—and goods to furnish them. In this way, domestic material culture tied home to the marketplace and male breadwinners even as it celebrated the private, feminine, noncommercial retreat. John Angell James emphasizes the home's role in preparing young men for business and the danger inherent in their transition from the private to the public sphere. As Andrew Jackson Downing describes, the architectural features of houses possessed a morality of their own—conveying simplicity, beauty, and truth. For James and Downing, the home is a reward for and antidote to men's economic struggle, which both authors associate with the dangers of urban life.

Even as home came to be celebrated as a woman's space, men continued to exert authority over it. Legally homes were men's property, and Downing addresses his text to his "countrymen" who would be making decisions about home construction. On the one hand, Herman Melville's defense of his protagonist's beloved chimney from feminine desires for a new entry hall suggests shifting authority within the home. On the other, the thwarted renovation affirms continued male authority over economic decisions shaping the domestic sphere.

Give Me the Delightful Occupation of Attending to You

In 1926, Mary and Henry Lee's granddaughter Frances Rollins Morse gathered and published selections of their personal writings in order to preserve for future generations the charm of life in eastern Massachusetts a hundred years earlier. As a young Boston businessman, Henry Lee traveled to Calcutta in 1811 and remained there during the War of 1812, returning home in 1816. The passages here are taken from a journal that Mary kept for him in his absence. The entries reveal an affectionate marriage and a network of family ties that included several notable New England families. Threaded through Mary's account are concerns about the relationship between labor and love within her marriage. While Henry is away, Mary struggles to find the value of her own domestic contributions, especially when contrasted against her husband's labor and financial support.

Feb. 28, 1813

Oh, my dear, dear husband, when we do meet I believe I shall hold you fast—for it appears to me that almost any labour, if together, would not be too hard for us. One great source of trouble to me now is that I am living a life of such corporeal ease. I think I should be better satisfied if I were obliged daily to make some efforts, either to gain or to avoid spending money—but my friends all think that I am spending as little as I can, and I suppose the pride of some of them would be sadly wounded if I were to do anything to gain—this is a pride I cannot conceive of. I know not why the wife should not work *a little* as well as the husband *labour so hard*, and did I feel a certainty that you would agree with me upon the subject, I should most certainly act upon the principle.

Aug. 12, 1814

. . . I only visit in our *clan*, very seldom beyond it except in the morning. I will give you an account of the last few days. Monday and Tuesday were passed very quietly at home, except Tuesday afternoon at Charles's; Wednesday I drank tea with the Searles, passed the evening at home alone; Thursday spent the day at my mother's [Mrs. Joseph Lee's], the evening at home. The Doctor was here for an hour, and I had a good deal of pleasant conversation with him about you and our child, etc. . . . I have just got home a good deal wearied and find a note from Ann Storrow, saying Stephen Higginson and wife are going to Andover tomorrow and have a vacant seat which they wish me to occupy. Though there is everything pleasant to anticipate from such a ride, I can hardly persuade myself to say "yes," yet as I have had no way of sending to them, I shall, I believe, go as I presume they will call. I believe it is because I have nothing to *prevent* my going that I feel so unpleasantly about it always, for I have no apprehension about leaving Molly—Do, my beloved husband, return to me and give me the delightful occupation of attending to you, and feeling my presence *at home* of some importance.

Oh when shall I have this happiness!

Sept. 1, 1813

I think you will notice throughout these pages an air of importance given to trifles which will amuse you, my dear husband: let it not render me insignificant in your eyes, my beloved Hal—if it does I am sure I shall deeply regret having solaced myself by writing them: the fact is, when one is placed in a situation removed from care and responsibility, trifles gain importance, and I so much desire to feel as if I was of *consequence* to someone that if the child has the finger-ache, or nurse looks pale, I immediately think I cannot possibly leave them and thus gain my point. I shall soon have to give up even this ideal importance, for Molly is getting to an age that will suffer from too much attention. The darling has been quite unwell for four days. I have had some moments of apprehension but they were wholly unnecessary, I believe—when I see an appearance of disease without anything very positive I shall always in future be alarmed—this was so much the case with our other darling. I had not an idea of her danger till very late and then it was excited by the appearance of those around me rather than observation of the child. I cannot be sufficiently thankful that I have James to guide me. You can scarcely conceive how much she talks of you. I have lately hit upon a method to make her feel her dependence upon you, and am very much pleased with the success of it. I had noticed that she understood the use of money, and one day when she wanted some for a cracker, or cakey as she calls it, I gave it to her and then asked if she knew who gave it to her. She, of course, answered—mama—I told her "yes, but who do you think gives it to mama?" This puzzled her and I told her "papa"—then enumerated the clothes, etc., purchased for her and me—she was highly delighted, and now never mentions buying anything without recollecting, and saying "papa buy."

Source: Henry Lee and Mary Lee, *Letters and Journals: With Other Family Letters, 1802–1860* (Boston: Privately printed, 1926), courtesy of the American Antiquarian Society.

Economy, like Grammar, Is a Very Hard and Tiresome Study, after We Are Twenty Years Old

Lydia Maria Child published *The Frugal Housewife* in 1829. Ultimately there were to be thirty-three American printings, with the 1832 edition announcing a new title, *The American Frugal Housewife*, to "differentiate it from an English work of the same name." One of the first domestic manuals for women on a budget, the book included recipes, household advice, and essays encouraging women's industry and economy. Its final chapter considered "how to endure poverty." This was not an abstract concern for Child. Her husband, David Lee Child, who was a lawyer and the editor of the *Massachusetts Whig Journal* and whom she married in 1828, was an unreliable breadwinner, and she struggled to support them both with her writing. In this passage, she offers advice on the "education of daughters," recommending that they be taught that marriage will not bring an end to labor. Instead girls must be trained in household skills that will support the success of husbands and stretch family resources.

One great cause of the vanity, extravagance and idleness that are so fast growing upon our young ladies, is the absence of *domestic education*. By domestic education, I do not mean the sending daughters into the kitchen some half dozen times, to weary the patience of the cook, and to boast of it the next day in the parlor. I mean two or three years spent with a mother, assisting her in her duties, instructing brothers and sisters, and taking care of their own clothes. This is the way to make them happy, as well as good wives; for, being early accustomed to the duties of life, they will sit lightly as well as gracefully upon them.

But what time do modern girls have for the formation of quiet, domestic habits? Until sixteen they go to school; sometimes these years are judiciously spent, and sometimes they are half wasted; too often they are spent in acquiring the *elements* of a thousand sciences, without being thoroughly acquainted with any; or in a variety of accomplishments of very doubtful value to people of moderate fortune. As soon as they leave school, (and sometimes before,) they begin a round of balls and parties, and staying with gay young friends. Dress and flattery take up all their thoughts. What time have they to learn to be useful? What time have they to cultivate the still and gentle affections, which must, in every situation of life, have such an important effect on a woman's character and happiness?

As far as parents can judge what will be a daughter's station, education should be adapted to it; but it is well to remember that it is always easy to know how to spend riches, and always safe to know how to bear poverty.

A superficial acquaintance with such accomplishments as music and drawing is useless and undesirable. They should not be attempted unless there is taste, talent, and time enough to attain excellence. I have frequently heard young women of moderate fortune say, "I have not opened my piano these five years. I wish I had the money expended upon it. If I had employed as much time in learning useful things, I should have been better fitted for the cares of my family."

By these remarks I do not mean to discourage an attention to the graces of life. Gentility and taste are always lovely in all situations. But good things, carried to excess, are often productive of bad consequences. When accomplishments and dress interfere with the duties and permanent happiness of life, they are unjustifiable and displeasing; but where there is a solid foundation in mind and heart, all those elegancies are but becoming ornaments.

Some are likely to have more use for them than others; and they are justified in spending more time and money upon them. But no one should be taught to consider them valuable for mere parade and attraction. Making the education of girls such a series of "man-traps," makes the whole system unhealthy, by poisoning the motive.

In tracing evils of any kind, which exist in society, we must, after all, be brought up against the great cause of all mischief—*mismanagement in education*; and this remark applies with peculiar force to the leading fault of the present day, viz, extravagance. It is useless to expend our ingenuity in purifying the stream, unless the fountain be cleansed. If young men and young women are brought up to consider frugality contemptible, and industry degrading, it is vain to expect they will at once become prudent and useful, when the cares of life press heavily upon them. Generally speaking, when misfortune comes upon those who have been accustomed to thoughtless expenditure, it sinks them to discouragement, or, what is worse, drives them to desperation. It is true there are exceptions. There are a few, an honorable few, who, late in life, with Roman severity of resolution, learn the long-neglected lesson of economy. But how small is the number, compared with the whole mass of the population! And with what bitter agony, with what biting humiliation, is the hard lesson often learned! How easily might it have been engrafted on *early habits*, and naturally and gracefully "grown with their growth, and strengthened with their strength!"

Yet it was but lately that I visited a family, not of "moderate fortune," but of no fortune at all; one of those people who live "nobody knows how," and I found a young girl, about sixteen, practising on the piano, while an elderly lady beside her was darning her stockings. I was told (for the mother was proud of bringing up her child so genteelly) that the daughter had almost forgotten how to sew, and that a woman was hired into the house to do her mending! "But why," said I, "have you suffered your daughter to be ignorant of so useful an employment? If she is poor, the knowledge will be necessary to her; if she is rich, it is the easiest thing in the world to lay it aside, if she chooses; she will merely be a better judge whether her work is well done by others." "That is true," replied the mother; "and I always meant she should learn; but she never has seemed to have any time. When she was eight years old, she could put a shirt together pretty well; but since that, her music, and her dancing, and her school, have taken up her whole time. I did mean she should learn some domestic habits this winter; but she has so many visiters, and is obliged to go out so much, that I suppose I must give it up. I don't like to say too much about it; for, poor girl! she does so love company, and she does so hate anything like care and confinement! *Now* is her time to enjoy herself, you know. Let her take all the comfort she can, while she is single!" "But," said I, "you wish her to marry some time or other; and, in all probability, she will marry. When will she learn how to perform the duties, which are necessary and important to every mistress of a family?" "Oh, she will learn them when she is obliged to," answered the injudicious mother; "at all events, I am determined she shall enjoy herself while she is young."

And this is the way I have often heard mothers talk! Yet, could parents foresee the almost inevitable consequences of such a system, I believe the weakest and vainest would abandon the false and dangerous theory. What a lesson is taught a girl in that sentence, "*Let her enjoy herself all she can, while she is single!*" Instead of representing domestic life as the gathering place of the deepest and purest affections; as the sphere of woman's *enjoyments* as well as of her *duties*; as, indeed, the whole world to her; that one pernicious sentence teaches a girl to consider matrimony desirable because "a good match" is a triumph of vanity, and it is deemed respectable to be "well settled in the world;" but that it is a necessary sacrifice of her freedom and her gayety. And then how many affectionate dispositions have been trained into heartlessness, by being taught that the indulgence of indolence and vanity were necessary to their happiness; and that to have this indulgence, they *must* marry money! But who that marries for money, in this land of precarious fortunes, can tell how soon they will lose the glittering temptation, to which they have been willing to sacrifice so much? And even if riches last as long as life, the evil is not remedied. Education has given a wrong end and aim to their whole existence; they have been taught to look for happiness where it never can be found, viz. in the absence of all occupation, or the unsatisfactory and ruinous excitement of fashionable competition.

The difficulty is, education does not usually point the female heart to its only true resting-place. That dear English word "*home*" is not half so powerful a talisman as "*the world.*" Instead of the salutary truth, that happiness is *in* duty, they are taught to consider the two things totally distinct; and that whoever seeks one, must sacrifice the other.

The fact is, our girls have no *home education.* When quite young, they are sent to schools where no feminine employments, no domestic habits, can be learned; and there they continue till they "come out" into the world. After this, few find any time to arrange, and make use of, the mass of elementary knowledge they have acquired; and fewer still have either leisure or taste for the inelegant, every-day duties of life. Thus prepared, they enter upon matrimony. Those early habits, which would have made domestic care a light and easy task, have never been taught, for fear it would interrupt their happiness; and the result is, that when cares come, as come they must, they find them misery. I am convinced that indifference and dislike between husband and wife are more frequently occasioned by this great error in education, than by any other cause.

The bride is awakened from her delightful dream, in which carpets, vases, sofas, white gloves, and pearl earrings, are oddly jumbled up with her lover's looks and promises. Perhaps she would be surprised if she knew exactly how *much* of the fascination of being engaged was owing to the aforesaid inanimate concern. Be that as it will, she is awakened by the unpleasant conviction that cares devolve upon her. And what effect does this produce upon her character? Do the holy and tender influences of domestic love render self-denial and exertion a bliss? No! They would have done so, had she been *properly educated*; but now she gives way to unavailing fretfulness and repining; and her husband is at first pained, and finally disgusted, by hearing, "I never knew what care was when I lived in my father's house." "If I were to live my life over again, I would remain single as long as I could, without the risk of being an old maid." How injudicious, how short-sighted is the policy, which thus mars the whole happiness of life, in order to make a few brief years more gay and brilliant! I have known many instances of domestic ruin and discord produced by this mistaken indulgence of mothers. *I never knew but one, where the victim had moral courage enough to change all her early habits.* She was a young, pretty, and very amiable girl; but brought up to be perfectly useless; a rag baby would, to all intents and purposes, have been as efficient a partner. She married a young lawyer, without property, but with good and increasing practice. She meant to be a good wife, but she did not know how. Her wastefulness involved him in debt. He did not reproach, though he tried to convince and instruct her. She loved him; and weeping replied, "I tried to do the best I can; but when I lived at home, mother always took care of everything." Finally, poverty came upon him "like an armed man;" and he went into a remote town in the Western States to teach a school. His wife folded her hands, and cried; while he, weary and discouraged, actually came home from school to cook his own supper. At last, his patience, and her real love for him, impelled her to exertion. She promised to learn to be useful, if he would teach her. And she did learn! And the change in her habits gradually wrought such a change in her husband's fortune, that she might bring her daughters up in idleness, had not experience taught her that economy, like grammar, is a very hard and tiresome study, after we are twenty years old.

Perhaps some will think the evils of which I have been speaking, are confined principally to the rich; but I am convinced they extend to all classes of people. All manual employment is considered degrading; and those who are compelled to do it, try to conceal it. A few years since, very respectable young men at our colleges, cut their own wood, and blacked their own shoes. Now, how few, even of the sons of plain farmers and industrious mechanics, have moral courage enough to do without a servant; yet when they leave college, and come out into the battle of life, they *must* do without servants; and in these times it will be fortunate if one half of them get what is called "a decent living," even by rigid economy and patient toil. Yet I would not that servile and laborious employment should be forced upon the young. I would merely have each one educated according to his probable situation in life; and be taught that whatever is his duty, is honorable; and that no merely external circumstance can in reality injure true dignity of character. I would not cramp a boy's energies by compelling him always to cut wood, or draw water; but I would teach him not to be ashamed, should his companions happen to find him doing either one or the other. A few days since, I asked

Figure 1.1. This advertisement for Hennessy's Cottage Furniture (1852; Library of Congress, Prints & Photographs Division, LC-USZ62-53908) offers a depiction of the variety of domestic furnishings available for purchase. The proliferation of furniture pieces and styles reflects growth not only in refinement but also in specialization of domestic spaces and functions. The settee in the center of the advertisement is designed to encourage good posture and conversation in the parlor, the public face of the private middle-class home.

a grocer's lad to bring home some articles I had just purchased at his master's. The bundle was large; he was visibly reluctant to take it; and wished very much that I should send for it. This, however, was impossible; and he subdued his pride; but when I asked him to take back an empty bottle which belonged to the store, he, with a mortified look, begged me to do it up neatly in a paper, that it might look like a small package. Is this boy likely to be happier for cherishing a foolish pride, which will forever be jarring against his duties? Is he in reality one whit more respectable than the industrious lad who sweeps stores, or carries bottles, without troubling himself with the idea that all the world is observing his little unimportant self? For, in relation to the rest of the world, each individual is unimportant; and he alone is wise who forms his habits according to his own wants, his own prospects, and his own principles.

Source: Lydia Maria Child, "Education of Daughters," in *The American Frugal Housewife* (Boston: Carter, Hendee, 1832).

For a Housekeeper's Business Is Not like That of the Other Sex

Like Lydia Maria Child, Catharine Beecher understood the home as a site of women's labor and that this work required considerable knowledge and skill. But as the never-married daughter of the famed Calvinist preacher Lyman Beecher, Catharine imbued this work with religious zeal and Christian mission. Her 1841 *Treatise on Domestic Economy* combined expertise in plumbing and preaching to enhance women's status in the home, putting them in charge of the moral well-being of their families and lending moral heft to mundane domestic tasks and goods. No detail of domestic life was insignificant if it could enhance women's positive influence. This was the ultimate value of a woman's domestic skills, and as Beecher suggests here, none was more important than a housewife's ability to regulate herself.

There is nothing, which has a more abiding influence on the happiness of a family, than the preservation of equable and cheerful temper and tones in the housekeeper. A woman who is habitually gentle, sympathizing, forbearing, and cheerful, carries an atmosphere about her, which imparts a soothing and sustaining influence, and renders it easier for all to do right, under her administration, than in any other situation.

The Writer has known families, where the mother's presence seemed the sunshine of the circle around her; imparting a cheering and vivifying power, scarcely realized, till it was withdrawn. Every one, without thinking of it, or knowing why it was so, experienced a peaceful and invigorating influence, as soon as they entered the sphere illumined by her smile and sustained by her cheering kindness and sympathy. On the contrary, many a good housekeeper, good in every respect but this, by wearing a countenance of anxiety and dissatisfaction, and by indulging in the frequent use of sharp and reprehensive tones, more than destroys all the comfort that otherwise would result from her system, neatness, and economy.

There is a secret, social sympathy, which every mind, to a greater or less degree, experiences with the feelings of those around, as they are manifested by the countenance and voice. A sorrowful, a discontented, or an angry, countenance, produces a silent sympathetic influence, imparting a somber shade to the mind, while tones of anger or complaint still more effectually jar the spirits.

No person can maintain a quiet and cheerful frame of mind, while tones of discontent and displeasure are sounding on the ear. We may gradually accustom ourselves to the evil, till it is partially diminished; but it always is an evil, which greatly interferes with the enjoyment of the family state. There are sometimes cases, where the entrance of the mistress of a family seems to awaken a slight apprehension, in every mind around, as if each felt in danger of a reproof, for something either perpetrated or neglected. A woman who should go around her house with a small stinging snapper, which she habitually applied to those she met, would be encountered with feelings very similar to those, experienced by the inmates of a family where the mistress often uses her countenance and voice to inflict similar penalties for duties neglected.

Yet there are many allowances to be made for housekeepers, who sometimes imperceptibly and unconsciously fall into such habits. A woman, who attempts to carry out any plans of system, order, and economy, and who has her feelings and habits conformed to certain rules, is constantly liable to have her plans crossed, and her taste violated, by the inexperience or inattention of those about her. And no housekeeper, whatever are her habits, can escape the frequent recurrence of negligence or mistake, which interferes with her plans. It is probable that there is no class of persons, in the world, who have such incessant trials of temper, and such temptation to be fretful, as American housekeepers. For a housekeeper's business is not like that of the other sex, limited to a particular department, for which previous preparation is made. It consists of ten thousand little disconnected items, which can never be so systemically arranged, that there is no daily jostling, somewhere. And in the best-regulated families, it is not unfrequently the case, that some act of forgetfulness or carelessness, from some member, will disarrange the business of the whole day, so that every hour will bring renewed occasion for annoyance. And the more strongly a woman realizes the value of time, and the importance of system and order, the more will she be tempted to irritability and complaint.

The following considerations may aid in preparing a woman to meet such daily crosses with even a cheerful temper and tones.

In the first place, a woman who has charge of a large household, should regard her duties as dignified, important, and difficult. The mind is so made, as to be elevated and cheered by a sense of far-reaching influence and usefulness. A woman, who feels that she is a cipher, and that it makes little difference how she performs her duties, has far less to sustain and invigorate her, than one who truly estimates the importance of her station. A man, who feels that the destinies of a nation are turning on the judgement and skill with which he plans and executes, has a pressure of motive, and an elevation of feeling, which are great safeguards from all that is low, trivial, and degrading.

So an American mother and housekeeper, who looks at her position in the aspect presented in the previous pages, and who rightly estimates the long train of influences which will pass down to hundreds, whose destinies, from generation to generation, will be modified by those decisions of her will, which regulated the temper, principles, and habits, of her family, must be elevated above petty temptations which would otherwise assail her.

Again, a housekeeper should feel that she really has great difficulties to meet and overcome. A person, who wrongly thinks that there is little danger, can never maintain so faithful a guard, as one who rightly estimates the temptations which beset her. Nor can one, who thinks that they are trifling difficulties which she has to encounter, and trivial temptations, to which she must yield, so much enjoy the just reward of conscious virtue and self-control, as one who takes an opposite view of the subject.

A third method, is, for a woman deliberately to calculate on having her best-arranged plans interfered with, very often; and to be in such a state of preparation that the evil will not come unawares. So complicated are the pursuits, and so diverse the habits of the various members of a family, that it is almost impossible for every one to avoid interfering with the plans and taste of a housekeeper, in some one point or another. It is therefore most wise, for a woman to keep the loins of her mind ever girt, to meet such collisions with a cheerful and quiet spirit.

Another important rule, is to form all plans and arrangements in consistency with the means at command, and the character of those around. A woman who has a heedless husband, and young children, and incompetent domestics, ought not to make such plans, as one may properly form, who will not, in so many directions, meet embarrassment. She must aim at just so much as it is probable she can secure, and no more; and thus she will usually escape much temptation, and much of the irritation of disappointment.

The fifth, and a very important, consideration, is, that *system, economy, and neatness,* are valuable, only so far as they tend to promote comfort and the well-being of those affected. Some women seem to act under the impression, that these advantages *must* be secured, at all events, even if the comfort of the family be the sacrifice. True, it is very important that children grow up in habits of system, neatness, and order; and it is very desirable that the mother give them every incentive, both by precept and example: but it is still more important, that they grow up with amiable tempers, that they learn to meet the crosses of life with patience and cheerfulness; and nothing has a greater influence to secure this, than a mother's example. Whenever, therefore, a woman cannot carry her plans of neatness and order, without injury to her own temper, or to the temper of others, she ought to modify and reduce them, until she can.

The sixth method, relates to the government of the tones of voice. In many cases, when a woman's domestic arrangements are suddenly and seriously crossed, it is impossible not to feel some irritation. But it *is* always possible to refrain from angry tones. A woman can resolve, that, whatever happens, she will not speak, till she can do it in a calm and gentle manner. *Perfect silence* is a safe resort, when such control cannot be attained as enables a person to speak calmly; and this determination, persevered in, will eventually be crowned with success.

Many persons seem to imagine, that tones of anger are needful, in order to secure prompt obedience. But observation has convinced the Writer that they are *never* necessary; that *in all cases*, reproof, administered in calm tones, would be better. . . .

Though some ladies, of intelligence and refinement, do fall unconsciously into such a practice, it is certainly very unlady-like, and in very bad taste, to *scold*; and the further a woman departs from all approach to it, the more perfectly she sustains her character as a lady.

Another method of securing equanimity, amid the trials of domestic life, is, to cultivate a habit of making allowance for the difficulties, ignorance, or temptations, of those who violate rule or neglect duty. It is vain, and most unreasonable, to expect the consideration and care of a mature mind, in childhood and youth; or that persons, of such limited advantages as most domestics have enjoyed, should practise proper self-control, and possess proper habits and principles.

Every parent, and every employer, needs daily to cultivate the spirit expressed in the Divine prayer, "forgive us our trespasses, as we forgive those who trespass against us." The same allowances and forbearance we supplicate from our Heavenly Father, and desire from our fellow-men, in reference to our deficiencies, we should constantly aim to extend to all who cross our feelings and interfere with our plans.

The last, and most important mode of securing placid and cheerful temper and tones, is, by a right view of the doctrine of a superintending Providence. All persons are too much in the habit of regarding the more important events of life as exclusively under the control of Perfect Wisdom. But the fall of a sparrow, or the loss of a hair, they do not feel to be equally the result of His directing agency. In consequence of this, Christian persons, who aim at perfect and cheerful submission to heavy afflictions, and who succeed, to the edification of all about them, are sometimes sadly deficient under petty crosses. If a beloved child is laid in the grave, even if its death resulted from the carelessness of a domestic, or a physician, the eye is turned from the subordinate agent, to the

Figures 1.2 and 1.3. Two versions of N. Currier's *Reading the Scriptures* (c. 1840 and 1838–1856; both courtesy of the American Antiquarian Society) merge genteel material culture and Christian morality. At the center, the hearth, lamp, and Bible illuminate the furnishings and establish the proper relationship between husband and wife. The lithographs themselves would be displayed in the parlors of middle-class Americans, again putting material culture in the service of moral uplift. The second, more richly decorated scene is no doubt from a later date and reflects the elaboration and refinement of parlor interiors.

Supreme Guardian of all, and to Him they bow without murmur or complaint. But if a pudding is burnt, or a room badly swept, or an errand forgotten, then vexation and complaint are allowed, just as if these events were not appointed by Perfect Wisdom, as much as the sorer chastisement.

A woman, therefore, needs to cultivate the *habitual* feeling, that all the events of her nursery and kitchen are brought about by the permission of our Heavenly Father, and that fretfulness and complaint, in regard to these, is, in fact, complaining and disputing at the appointments of God, and are really as sinful, as unsubmissive murmurs amid the sorer chastisements of His hand. And a woman, who will daily cultivate this habit of referring all the events of her life to the wise and benevolent agency of a Heavenly Parent, will soon find it the perennial spring of abiding peace and content.

Source: Catharine Beecher, "On the Preservation of a Good Temper in a Housekeeper," in *A Treatise on Domestic Economy* (Boston: Marsh, Capen, Lyon and Webb, 1841).

You Cannot Always Remain at Home

While the ideal middle-class home provided a respite from the competitive world of commerce, its influence was meant to follow men out into their public dealings and protect them from temptation and vice. In this passage, English Nonconformist minister John Angell James advises young men of the dangers they will face as they prepare to leave their parents' homes. James's warnings about untrustworthy strangers and attenuated community bonds highlight that the moral home emerged in the context of growing urbanization and increased geographic mobility. Away from home, a man's good character was his best defense, but the proliferation of works such as James's emphasizes the feared inadequacy of this strategy.

A Youth leaving home! There is something not a little melancholy in the idea. Home is one of the most delightful of words, and it is no wonder that it should have become the subject of poetry and song. There is music in the sound, and in every heart that is not yet corrupted, there is a chord that vibrates to the note. It will ever awaken a long train of associations and recollections, painful or pleasant, as may have been the conduct of the individual by whom the word is repeated. It is at home that parents and children, brothers and sisters, as long as Providence permits them to dwell together, mingle in the sweet fellowship of domestic bliss. But you, whose eye is ranging over these pages, are leaving, or have left your father's house. You are going, or have gone away from home. I sympathize with you in the sorrows of that tearful hour of your existence. Well do I remember, even at this distance from the time, the scene which my own home presented, when I finally quitted it, to embark on life's stormy and dangerous ocean. My mother, one of the kindest and tenderest that ever bore that dear relationship, unable to sustain the parting, had retired to the garden; my sisters wept; my father walked silently by my side to the edge of the town, where I was to take horse and ride to meet the coach that was to carry me to London; while my own heart was almost overwhelmed with emotion, under the idea that I was leaving home, to encounter the anxieties, dangers, and responsibilities of a new and untried course.

In any aspect of the event, it is no trifling or inconsiderable transaction, to quit the scenes, the friends, and the guardians of our childhood; to leave that spot, and its dear inhabitants, with which are associated all our earliest reminiscences; to go from beneath the immediate inspection of a mother's anxious love, and the protection of a father's watchful care, and expose ourselves to the perils, privations, and sorrows that await the traveller on his journey through this world. You *ought*, as a child, to feel a pang as your mother presses you to her bosom, and sobs out her parting exclamation, "Adieu, my son." You *ought* to feel pensive and sad, as your father squeezes your hand, and turns from you with a heart too full to speak. You *ought*, as you cross the threshold of that habitation where you have been nurtured so tenderly, to cast a longing, lingering look behind. You would be unworthy of your parents' love, and of home's endearments, if you could leave them without emotion.

Still, however, these feelings are to be guided and limited by reflection. You cannot always remain at home, to be nursed in the lap of domestic enjoyment. You have a part to act in the great drama of life, and must leave home to prepare to act it well. It is the appointment of God that man should not live in idleness, but gain his bread by the sweat of his brow; and you must be placed out in the world to get yours by honest industry. In some few cases, the son remains with the father, and prepares for his future calling *at* home; but in by far the greater number of instances it is necessary for young men to learn their trade or profession, and to procure their livelihood by being placed with strangers at a distance *from* home. This is your case, and in kind solicitude for your welfare, this little volume has been prepared, and is now presented to you, with the prayers and best wishes of the author. . . .

. . . You are aware that, besides your attention to business and acquiring a knowledge of that trade or profession to which your attention is directed, there is such a thing as the formation of character, or fixed habits of action, arising out of fixed principles. A man may be a good tradesman, and yet a bad man; though generally, good moral character has a very favorable influence in forming the good tradesman. I wish you to direct your most serious attention to the importance of character—*moral* and *religious* character. What is everything else without character? How worthless is any man without this! He may have wealth, but he can neither enjoy it, improve it, nor be respected for it, without character. But it very rarely happens that they who begin life with a bad character, succeed in the great competition of this world's business. Multitudes, with every advantage at starting, have failed through bad conduct, while others, with every disadvantage, have succeeded by the aid and influence of good character.

Character for life, and for eternity too, is usually formed in youth. Set out with this idea written upon your very hearts, in order that it may be ever exerting its powerful influence on your conduct. As is the youth, such, in all probability, will be the man, whether he be good or bad. And as character is generally formed in youth, so it is not less generally formed at that period of youth when young people leave home. The first year or two after quitting his father's house, is the most eventful period of all a young man's history, and what he is at the expiration of the second or third year after leaving the parental abode, that in all probability he will be, as a tradesman for this world, and as an immortal being in the next. This should make you pause and consider. Before you read another line, I entreat you to think of it. Perhaps you doubt it. Attend then to what I have to offer in support of the assertion.

Does not reason suggest that such a transition as leaving home, cannot be negative in its influence? You cannot quit so many restraints, so much inspection and guardianship, and come into such new circumstances, at an age when the heart is so susceptible and the character so pliable, without receiving a bias: it is impossible. New temptations assail you, which, if not at once and successfully resisted, will acquire a permanent ascendency.

Your parents, who have gone before you in the path of life, know the fact and tremble. It makes their hearts ache to think of sending you away from home. You know not, you cannot know, what was the deep and silent trouble of your father's heart, the painful solicitude of your mother's gentle spirit, in the prospect of your leaving them. They sat hour after hour by the fireside, or lay awake at night talking on the subject, and mingled their tears as they thought of the youths of their acquaintance, whose ruin was dated from the hour of their departure from home: "Oh!" they exclaimed in anguish, "if this our son should be like them, and become a prodigal too, and thus bring down our gray hairs in sorrow to the grave! Would that we could keep him at home under our own care, but we cannot." They then fell upon their knees, and by united prayer, gained relief and comfort to their aching hearts, while commending you to Him, who has in ten thousand instances been the guide and protector of youth. While your mother, good woman! as she packed your trunk, dropped her fast flowing tears upon your clothes, placed the Bible among them, and sighed out the petition, "Oh my son, my son! Great God, preserve him from all evil."

Ministers have seen the danger of youths leaving home, most painfully exemplified in young men who have come from a distant town, recommended perhaps by parents to their care, and who for a while attended their ministry. At first their places in the sanctuary were regularly filled twice a day, and while the novelty lasted, they appeared to hear with attention and interest: this soon diminished, and they became listless and neglectful; then their seat was occasionally empty on a sabbath evening; then habitually so; till at length giving up the morning, or only strolling in occasionally with some gay companion, they proclaimed the dreadful fact, that they had fallen into the dangers incident to young men upon leaving home: and the next intelligence concerning them, perhaps was a letter from a heart-broken parent, confirming the worst fears of the minister, by asking him to make an effort to snatch their son from his evil companions and profligate courses.

Instances innumerable have occurred, in which youths, who, while dwelling under their father's roof, have been the joy and the hope of their parents, have, on leaving home and entering into the world, exhibited a melancholy and awful transformation of character. Some by slow degrees have passed from virtue to vice, while others have made the transition so suddenly, as if by one mighty bound they had resolved to reach the way of the ungodly; in either case, the bitterest disappointment has been experienced by those who have had to contrast the prodigal abroad with the sober youth at home.

Youthful reader, I assure you that this is no uncommon case, but, on the contrary, so frequent, as to make every considerate parent tremble at sending away his son, especially to the large provincial towns, and most of all to that mighty sink of iniquity, the metropolis.

What, then, should be the state of your mind, and your reflections upon reading such an account as this? "Is it so, that on leaving their father's house, so many young men who were once virtuous and promising, have become vicious and profligate, how much does it become me to pause and reflect, lest I add another to the number! What was there in their circumstances and situation so dangerous to virtue, that I may not expect to find in mine? or what is there in my habits and resolutions, which was not, in their better days, in them? Did they fall, and shall I be so confident of steadfastness as to dismiss fear and despise caution? Do I recoil from vice? so did they, when, like me, they were at home. Do I shudder at grieving my parents by misconduct? so did they, when, like me, they had their parents continually before them. Am I going forth high in the confidence of my parents, and the esteem of my friends? so did they. Yet how cruelly have they disappointed every hope that was formed concerning them! and what is there in my habits and purposes that shall prevent me from imitating their example? Oh if this *should* be the case! If *I* should add another to the victims of leaving home! If *my* reputation, now happily so fair, should be tarnished, faded, lost! If *I*, of whom hopes are entertained that I am becoming a Christian, should turn out a prodigal, a profligate! Dreadful aposta[s]y. Great God, prevent it!"

Could I induce you thus to reflect, I should have hope of you; while a contrary spirit of self-dependence and confidence, would lead me to expect in *you* another proof that the time of a youth's leaving home is most critical.

Source: John Angell James, *The Young Man from Home* (New York: American Tract Society, 1838).

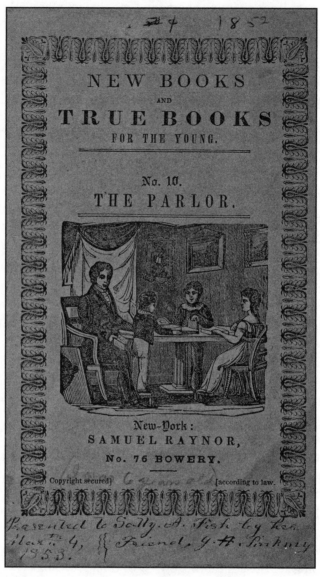

Figure 1.4. *The Parlor, New Books and True Books for the Young* (1853; courtesy of the American Antiquarian Society) underscored the home's didactic role in shaping children's character as well as the specialized role of the parlor, the setting for formal family life and uplift. The book's illustrations show typical parlor furnishings, and the text explains the lessons they teach. For example, an image of a sideboard is followed by the observation that many people keep liquor in their sideboards: "but I would not have a drop of such bad things in the sideboard or the house."

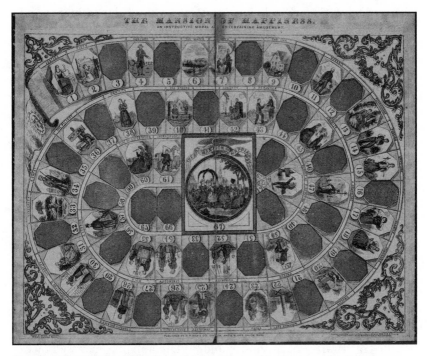

Figure 1.5. The Mansion of Happiness (1843; courtesy of the American Antiquarian Society) was the first board game produced in the United States. Players must move along the path to the Mansion of Happiness, but the route is fraught with moral pitfalls. Virtues are rewarded and vices punished. According to the rules, "Whoever possesses Piety, Honesty, Temperance, Gratitude, Prudence, Truth, Chastity, Sincerity, Humility, Industry, Charity, Humanity, or Generosity is entitled to advance six numbers toward the Mansion of Happiness. . . . Whoever gets into Idleness must come to Poverty. . . . Whoever becomes a Cheat must be sent to the House of Corrections for one month, and when at liberty begin the game again." Although the game was intended to teach moral lessons, players spun a top to determine their moves, leaving their fates to chance rather than character.

Where Do We Find Our Ever-Returning and Indispensible Wants Satisfied . . . ?

Founded in 1830 by the publisher Louis Godey, *Godey's Lady's Book* did not find its true voice until Sarah Josepha Hale became its editor in 1837. She edited the magazine until 1877, retiring at the age of ninety. Under Hale's direction, the women's magazine thrived, reaching 150,000 subscribers by midcentury. Under the direction of "The Lady Editor" (Hale's preferred title), *Godey's* included departments devoted to fashion, beauty and health, architecture and home decoration, cooking, and gardening. A strong and consistent advocate for feminine domesticity and piety, Hale also sought to provide her readers with an education appropriate to their roles as wives and mothers. In addition to sentimental and didactic fiction, the magazine sought to publish literary works of high quality—especially those by American authors. Although the passage here is by Goethe, the German author's sentiments reflect Hale's own beliefs about the importance of woman's domestic role and its service to both family and nation.

Women often complain that men are unjust towards their sex, in withholding from them higher mental culture, and in not allowing them full access to the sciences, thus Keeping them down to mere household duties, and to the government of the domestic circle. It is, however, unjust that man, on this account, should be the subject of complaint. For has he not placed his wife in the highest and holiest position she can occupy when he places her at the head of his domestic relations, and intrusts to her the government of his household? When a man is harassed by external duties and relations, when anxiously employed in procuring the means of subsistence, and when he even takes part in the government of the state—in all these conditions of life he is dependent on circumstances, and can scarcely be said to govern anything, but is often reduced to the necessity of acting from motives of *policy*, when he would gladly act from his own rational convictions—to conceal his real principles when he would delight to act frankly and openly; and even to act out the suggestions of fallacy and falsehood, when he would gladly act from sincerity and uprightness. To all this the man, in his external life in the world, is subject, and at the same time rarely attains the end for which he labors, but loses that harmony with himself, in which, nevertheless, the true ends and the true enjoyment of life consist. Whereas, the prudent woman reigns in her family circle, making happiness and every virtue possible, and spreading harmony and peace through her domain. What is the highest happiness of man, but to carry out what he knows to be right and good, and to have full control over the means to this end? And where are our dearest and inmost ends in life, but in the household? Where do we find our ever-returning and indispensable wants satisfied,

THE SPHERE OF WOMAN.

Figure 1.6. "The Sphere of Woman" (1850; courtesy of the American Antiquarian Society) accompanied the passage by Goethe in *Godey's Lady's Book*. Celebrating familial affection and character formation, it illustrates woman's role in overseeing the refined setting and appropriate leisure of domestic life. The scene is peaceful and relationships harmonious, with both femininity and literacy at the center; even the dog seems to be participating.

but in the beloved spot where we rise up and lie down? What regular activity is required to carry out this ever-returning order of things. To how few men is it granted to return regularly like a star, and to preside both over the day and the night! But the woman who arranges her household, forms her domestic plans, watches over the economy of her house, and wisely dispenses her means, spreads harmony, love, and peace throughout the circle, and makes her husband, whom she loves, a happy prince over the happiest domain. Her attention gathers all the knowledge she requires, and her activity knows how to employ it. She is dependent on nothing, save the love and attachment of her husband, for whom she procures true independence—that which is internal and domestic. That which his labor has acquired, he sees properly secured and employed. Thus, in a spirit of true independence, he can devote his energies to great objects—and become to the state (by promoting its prosperity) what his wife is to the household over which she presides.

Source: "The Sphere of Woman, Translated from the German of Goethe," *Godey's Lady's Book*, March 1850.

Making a Little World of the Family Home

In 1848, Andrew Jackson Downing published an article titled "On the Moral Influence of Good Houses." The title is an ideal encapsulation of the landscape architect's beliefs. For Downing, "good houses" accommodated single families in rural settings, reflected their functions, and used materials and ornamentation honestly. These qualities were the basis of beauty, which, in turn, uplifted the morality of individual homeowners and the nation more broadly. His plans called special attention to design features marking the separation of domestic and public spaces— doorways, porches, and bay windows. In *The Architecture of Country Houses*, excerpted here, Downing sought to make "good houses" available to Americans of varied classes by including drawings, floor plans, building directions, and estimated construction costs for cottages, farmhouses, and villas in varied architectural styles.

There are three excellent reasons why my countrymen should have good houses.

The first is, because a good house (and by this I mean a fitting, tasteful, and significant dwelling) is a powerful means of civilization. A nation, whose rural population is content to live in mean huts and miserable hovels, is certain to be behind its neighbors in education, the arts, and all that makes up the external signs of progress. With the perception of proportion, symmetry, order, and beauty, awakens the desire for possession, and with them comes that refinement of manners which distinguishes a civilized from coarse and brutal people. So long as men are forced to dwell in log huts and follow a hunter's life, we must not be surprised at lynch law and the use of the bowie knife. But, when smiling lawns and tasteful cottages begin to embellish a country, we know that order and culture are established. And, as the first incentive towards this change is awakened in the minds of most men by the perception of beauty and superiority in external objects, it must follow that the interest manifested in the Rural Architecture of a country like this, has much to do with the progress of its civilization.

The second reason is, because the *individual home* has a great social value for a people. Whatever new systems may be needed for the regeneration of an old and enfeebled nation, we are persuaded that, in America, not only is the distinct family the best social form, but those elementary forces which give rise to the highest genius and the finest character may, for the most part, be traced back to the farm-house and the rural cottage. It is the solitude and freedom of the family home in the country which constantly preserves the purity of the nation, and invigorates its intellectual powers. The battle of life, carried on in cities, gives a sharper edge to the weapon of character, but its temper is, for the most part, fixed amid those communings with nature and the family, where individuality takes its most natural and strongest development.

The third reason is, because there is a moral influence in a country home—when, among an educated, truthful, and refined people, it is an echo of their character—which is more powerful than any mere oral teachings of virtue and morality. That family, whose religion lies away from its threshold, will show but slender results from the best teachings, compared with another where the family hearth is made a central point of the Beautiful and the Good. And much of that feverish unrest and want of balance between the desire and the fulfilment of life, is calmed and adjusted by the pursuit of tastes which result in making a little world of the family home, where truthfulness, beauty, and order have the largest dominion.

The mere sentiment of home, with its thousand associations, has, like a strong anchor, saved many a man from shipwreck in the storms of life. How much the moral influence of that sentiment may be increased, by making the home all that it should be, and how much an attachment is strengthened by every external sign of beauty that awakens love in the young, are so well understood, that they need no demonstration here.

All to which the heart can attach itself in youth, and the memory linger fondly over in riper years, contributes largely to our stock of happiness, and to the elevation of the moral character. For this reason, the condition of the family home—in this country where every man may have a home—should be raised, till it shall symbolize the best character and pursuits, and the dearest affections and enjoyments of social life. . . .

It is, therefore, as clear as noonday, that cottages of this class should be arranged with a different view, both as regards utility and beauty, from either farm-houses or villas. An industrious man, who earns his bread by daily exertions, and lives in a snug and economical little home in the suburbs of a town, has very different wants from the farmer, whose accommodation must be plain but more spacious; or the man of easy income, who builds a villa as much to gratify his taste, as to serve the useful purposes of a dwelling.

We would gladly enforce this point in the outset, because it is but too plainly demonstrated that many of the worst failures in cottages all over the country, have arisen from a want of appreciation of *truthfulness of character* in Rural Architecture. Any intrinsic difference between the cottage, the farm-house, or the villa, between a dwelling for one family of simple habits and limited means, and another, whose tastes and habits of life are as complex as their means are more abundant, seems to be entirely unrecognized. The cottage is not made to express, as much as possible, the simplicity of cottage life, joined with the greatest comfort, intelligence, and taste of which that life is capable, but to imitate as closely as cheap and flimsy materials and a few hundred dollars will permit, the style and elaborate ornament of the villa, with its expenditure of thousands. . . .

All ornaments which are not simple, and cannot be executed in a substantial and appropriate manner, should be at once rejected; all flimsy and meager decorations which have a pasteboard effect, are as unworthy of, and unbecoming for the house of him who understands the true beauty of a cottage life, as glass breastpins or gilt-pewter spoons would be for his personal ornaments or family service of plate.

As much taste, as much beauty, as can be combined with the comparatively simple habits of cottage life, are truly admirable and delightful in a cottage. But everything beyond this, everything only imitated, everything that is false, forced or foreign to the real feelings or intelligence of the inmates, is not worthy of the least approbation in a cottage.

We do not mean by this to say that it is impossible to build a highly ornamented cottage which shall be in good taste—what novel writers delight to call "a perfect bijou of a house." The thing is quite possible; but it must either be a cottage as a plaything for wealthy people, not for them to live in, or it must be a villa disguised in cottage form, and not a true cottage; that is to say, a small house for a simple manner of living. You may cover such a small house with very beautiful ornamental work if you please, but its beauty will not be satisfactory to the reason, because it is not expressive of the life of its inmates, and because, therefore, it is destitute of truthfulness or significance; and the human mind is so constituted, that the beautiful must overlay the true, to give permanent satisfaction.

Admitting the justness of this proposition, we may state it as the highest principle in designing or building a cottage, that it should be truthful, that is, it should clearly express the modesty and simplicity of cottage life. Hence, not only should the cottage aim to look like a cottage, but it should avoid all pretension to what it cannot honestly and faithfully be. And as its object is first utility, and then beauty, the useful should never be sacrificed to the ornamental, but the latter should more obviously be connected with, and grow out of the former, in a cottage than in a more elaborate dwelling.

Among the first principles of utility in building or designing a cottage, we may state the following:

The principal entrance or front door should never open directly into an apartment of any kind, but always into a porch, lobby, or entry of some kind. Such a passage not only protects the apartment against sudden draughts of air, but it also protects the privacy and dignity of the inmates.

The roof should always be steep enough to carry off the snow freely, and there should be means of ventilation provided, in order to secure comfort in the upper sleeping apartments.

The level of the first floor should never be less than one foot above the level of the surrounding surface of the ground, to secure dryness.

In all small cottages the kitchen should always be on the first floor, because, in such dwellings, the kitchen must be kept under the eye of the mistress. The only exception to this would be in cases where the cost of additional service, and the inconvenience of ascending and descending stairs are of less consequence than the additional room gained at a certain first cost in building.

In all cottages constructed of brick or stone (when the walls are not built hollow), the inside (lath and plaster) walls should be "firred off," to prevent dampness.

In all cottages built of wood, in the colder portions of the country, there should either be a double weather-boarding, as is common in New England, or the space between the weatherboarding and the inside should be "filled in" with cheap brick, as is common in the Middle States. Or, when the latter is too expensive, unburnt bricks, of clay and straw, may be used instead. The warmth of the cottage in winter and its coolness in summer are so greatly increased by this trifling additional cost, that it should never be neglected in the Northern States. In endeavoring to give beauty to cottages, the following principles must be remembered:

First, that, as beauty of outline (absolute beauty) belongs to the simplest as well as to the most complex outlines, where beauty of decoration or ornamental members does not agree with simplicity, the former is mainly and especially to be employed in cottage architecture. Hence regularity, uniformity, proportion, symmetry, are beauties of which every cottage is capable, because they are entirely consistent with the simple forms of the cottage, while irregularity and variety are usually possible, with good effect, in a dwelling of larger size, and consisting of a great number of parts. Small cottages can scarcely be very irregular in form and outline, unless they are built in highly picturesque situations, such as a mountain-valley, or a wooded glen, when they form part of the irregular whole about them, rather than single objects, as is usually the case.

As a cottage may have all the beauty which results from proportion and symmetry, without adding a farthing to its cost, and without detracting in the least from its simplicity and truthfulness, it is evident that these two elements should be considered before any ornaments are introduced. Not only should the general outlines be well proportioned and symmetrical, but also the forms of all the smaller portions—such as doors, windows, chimneys, etc.

When the means of the builder enable him to go beyond these simple beauties of form, his first thought, on elevating the expression of the cottage, should be to add ornament to the most important parts of the dwelling. These are the entrance door, the principal windows, the gables, and the chimneys. The front door and the principal or first floor windows should be recognized as something more than mere openings, by lintels, hoods, or borders (dressings); the gables by being very simply moulded or bracketed about the junction with the roof; the chimneys, by a pleasing form or simple ornaments, or merely by having the usual clumsy mass lightened and separated into parts.

After this, the next step is to add something to the expression of domestic enjoyment in cottage life—such as a simple porch, or veranda, or simple bay-window. A much higher character is conferred on a simple cottage by a *veranda* than by a highly ornamented gable, because one indicates the constant means of enjoyment for the inmates—something in their daily life besides ministering to the necessities—while a more ornamental verge-board shows something, the beauty of which is not so directly connected with the life of the owner of the cottage, and which is therefore less expressive, as well as less useful.

After all these elements of beauty are attained in the cottage (in any style of architecture), one ought to pause before attempting much more ornament or architectural decoration. Beyond this it is difficult to go without endangering simplicity, and it is therefore difficult to lay down any other rules than the following:

Never introduce in a cottage any elaborate or complex ornament (however beautiful intrinsically or in higher architecture) which is not entirely consistent with that simple, truthful character which is the greatest source of pleasure in Cottage Architecture.

Never attempt any ornamental portions in a cottage, which cannot be executed in a substantial and proper manner, so that the effect of beauty of design may not be weakened by imperfect execution or flimsy materials.

As the effect of Rural Architecture is never a thing to be considered wholly by itself, but, on the contrary, as it always depends partly upon, and is associated with, rural scenery, trees, shrubbery, and vines, we should not, as many architects do, wholly overlook the aid of such accessories. Cottage Architecture, especially, borrows the most winning and

Accommodation.—This is a simple, economical, and comfortable dwelling, without pretensions either to ornament or style. It contains an entrance lobby, *a*; kitchen, *b*; back kitchen, *c*; children's bed-room, *d*; bed-room for the father and mother, and the infant children, *e*; tool-house, *f*; pantry, *g*; place for fuel, *h*; privy, *i*; cow-house, *k*; and dairy, *l*. There is a yard behind the house containing a pig-sty and the manure well. This yard is entered from the back kitchen, *c*; and also by doors in its boundary fence, *m*.

Construction.—The walls may be of stone, brick, or earth; the two former materials will not only be found more suitable in reality, but more satisfactory to the eye; for walls of earth, when not white-washed, have always a mean appearance, from the inferiority of the material; and when whitewashed, this meanness, though concealed, is still known to exist; for no building was ever whitewashed, but for the purpose of concealing something, and every one must feel, with Wood, that the grandeur or the beauty of any building is never heightened by this operation. " The world in general," says this philosophical artist, " is exceedingly unwilling to acknowledge beauty of form when the material is bad; and, on the other hand, where the materials are good, it is ready to praise the form also; the one is a much more obvious and indisputable merit than the other." (*Letters,* &c., vol. ii. p. 96.) Where white-washing, or lime-washing, a building, with any color, contributes to the preservation of the wall, it is justifiable; but no genuine lover of truth will

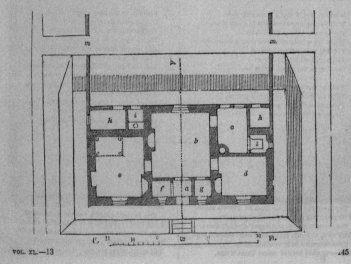

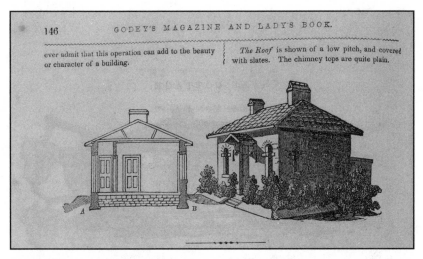

Figures 1.7a and 1.7b. Plans for "A Cheap Cottage" (*Godey's Lady's Book*, 1850; courtesy of the American Antiquarian Society) appeared as part of "Godey's Model Cottages," a regular feature introduced in 1846. At the time, publishing house plans in a magazine was an innovation, and their inclusion in *Godey's* reflected Sarah Hale's multifaceted commitment to fostering domesticity in her female readers. As in Downing's plans, those depicted here emphasize the simplicity and honesty of the materials employed as well as the home's separation from the public world.

captivating expression from foliage. If we analyze the charm of a large part of the rural cottages of England—the finest in the world—we shall find, that strip them of the wealth of flowing vines that adorn them, and their peculiar poetry and feeling have more than half departed. And, since no architectural decorations, however beautiful or costly, can give the same charm of truthful decoration to a cottage, as flowering vines and creepers, we shall, in another page, point out the most hardy, valuable, and beautiful species for this purpose.

Source: Andrew Jackson Downing, *The Architecture of Country Houses: Including Designs for Cottages, Farmhouses, and Villas, with Remarks on Interiors, Furniture, and the Best Modes of Warming and Ventilating* (New York: D. Appleton, 1850).

All This Ellen Did with the Zeal That Love Gives

Susan Warner's *The Wide, Wide World* was published in December 1850 to unprecedented sales. The sentimental novel follows the growth and devel-

opment of Ellen Montgomery. Ellen is ten years old when she learns that she will be left behind while her parents travel to Europe for the sake of her mother's health. Neither Mrs. Montgomery nor Ellen has the power to change these plans, and each understands that she will never see the other again. In the excerpt here, Ellen struggles to regain her composure while her mother tries to teach her Christian submission—a challenge Ellen will face repeatedly as she moves into the world beyond her mother's protective influence. Warner emphasizes the emotional content of Ellen's domestic tasks and Mrs. Montgomery's role as moral guide. Later in the novel, Ellen will live with her Aunt Fortune, a masterful housekeeper who labors without affection, underscoring all Ellen has lost and testing her ability to learn her mother's last lesson.

Ellen had plenty of faults, but amidst them all love to her mother was the strongest feeling her heart knew. It had power enough now to move her as nothing else could have done; and exerting all her self-command, of which she had sometimes a good deal, she *did* calm herself; ceased sobbing; wiped her eyes; arose from her crouching posture, and seating herself on the sofa by her mother, and laying her head on her bosom, she listened quietly to all the soothing words and cheering considerations with which Mrs. Montgomery endeavoured to lead her to take a more hopeful view of the subject. All she could urge, however, had but very partial success, though the conversation was prolonged far into the evening. Ellen said little, and did not weep any more; but in secret her heart refused consolation.

Long before this the servant had brought in the tea-things. Nobody regarded it at the time, but the little kettle hissing away on the fire now by chance attracted Ellen's attention, and she suddenly recollected her mother had had no tea. To make her mother's tea was Ellen's regular business. She treated it as a very grave affair, and loved it as one of the pleasantest in the course of the day. She used in the first place to make sure that the kettle had really boiled; then she carefully poured some water into the tea-pot and rinsed it, both to make it clean and to make it hot; then she knew exactly how much tea to put into the tiny little tea-pot, which was just big enough to hold two cups of tea, and having poured a very little boiling water to it, she used to set it by the side of the fire while she made half a slice of toast. How careful Ellen was about that toast! The bread must not be cut too thick, nor too thin; the fire must, if possible, burn clear and bright, and she herself held the bread on a fork, just at the right distance from the coals to get nicely browned without burning. When this was done to her satisfaction (and if the first piece failed she would take another), she filled up the little tea-pot from the boiling kettle, and proceeded to make a cup of tea. She knew, and was very careful to put in, just the quantity of milk and sugar that her mother liked; and then she used to carry the tea and toast on a little tray to her mother's side, and very often held it there for her while she ate. All this Ellen did with the zeal that love gives, and though the same thing was to be gone over every night of the year, she was never wearied. It was a real pleasure; she had the greatest satisfaction in seeing that the little her mother could eat was prepared for her in the nicest possible manner; she knew her hands made it taste better; her mother often said so.

But this evening other thoughts had driven this important business quite out of poor Ellen's mind. Now, however, when her eyes fell upon the little kettle, she recollected her mother had not had her tea, and must want it very much; and silently slipping off the sofa, she set about getting it as usual. There was no doubt this time whether the kettle boiled or no; it had been hissing for an hour and more, calling as loud as it could to somebody to come and make the tea. So Ellen made it, and then began the toast. But she began to think, too, as she watched it, how few more times she would be able to do so,—how soon her pleasant tea-makings would be over,—and the desolate feeling of separation began to come upon her before the time. These thoughts were too much for poor Ellen; the thick tears gathered so fast she could not see what she was doing; and she had no more than just turned the slice of bread on the fork when the sickness of heart quite overcame her; she could not go on. Toast and fork and all dropped from her hand into the ashes; and rushing to her mother's side, who was now lying down again, and throwing herself upon her, she burst into another fit of sorrow; not so violent as the former, but with a touch of hopelessness in it which went yet more to her mother's heart. Passion in the first said, "I cannot;" despair now seemed to say, "I must."

But Mrs. Montgomery was too exhausted to either share or soothe Ellen's agitation. She lay in suffering silence; till after some time she said faintly, "Ellen, my love, I cannot bear this much longer."

Ellen was immediately brought to herself by these words. She arose, sorry and ashamed that she should have given occasion for them; and tenderly kissing her mother, assured her most sincerely and resolutely that she would not do so again. In a few minutes she was calm enough to finish making the tea, and having toasted another piece of bread, she brought it to her mother. Mrs. Montgomery swallowed a cup of tea, but no toast could be eaten that night.

Both remained silent and quiet after this, till the clock struck ten. "You had better go to bed, my daughter," said Mrs. Montgomery.

"I will, mamma."

"Do you think you can read me a little before you go?"

"Yes, indeed, mamma;" and Ellen brought the book: "where shall I read?"

"The twenty-third psalm."

Ellen began it, and went through it steadily and slowly though her voice quavered a little.

"'The Lord is my shepherd, I shall not want.

"'He maketh me to lie down in green pastures: He leadeth me beside the still waters.

"'He restoreth my soul: He leadeth me in the paths of righteousness for His name's sake.

"'Yea, though I walk through the valley of the shadow of death, I will fear no evil; for Thou art with me; thy rod and thy staff they comfort me.

"'Thou preparest a table before me in the presence of mine enemies: Thou anointest my head with oil; my cup runneth over.

"'Surely goodness and mercy shall follow me all the days of my life; and I will dwell in the house of the Lord for ever.'"

Long before she had finished Ellen's eyes were full, and her heart too. "If I only could feel these words as mamma does!" she said to herself. She did not dare look up till the traces of tears had passed away; then she saw that her mother was asleep. Those first sweet words had fallen like balm upon the sore heart; and mind and body had instantly found rest together.

Ellen breathed the lightest possible kiss upon her forehead, and stole quietly out of the room to her own little bed.

Source: Susan Warner (pseud. Elizabeth Wetherell), *The Wide, Wide World* (1850; repr., New York: Putnam, 1853).

I Never Was a Very Forward Old Fellow

Herman Melville is not usually associated with domestic fiction, but his humorous "I and My Chimney" suggests what the new domestic ideal might have meant to some men. Melville's protagonist resists the cultural redefinition and spatial reorganization of home as a woman's space committed to moral uplift and refined tastes. Here home is a place of shelter and comfort as well as a site of male camaraderie in the form of an unusually large and awkwardly shaped center chimney, which like the protagonist is behind the times and enjoys smoking. Melville's narrator defends his chimney against his wife's plans for a new entrance hall, a popular design element marking the transition from public to domestic space. By giving the chimney a human personality, Melville both echoes and mocks his contemporaries' penchant for giving architectural features moral qualities.

I and my chimney, two grey-headed old smokers, reside in the country. We are, I may say, old settlers here; particularly my old chimney, which settles more and more every day.

Though I always say, *I and My Chimney*, as Cardinal Wolsey used to say, "*I and My King*," yet this egotistic way of speaking, wherein I take precedence of my chimney, is hereby borne out by the facts; in everything, except the above phrase, my chimney taking precedence of me.

Within thirty feet of the turf-sided road, my chimney—a huge, corpulent old Harry VIII of a chimney—rises full in front of me and all my possessions. Standing well up a hillside, my chimney, like Lord Rosse's monster telescope, swung vertical to hit the meridian moon, is the first object to greet the approaching traveler's eye, nor is it the last which the sun salutes. My chimney, too, is before me in receiving the first-fruits of the seasons. The snow is on its head ere on my hat; and every spring, as in a hollow beech tree, the first swallows build their nests in it.

But it is within doors that the pre-eminence of my chimney is most manifest. When in the rear room, set apart for that object, I stand to receive my guests (who, by the way call more, I suspect, to see my chimney than me) I then stand, not so much before, as, strictly speaking, behind my chimney, which is, indeed, the true host. Not that I demur. In the presence of my betters, I hope I know my place.

From this habitual precedence of my chimney over me, some even think that I have got into a sad rearward way altogether; in short, from standing behind my old-fashioned chimney so much, I have got to be quite behind the age too, as well as running behindhand in everything else. But to tell the truth, I never was a very forward old fellow, nor what my farming neighbors call a forehanded one. Indeed, those rumors about my behindhandedness are so far correct, that I have an odd sauntering way with me sometimes of going about with my hands behind my back. As for my belonging to the rear-guard in general, certain it is, I bring up the rear of my chimney—which, by the way, is this moment before me—and that, too, both in fancy and fact. In brief, my chimney is my superior; my superior, too, in that humbly bowing over with shovel and tongs, I much minister to it; yet never does it minister, or incline over to me; but, if anything, in its settlings, rather leans the other way.

My chimney is grand seignior here—the one great domineering object, not more of the landscape, than of the house; all the rest of which house, in each architectural arrangement, as may shortly appear, is, in the most marked manner, accommodated, not to my wants, but to my chimney's, which, among other things, has the centre of the house to himself, leaving but the odd holes and corners to me.

But I and my chimney must explain; and as we are both rather obese, we may have to expatiate.

In those houses which are strictly double houses—that is, where the hall is in the middle—the fireplaces usually are on opposite sides; so that while one member of the household is warming himself at a fire built into a recess of the north wall, say another member, the former's own brother, perhaps, may be holding his feet to the blaze before a hearth in the south wall—the two thus fairly sitting back to back. Is this well? Be it put to any man who has a proper fraternal feeling. Has it not a sort of sulky appearance? But very probably this style of chimney building originated with some architect afflicted with a quarrelsome family.

Then again, almost every modern fireplace has its separate flue—separate throughout, from hearth to chimney-top. At least such an arrangement is deemed desirable. Does not this look egotistical, selfish? But still more, all these separate flues, instead of having independent masonry establishments of their own, or instead of being grouped together in one federal stock in the middle of the house—instead of this, I say, each flue is surreptitiously honey-combed into the walls; so that these last are here and there, or indeed almost anywhere, treacherously hollow, and, in consequence, more or less weak. Of course, the main reason of this style of chimney building is to economize room. In cities, where lots are sold by the inch, small space is to spare for a chimney constructed on magnanimous principles; and, as with most thin men, who are generally tall, so with such houses, what is lacking in breadth, · must be made up in height. This remark holds true even with regard to many very stylish abodes, built by the most stylish of gentlemen. And yet, when that stylish gentleman, Louis le Grand of France, would build a palace for his lady, friend, Madame de Maintenon, he built it but one story high—in fact in the cottage style. But then, how uncommonly quadrangular, spacious, and broad—horizontal acres, not vertical ones. Such is the palace, which, in all its one-storied magnificence of Languedoc marble, in the garden of Versailles, still remains to this day. Any man can buy a square foot of land and plant a liberty-pole on it; but it takes a king to set apart whole acres for a grand triannon [sic]. . . .

But stately as is the chimney—yea, grand high altar as it is, right worthy for the celebration of high mass before the Pope of Rome, and all his cardinals—yet what is there perfect in this world? Caius Julius Caesar, had he not been so inordinately great, they say that Brutus, Cassius, Antony, and the rest, had been greater. My chimney, were it not so mighty in its magnitude, my chambers had been larger. How often has my wife ruefully told me, that my chimney, like the English aristocracy, casts a contracting shade all round it. She avers that endless domestic inconveniences arise—more particularly from the chimney's stubborn central locality. The grand objection with her is, that it stands midway in the place where a fine entrance-hall ought to be. In truth, there is no hall whatever to the house—nothing but a sort of square landing-place, as you enter from the wide front door. A roomy enough landing-place, I admit, but not attaining to the dignity of a hall. Now, as the front door is precisely in the middle of the front of the house, inwards it faces the chimney. In fact, the opposite wall of the landing-place is formed solely by the chimney; and hence-owing to the gradual tapering of the chimney—is a little less than twelve feet in width. Climbing the chimney in this part, is the principal staircase—which, by three abrupt turns, and three minor landing-places, mounts to the second floor, where, over the front door, runs a sort of narrow gallery, something less than twelve feet long, leading to chambers on either hand. This gallery, of course, is railed; and so, looking down upon the stairs, and all those landing-places together, with the main one at bottom, resembles not a little a balcony for musicians, in some jolly old abode, in times Elizabethan. Shall I tell a weakness? I cherish the cobwebs there, and many a time arrest Biddy in the act of brushing them with her broom, and have many a quarrel with my wife and daughters about it. . . .

The truth is, my wife, like all the rest of the world, cares not a fig for philosophical jabber. In dearth of other philosophical companionship, I and my chimney have to smoke and philosophize together. And sitting up so late as we do at it, a mighty smoke it is that we two smoky old philosophers make.

But my spouse, who likes the smoke of my tobacco as little as she does that of the soot, carries on her war against both. I live in continual dread lest, like the golden bowl, the pipes of me and my chimney shall yet be broken. To stay that mad project of my wife's, naught answers. Or, rather, she herself is incessantly answering, incessantly besetting me with her terrible alacrity for improvement, which is a softer name for destruction. Scarce a day I do not find her with her tape-measure, measuring for her grand hall, while Anna holds a yardstick on one side, and Julia looks approvingly on from the other. Mysterious intimations appear in the nearest village paper, signed "Claude," to the effect that a certain structure, standing on a certain hill, is a sad blemish to an otherwise lovely landscape. Anonymous letters arrive, threatening me with I know not what, unless I remove my chimney. Is it my wife, too, or who, that sets up the neighbors to badgering me on the same subject, and hinting to me that my chimney, like a huge elm, absorbs all moisture from my garden? At night, also, my wife will start as from sleep, professing to hear ghostly noises from the secret closet. Assailed on all sides, and in all ways, small peace have I and my chimney.

Were it not for the baggage, we would together pack up and remove from the country.

What narrow escapes have been ours! Once I found in a drawer a whole portfolio of plans and estimates. Another time, upon returning after a day's absence, I discovered my wife standing before the chimney in earnest conversation with a person whom I at once recognized as a meddlesome architectural reformer, who, because he had no gift for putting up anything was ever intent upon pulling them down; in various parts of the country having prevailed upon half-witted old folks to destroy their old-fashioned houses, particularly the chimneys.

But worst of all was, that time I unexpectedly returned at early morning from a visit to the city, and upon approaching the house, narrowly escaped three brickbats which fell, from high aloft, at my feet. Glancing up, what was my horror to see three savages, in blue jean overalls in the very act of commencing the long-threatened attack. Aye, indeed, thinking of those three brickbats, I and my chimney have had narrow escapes.

It is now some seven years since I have stirred from my home. My city friends all wonder why I don't come to see them, as in former times. They think I am getting sour and unsocial. Some say that I have become a sort of mossy old misanthrope, while all the time the fact is, I am simply standing guard over my mossy old chimney; for it is resolved between me and my chimney, that I and my chimney will never surrender.

Source: Herman Melville, "I and My Chimney," *Putnam's Monthly Magazine*, March 1856.

2

The Persistence of Domestic Labor

Despite the celebration of home's isolation from the public world of paid labor and commerce, the two realms remained intertwined. This was true for poor, working-class and middle-class women who took in boarders and for the men and women who, like the Lowell mill girls or journalist Nellie Bly in this chapter, lived in boarding houses. Even in private single-family homes of the middle class, domestic chores did not take care of themselves simply because their inhabitants strove to be moral or refined—a reality Louisa May Alcott depicts with good humor in *Little Women*.

After the emergence of the new domestic ideal, middle-class women continued to cook, sew, and clean for their families, often beside hired domestic servants—a juxtaposition that revealed the economic nature of women's domestic labor and transformed housewives into employers. Catharine Beecher's letters to servants reframe domestic service as moral work, but the writings of Clarissa Packard and Lizzie Goodenough reveal that the relationship between mistress and servant, even when tempered by affection, remained at heart an economic one. In short, nineteenth-century Americans lived with inconsistencies between their values and their experiences of home life.

Although domestic labor persisted in the age of the moral home, its meaning was altered by the new ideal, ultimately serving as a marker of class and racial difference. Middle-class culture (if not reality) deemphasized women's labor and, in turn, viewed women who worked for wages as morally suspect. Likewise, homes that failed to conform to the rising standards of privacy and refinement came to be seen as moral problems—threats to proper family life, values, and social order. Ironically then, the same values that imagined middle-class homes as more private transformed poor and working-class homes into public concerns.

Collapsing morality and economics, benevolent reformers such as Ward Stafford believed that Christian restraint and conduct would not only ease the sufferings of poverty but eliminate poverty by instilling proper habits among the poor. His account and Catharine Maria Sedgwick's fictional portrayal of urban poverty reveal the ways in which the poor and working class were simultaneously included and excluded from the middle-class norm of domestic privacy and refinement—expected to meet new domestic ideals and to incorporate productive labor into their homes. This same double standard was stretched so far that some slaveholders designed cabins to refine and uplift slaves while lending a moral cast to slavery itself. Solomon Northup's description of his life in the slave quarters underscores the failure of this ideal to conform to reality.

They Have Entered the Habitations of the Poor—Have Sought Out the Destitute

In the second decade of the nineteenth century, as middle-class Americans recast home as a site of moral uplift and training, they often lost sight of the economic underpinnings of home life. This was particularly evident in depictions of the urban poor that collapsed poverty and immorality. Benevolent societies, striving to distinguish between the deserving and undeserving poor, now sent "friendly visitors" into urban slums: they arrived armed with Bibles and tracts rather than food and firewood. The Reverend Ward Stafford's account reveals how such efforts opened up poor neighborhoods and homes to middle-class men and women intent on uplift. Emphasizing his belief that Christian teaching would foster the sobriety, industriousness, and morality needed to avoid poverty, he also highlights the ways in which too much domestic privacy exacerbated the problems of the urban poor.

It is about nine months since I first engaged in the service of the Society. Having had some previous knowledge of the state of the poor, and being fully persuaded, that hundreds of families were destitute of the Bible, as well as all other means of religious instruction, I determined to devote a considerable part of my time to exploring sections of the city, for the purpose of obtaining further information concerning them, of distributing Bibles and Tracts, and of promoting their spiritual welfare in other ways. By this means, I have had opportunity to address, on the most important subjects of religion, thousands, who had never before seen a minister within their dwellings, and many of whom had never seen one in the house of God. . . .

A great proportion of the people are crowded together, as we have seen, from four to twelve families in a house, often two or three in a room, and those of all colours; are deplorably ignorant and destitute of all the means of grace, and consequently are not under the restraining influence of religion. Such is the natural corruption of the human heart, such the ease with which the vile passions are kindled into a flame, and the whole course of nature set on fire of hell, that the simple fact, that people live together in the manner described, and without the restraints of religion, is strong evidence that they are immoral. But we have other evidence of this painful, this humiliating truth; a mass of evidence, but a small portion of which can be exhibited in this place. . . .

The value of the Bible is discovered by experiment. We have made this discovery; and if we neglect to make it known to our fellow-men, "how dwelleth the love of God in us?" Let it be remembered, that where the Bible is known and believed to be the word of God, it is often, and if its humbling truths come home with power to the conscience, is always, hated. It is the sun of the moral world. It is that light to which natural man will not come, "lest their deeds should be reproved." We must carry it to them; we must cause it to shine in the dark abodes. If they flee from it into a cavern more dark, we must follow them; till there shall be no place in the city or in the world to which they can retreat. When this is done, we shall have performed our duty, in relation to distributing Bibles, and we may then hope that God, by his spirit will open the eyes of the understanding, and purify the heart, so that men shall not only see but love that light, and rejoice in it.* . . .

Such a system would directly promote the temporal, and in that way indirectly, the spiritual welfare of the poor. . . . A respectable lady, a few weeks ago, went into the house of a poor neighbour, and found, to her

---

* The managers and members of the Female Bible Society, we rejoice to state, have actually commenced the work. Not satisfied with aiding, by their funds and approbation, the parent and other Bible institutions, nor with purchasing Bibles, and depositing them in the usual manner, they have entered the habitations of the poor—have sought out the destitute, and, with their own hands, have given them the word of life. We trust their truly christian example will be extensively followed, not only in this, but in other places.

great surprise, a woman lying sick, and in the cradle by her side, the remains of a lovely child. On inquiry she learned, that the woman had
been reduced so low, that she could not go out to obtain relief, or make
known her situation. The child had died with hunger, and would, doubt-
less, soon have been followed by its mother to the world of spirits, had it
not been for this providential discovery. Those who are acquainted with
the circumstances of the poor, know that occurrences of the same general nature are not uncommon. With such facts in view, who will pretend that some system like the one proposed, is not indispensible? It
would not only prevent the poor from suffering and dying for want of
timely aid, but it would prevent the necessity of that aid. To manage their
temporal concerns to advantage, many need information, advice, and
direction, which, without the least difficulty, might be given by a kind
and judicious neighbor. This remark is more especially applicable to
strangers, who are unacquainted with the customs of the city. In consequence of disappointment or misfortune, many are disheartened, and
settle down into a state of gloom and sloth, which are the precursors of
personal and family vice, disgrace, and ruin. This might frequently be
prevented, should some friend take them by the hand, assist them in
finding employment, and encourage them to make every effort. Their
characters being known, there would be no difficulty in obtaining employment, and other necessary aid, for the respectable poor. But at present they are mixed with the vicious, are regarded in the same light, and
are treated in the same manner. . . .

. . . Let every man's character and conduct be known to the moral and
pious, and a change in society will be effected; for there are but few, who
are insensible to the opinion of their fellow men, however they may dis-
regard the command of God. The very sight of the moral and the pious
is a check to the wicked. Should respectable persons simply pass through
particular streets every day, and look at those who now exhibit in those
streets all the degradation of their character, it would soon cause them
to hide their heads. The voice of the pious wakes the internal monitor,
and their presence encourages him to do his duty. Christians may greatly
promote the spiritual welfare of the poor, by holding small meetings
among them, for the purpose of prayer and the reading of scriptures.
The exertions of such associations would induce many to attend public
worship, particularly those who are not grossly vicious, and strangers

who have been accustomed to attend previous to their residence in the city. When they first come, they generally wander from place to place. Having no seat of their own, and being frequently unable to find one, it becomes unpleasant. They occasionally stay at home; it agrees with the practice of many around them; it gratifies the natural heart, and soon, instead of the old and good habit, a new and bad one is formed. This is true not merely of the poorer class of people, but also of a large class in comfortable circumstances. . . .

. . . With such a prospect before him, what christian will not wrestle day and night at the throne of grace? What christian will not consecrate his property, his time, his talents, his life, to this glorious work? . . . What christian is there who cannot devote two hours a week, or two hours out of one hundred and sixty-eight, in "*going about* doing good," directly to his fellow-men? Will it be said, that those in the humble walks of life cannot engage in this work? Let me ask, what christian is so humble, so ignorant, so poor, that he cannot give to a neighbour a word of good advice; set before that neighbour a holy example; or invite that neighbor to go to a sanctuary or a religious meeting; or give a Bible or a Tract, when furnished to his hands? What christian cannot pray? What child cannot give to another child a Catechism, or lead him to a Sabbath School, or to the house of God?

There is another consideration, which every one must have anticipated. In this field we have the advantage of a numerous class of christians, who will regard this work as among the domestic concerns which claim their attention. Their leisure, their characteristic sensibility, and the successful efforts which they have already made, need no remark: it is sufficient to say, that in this good work, may be employed thousands of PIOUS FEMALES.—Instead of being scattered over a wide extent of country, these people live together; and may, therefore, be approached without loss of time, and expense, and all employed may act in CONCERT.

We have reason to believe success will attend our efforts, from what is said in the word of God. The parable of the Great Supper exhibits our Saviour's view on this subject. The rich refused the invitation; but the poor, those in the highways and hedges, were brought in. Lazarus is in heaven, Dives in hell. "It is easier for a camel to go through the eye of a needle, than for a rich man to enter into the kingdom of heaven." It was among the poor that our Saviour labored, and it was the poor, "the common people," that heard him gladly. Such has been the success of the gospel among the poor in every age of the church.

Source: Ward Stafford, *New Missionary Field: A Report to the Female Missionary Society for the Poor of the City of New York, and Its Vicinity* (New York: J. Seymour, 1817).

Better, My Child, to Trust to Diligent, Skilful Hands

Published in 1836, Catharine Maria Sedgwick's *The Poor Rich Man, and the Rich Poor Man* was a popular work by the already-successful author of domestic fiction. Meant as a didactic sketch of everyday life, the story contrasts the hardworking but humble Harry and Susan Aikin with an old friend of extravagant tastes and unreliable morals. The passage here describes a domestic scene permeated by unpaid and paid labor, as child rearing, cooking, and home manufacturing take place side by side. Compare this scene with the depiction of the "Sphere of Woman" in the previous chapter. While here labor is the source of its own morality, Sedgwick makes sure the Aikins' home includes a few trappings of domestic refinement, giving them a clean carpet and closed blinds to distinguish them from the undeserving poor.

Seven years had not passed over without those precious accumulations to Aikin that constitute the poor man's wealth; for, save a conscience void of offence, there is no treasure comparable to healthy, bright, well-trained children. Our friend Harry and his wife had kept the even tenour of their way—no uncommon event had happened to them; but, as the river of life glides through a varied country, the aspect of theirs now varied from what it was when we last saw them.

The floor of the room was partly covered with a carpet, and the part visible as clean as hands could make it. It was summer, and the blinds were closed, admitting only light enough to enable the persons within to carry on their occupations. Uncle Phil is sitting by the half-opened window, with a year-old baby on his lap, telling over on its toes that charming lyric, "this pig went to market, and that pig stayed at home"—Aunt Lottie was preparing a pot of wholesome soup, which, like a judicious housewife, having boiled the day before, she was freeing from every particle of fat—a little girl, six years old, was tacking worsted binding together for Ven[e]tian blinds, whereby she got from a manufacturer (working only at odd intervals) half a dollar per week; and at the same time teaching a sister, something more than two years younger, the multiplication-table—Susan Aikin sat by, her vigilant eye seeing every thing, and her kind voice interposing, as often as the wants or claims of the children rendered her interference necessary. Her most difficult duty seemed to be to keep in due order a restless, noisy little fellow, William, the twin brother of her eldest girl, whom she was teaching to write, while at the same time she was tailoring and instructing in her art a young girl, who had just set the last stitch in a vest of the most costly material, and was holding it up for inspection; a slight anxiety, till she heard the approving word, tempering her conscious success. Susan scrutinized every part of it, every seam, button-hole, and button; and then said—

"There's not a fault in it—I could not do one better myself, Agnes."

Agnes burst into tears; Anne looked up from her work inquiringly; little Mary exclaimed, "Such a big girl cry!" Willie said, " She is not *really* crying;" and the baby stretched out its neck, and put up its lips to offer a kiss of consolation, which Agnes took, smiling through her tears, and saying, "Oh, I'm only crying because your mother has been so good to me!"

"Well," shouted Willie, "that's a funny thing to cry for!"

"That was not all, Willie," said his mother; "Agnes cries because she has been good herself."

"That's funnier yet; we never cry only when we are naughty."

Mrs. Aikin solved the riddle, and so will we, Agnes was the eldest child of a worthy and very poor neighbour of Mrs. Aikin. Her father had been disabled for some months, by falling from a building, and had recently died; her mother had lost her health from over-exertion. Agnes had an idiot sister, and two brothers too young to render the family any assistance. Mrs. Aikin, foreseeing the distress of the family after they should have exhausted the father's earnings, and knowing that Agnes was a diligent and good girl, and had been well taught plain sewing in a public school, offered to instruct her in making vests, a very profitable business to those who are skilled in it, and can command work from the first merchant tailors. There were some obstacles in the way: Agnes could only be spared from home at odd intervals, and often only at times very inconvenient to Susan Aikin; but who, as Susan said, would ever do any good in this world if they made mountains of mole hills? Those who saw her multiplied cares, her bee-like industry, would rather have said she made molehills of mountains. She always received Agnes with a smile, always found a quiet corner for her, and made leisure to attend to her. Agnes, seeing the efforts and sacrifices her kind friend made for her, set the right value upon the good she was obtaining, and performed her part with fidelity.

Many complaints are made of the low rates of women's wages—some just, no doubt; but, for the most part, they are paid according to their capacity. A well-qualified seamstress, tailoress, or milliner, can, except in very rare cases, obtain certain employment and good pay: a half-taught and careless worker must take her chance for slop work, at low wages. Susan Aikin could at all times command work from the most respectable houses, was sure of the highest wages, and incidental favours that she knew how to turn to account. "Now, Agnes, my child," she had said on the day previous to this on which we have introduced her young friend, "here is a trial vest for you; I have got leave from my employers to put it into your hands; you must set every stitch in it and, if it is done to their satisfaction, you are to have as much of their best work as you can do, which is as good as a promise of six dollars a week to you—a sure support for your poor mother, and helpless sister, and little brothers. Better, my child, to trust to diligent, skilful hands, than to widows' societies, and assistance societies, and so on; leave those for such as can get nothing better, while we use the means of independence that Providence has given us."

"But if I should fail, Mrs. Aikin?"

"Why, then there is one comfort left, we can try again; but you will not fail."

Thus stimulated and encouraged, Agnes set to work, and, as has been seen, accomplished her task, and no wonder that she shed tears of joy when it was done. Which, we would ask, was happiest—which *richest*; he who paid fifteen dollars for the vest, or she who earned the dollar by making it, and thereby cheered the hearts of the desolate, and brought comfort and light to a dreary home? or, which is happiest—*richest*; she who is lapped in luxury, and is every day seeking some new and expensive pleasure, or those who, like our friend Mrs. Aikin, in some obscure place, are using their faculties and seizing their opportunities of doing good, never to be known and praised by the world, but certainly recorded in the book of life?

Source: Catharine Maria Sedgwick, *The Poor Rich Man, and the Rich Poor Man* (New York: Harper, 1837).

WASHING ESTABLISHMENT.

AT THE
INSTITUTION FOR EMPLOYING FEMALE POOR.
No. 7 HIGH STREET—BOSTON.

☞ WASHING, IRONING AND MENDING, ☜
DONE WITH NEATNESS, PROMPTNESS & FIDELITY.

☞ *The Society is responsible for all work sent to the Institution.*☜

FOR SALE AS ABOVE
A variety of articles of Apparel and Clothing for the Poor.

Shirts made and other sewing done with neatness—Coarse Sewing
solicited for the employment of the Poor.

RATES OF WASHING.

GENTLEMEN'S CLOTHES.	CTS.	LADIES' AND CHILDREN'S	CTS.	HOUSE AND BED LINEN.	CTS.
Plain Shirts	6¼	Gowns,	6 a 150	Breakfast Cloths,	5
Full Bosomed, do.	7	Flannel do.	8 a 12½	Table Cloths,	6 a 50
Ruffled do. without plaits,	8	Night gowns and caps		Sheets, per pair	8 a 14
Do. do. with box plaits,	9	Dimoty & other skirts,	4 a 12½	Towels and Napkins,	
Do. do. with fine plaits,	12½	Linen and Stays,		per dozen,	12 a 30
Collars,	3	Plain Ruffs in stripes,	3 a 4	Blankets, per piece,	8 a 30
Cravats,	4 a 6	Worked, or Lace do.	5 a 8	Pillow Cases, per pair,	4 a 6
Stockings & Socks per pr.	4 a 6	Caps or Ruffs plaited,	10 a 25	Counterpanes,	8 a $1
Pantaloons,	8 a 16	Stockings,	4 a 6	Suits of Curtains, com-	
Pocket Handkerchiefs,	2	Pocket Handkerchiefs,	2 a 4	plete,	$1 a 3
Flannels,	4	Small children's clothes,	5 a 10		
Waistcoats,	6¼	Vandykes or Capes,	4 a 50	20 per cent added to the above	
Surplices	75			rates for Sea clothes.	

☞ *Those persons who have washing done by the quarter, will be entitled to a discount of ten per cent.
on all their payments, provided they send their clothes, or will be subject to the expense of sending for
them, and returning them. A discount also made on all bills amounting to $7 and upwards.*
☞ *Persons sending particular directions, are requested to put them in writing.*☜

Printed at W W CLAPP's Office, 4 Congress-Street.

Figure 2.1. The broadside "Washing Establishment at the Institution for Employing the Female Poor" (Boston, 1825; courtesy of the American Antiquarian Society) emphasizes the persistence of domestic labor in the lives of poor women and its ongoing connection to household economics. Benevolent reformers believed that the willingness to work for wages separated the deserving and undeserving poor by revealing or instilling "neatness, promptness, and fidelity." The Society for Employing the Female Poor encouraged middle-class women to send out their laundry at below-market rates with the knowledge that they were supporting poor women. Such work in turn required poor women, usually widows with young children, to bring additional labor into their homes, belying the middle-class ideal that home offered a respite from the marketplace.

The Perfection of Society Consists in the Division of Labour

Writing in the early 1830s, Clarissa Packard chose to tell the story of her life through her experiences with a series of domestic servants, starting from her childhood training in household labor to her running her own household as a wife and mother. Throughout she underscores the amount of domestic work she did as well as the challenges of training servants in the requisite skills. Like Lydia Maria Child, she emphasizes the usefulness of domestic work while underscoring the ways in which constant labor undermined housekeepers' abilities to be the moral caretakers of their families, as advocated by Catharine Beecher. In the concluding chapter, excerpted here, she offers a novel solution—calling for specialization and outsourcing of the varied domestic tasks usually done by middle-class housekeepers and their servants within the home.

The successor of Mrs. Sliter was Sukey Hopkins, an untamed damsel from Nantucket; and as Edward required some attendance at the office, he engaged a friend of hers, Aaron Wheeler, who had *driv her down*, to remain with us. I passed every forenoon for a month in the kitchen, to initiate her in cookery; and even after that period was obliged to be with her whenever I had guests, of course at the period when I ought to have been most unincumbered with care. I was obliged to watch the last turn of the spit, and the last bubble of the boiling gravy, and even lay the meats in their right position; for know, inexperienced reader, that a lady may as excusably stand on her own head at her table, as have her turkey or goose in an unauthorized posture. One bleak autumnal day we had company to dine; but I became so much heated with my business and anxiety as not to dream of the necessity of a fire. Just five minutes before dinner was carried in, I ran up stairs, changed my dress, and seizing a fan, descended to the drawing-room. My zeal in fanning was proportioned to the kitchen thermometer; and it was not until I detected a shiver in a lady who sat within the influence of my Æolus, as Edward prettily called a fan, that I perceived my *faux pas*.

The day after Aaron's induction into his duties, I went to Cornhill, shopping; and Edward left word with him that if a certain gentleman called, he must ask him to sit until he came. When Edward opened the door, what should he behold but Aaron, sitting with his feet on the fender, entertaining Mr. —— with the last Nantucket news!

A few evenings succeeding I invited company to tea. I was the whole morning drilling Sukey and Aaron, and as I went to make my toilet, I said, "be very careful, Aaron, that the ladies and gentlemen are all supplied with sugar and cream in their coffee." When the company had assembled, and the very last visiter, according to the old and formidable rule, had arrived and was seated, Aaron entered with his tea tray, followed by Sukey with the cream and sugar. He walked round as carefully as if he were treading on eggs. When the circuit was over, and he had reached the door, his mind seemed to misgive him; and with an anxious look, standing on tiptoe, he said, "I say, how are ye on't for sugar and cream in that corner?"

On that memorable evening a lady spilled some quince syrup on the carpet, when, to my utter dismay, Sukey set the waiter on the floor, rushed out, and brought in the mop to wipe it up.

I have inserted these lingering reminiscences in this chapter, to show that the most skillful housewifery cannot counteract the mortification and embarrassment of our present system. I took infinite pains to make my daughter useful. She was a sweet, docile girl, and at the age of eleven often made our tea, arranged the table, and assisted in handing it when we had company; but notwithstanding this early discipline, the awkward blending of lady and housewife led to countless anxieties; indeed, it requires an omnipresent eye to meet one's guests with the personal welcome they demand, while providing for their grosser wants. How many girls like Sukey have I passed months in drilling, when, just as I began to realize the effects of my care, they have taken a sudden whim and departed! How many were there whom I never *could* teach, whose inattention or willfulness rendered me miserable! How much hard labour have I performed while paying high prices for that of others! What then can be done to remedy this evil? It is the opinion of Adam Smith, and an humble housekeeper agrees with him, that the perfection of society consists in the division of labour.

Is it not monstrous that educated, intelligent women, should be obliged to give over their children to the care of servants, and pass their days in the most menial occupation? And must our lovely daughters be called from intellectual or graceful accomplishments, to associate with the vulgar inmates of the kitchen?

We have a partial system, which it appears to me might easily be carried through the whole order of social life. We have our chimney-sweeps, our wood-sawyers, our bakeries; why not have our grand cooking establishments, our scourers, our window-cleaners, etc.? I will give one example, a direct one however, of the helplessness of a housekeeper on the present plan of life. She perceives, and none but those who have witnessed it can tell how irritating is the feeling, that about five hundred panes of glass in her house require washing. How can they be cleansed? It is properly a man's business, but she must put an inexperienced female to the work who is required for a hundred other things; one, too, who perhaps never wiped a glass before. A particular set of cloths is required, step-ladder, hammer, and a knack at *cleaning* glass. By the time she has accomplished her task, which is probably imperfectly done, broken a few panes, and left the sashes loose and clattering, dust and flies have been equally active, and the *gude man* begins to say "my dear, our windows require a little cleaning." What a cheering sound would it be to a lady so circumstanced, if she could hear in the street "any windows to clean to-day?" or, what is better, know where to send to an establishment for a person devoted to that object.

What a desideratum is a cooking establishment, where families can be provided with prepared food, and a still greater to have our meals brought to us, now that the improvements in steam can give them hotter than from our own hearths. They could probably be furnished cheaper than on the present plan. Our husbands would no longer be seen haggling with butchers at their stalls, or balancing raw meat in the open streets; nor should we see decent women, in utter uncertainty of their dinners, throwing up their window-sashes to the passing countrymen, with "Mister, what's you got to-day?" A friend could *drop in* without disconcerting a family, and the lady of the house sit without a thorn. How many more smiles would kindle up around the domestic board, could the wife be assured of her husband's comfort. She has enough to do in the agitating responsibility of her maternal cares; her little ones may be sickly, her own health feeble. Many a woman breaks and sinks beneath the wear and tear of the frame and the affections. She rallies before the world, and "her children rise up and call her blessed," and she is blessed in the conscious attempt to discharge her duty; but cares eat away at her heart; the day presses on her with new toils, the night comes, and they are unfulfilled; she lies down in weariness, and rises with uncertainty; her smiles become languid and few, and her husband wonders at the gloominess of his home.

How great a duty is it, then, to study modes of comfort, and preserve the song of cheerfulness in the routine of domestic industry. It is not below the task of legislation, if legislation is a study of the order and happiness of a community, or if legislators would have neat houses, good dinners, and smiling wives.

Source: Clarissa Packard, *Recollections of a Housekeeper* (New York: Harper, 1834).

I Shall Prove That the Station of a Domestic Is an Honourable and Respectable One

After publishing *A Treatise on Domestic Economy*, Catharine Beecher noted that there was a considerable body of prescriptive literature for middle-class and elite women who supervised servants but virtually none for domestics themselves. To rectify this imbalance, she offered advice in the form of letters addressed to women engaged in domestic service. She directed her introductory remarks, however, to the ladies who employed them: "The persons for whom I write, have few opportunities to know what issues from the press, and seldom buy books. It is others, who, from a spirit of philanthropy and benevolence, must procure such advantages for them, or they will seldom be secured." She encouraged mistresses to purchase her volume for their servants, even suggesting it as a Christmas gift. Despite her tone of condescension, Beecher depicts domestic servants engaged in the same type of moral housekeeping as their mistresses. In fact, she seems to ignore the issues of labor and wages altogether. How might domestic servants have responded to Beecher's letters?

Reasons for regarding the station of a domestic as honourable and respectable.

My Friends:

The preceding letters were designed to give you some general views of the state of things in this country, and of the station which you are called to occupy. I will now point out reasons for regarding your station and employment as honourable and respectable.

It is sometimes the case that persons will speak of the place of a domestic as the humblest and least desirable of any; and some young girls will go into shops and manufactories, and work much longer, and for lower wages, because they fancy that it is more respectable than the place of a domestic. And not unfrequently "shop girls" and "factory girls" will show much pride and folly, in shunning the society of domestics, and in treating them with disrespect and contempt, as if they were very much below themselves. All these things are owing to a want of correct notions as to the real usefulness and respectability of this important station in life. And I will now point out the reasons for considering your situation as far more honourable, desirable, and useful than that of a sempstress, a shop girl, or a factory girl; and even as superior in respectability to that of many persons who consider themselves as belonging to the "very first society."

There are two things that make a station honourable; one is the *power to do good*, and the other is *using this power in the right manner*.

Why is the office of a king or queen the most honourable of any in the nation? Because it secures the most power to confer benefits and enjoyment on others? Why is the station of a president, a governor, or a judge so honourable? Because they have great power given them to use for the happiness of others. Why is the office of a minister of the gospel honourable? Because his education, character and office give him great powers to do good. Why are rich men considered more honourable than poor? Because their money gives them power to increase the happiness of others. They can give employment to the poor, can give custom to the shop-keepers and tradesmen, can bestow money on charitable objects, can secure a superior education, and many other agreeable things that make it pleasant to others to associate with them. Why are persons of talent and learning honourable? Because their talents and knowledge give them power in various ways to promote their own interest and to do good to others.

The mere possession, then, of a power to do good, is what makes one station more honourable than another. But another thing that makes a station honourable, is the actual *using of this power* in doing good.

If kings and queens are selfish and wicked, and use their power to oppress their people, they are never as much honoured as when they use it to do good.

If presidents, governors, and judges use their power to do evil, they are not honoured like those who use it to do good. If a minister of the gospel uses his influence to do harm rather than good, he is more despised than he is honoured. If rich people spend their wealth in selfish indulgences, or in harmful vices, they are not honoured as they would be, if they spent it for useful and benevolent purposes. If persons who have talents and learning, spend their time and influence to do evil, they are not honoured or respected as they would be, if they employed them to do good.

Now I think you clearly see, that the two things which make a station honourable are, the power to do good, and the use of this power in a proper manner. If, then, I can show that domestics have great power to do good given them, and that they really use this power in doing good, I shall prove that the station of a domestic is an honourable and respectable one. And if I can show that domestics have more power, and actually do more good, than many who think themselves above them, I shall prove, too, that they have the more honourable and respectable station. I will therefore point out the power of doing good which is given to domestics. In the first place, then, they do more than any other class of persons to sustain that most important institution of God, *the family state.* How much benefit and comfort mankind receive through this institution, few of us can realize. To help you to do so, just imagine the state of things in this country, if all the *homes* in the land were broken up, and all classes of persons herded together in common, like flocks of animals.

In this case the father and husband would have no quiet home to go to for comfort, and the mother would have no house of her own where she could train her children. Every child, too, would be turned out into the community to take care of itself, with no parents to watch over it by day and night, no brothers and sisters to sleep and play with, no regular meal to call all the children together around their kind parents.

In a cold and selfish world, without guardians, without a home, without parental restraint and tenderness, each young child would go into the common herd, to grow up selfish, unhappy, unloving and unloved.

Instead of this, God ordains that parents shall have a home of their own, where they can have their children to themselves, to train them up in love and peace and plenty. And one main support of this blessed institution of family and home is, those domestics who are hired to do the chief labours of the family. Just take away from this country all the cooks, chambermaids, waiters, washers, and house cleaners, and what would be the result? The fathers could not leave their business to do the family work, the mothers would not have strength to do it, and the family state would be broken up. And thus unnumbered miseries and crime would come in floods upon the land. The position and the work of a domestic, then, are among the most useful, the most important and the most honourable. They have a power given them to do good and to save from evil, not surpassed by that of any other class in the community. Let any one select the class of persons that could be dispensed with *last of all*, and it would be found that lawyers, merchants, doctors, and ministers would all be given up, before every family would agree to give up all aid from cooks, washers, nurses and every kind of hired service in the family.

But, in addition to the power thus given to domestics in sustaining the family state, they have another most important position of usefulness. This relates to the power they exercise in forming the characters of young children. The period of life from infancy to twelve years old, is the time in which the foundations of future character are laid. During this time, children are in the society of domestics almost as much as they are with their parents, and in many cases, they talk with those hired to take care of them much more than they do with their parents. Children are creatures of imitation and sympathy, and they soon learn to think, and feel and act like those around them. Of course domestics are constantly exerting a powerful influence in forming the opinions, tastes, habits, and character of children, more so, probably, than any other class in the community. To estimate this power properly, we must remember that the happiness of children depends almost entirely on the character they form. If they learn to control their appetites, to be honest, truthful, benevolent, and industrious, they will be useful and happy in future life. If they do not learn to control their appetites, if they learn to be deceitful, dishonest, selfish and irritable, they certainly will be unhappy and unprosperous. And our whole nation is to be made up of children, whose happiness and prosperity will depend, to a great degree, on the influences exerted over them by domestics in early life. And the next generation is to depend, for happiness and prosperity, on the manner in which the present generation is trained. And the next after that, depends in like manner, on the one before it, so that the influence which domestics exert on one generation of children is to go down to generation after generation, for hundreds of years.

And yet, this is not half of the mighty power, which is given to domestics to use, either for good or for evil. All these children, who from generation to generation are thus influenced in character, by domestics who take care of them, are to *live forever*, and their happiness for endless ages, is to depend on the character which they form in this life! Oh eternity! eternity! who can estimate the power of those who are doing so much, in forming the character of beings who can *never, never die!*

Another particular in which domestics have great power is, the influence they exert in making home pleasant to husbands and sons. In a family where most of the work is done regularly and well, by domestics, the mother has time to take good care of her children, and her mind is cheerful and free from excessive cares. In this case, the husband and sons find a comfortable and pleasant home, and are not tempted to resort to dangerous amusements abroad. But when every thing is going wrong in the kitchen and nursery, the wife and mother is perplexed and harassed, and often is low-spirited or irritable. The father and sons, when they come home, find the house in disorder, their food ill cooked and served, their linen out of order, their beds uncomfortable, the housekeeper gloomy, the children unregulated, and every thing seems to drive them off to look for a more cheerful and comfortable resort. Many and many a husband and son has thus been driven to temptations and snares, that have drawn them and their families to misery and ruin.

Another power for doing good given to domestics is, their opportunities for comforting and relieving the sick. Sickness always makes a great deal of work, and were it not for domestics, the sick would suffer greatly for want of nursing and many comforts. No persons owe more to domestics than those who, by sickness, are deprived of all power to take care of themselves. I might point out other particulars in which domestics have it in their power to do great good, but surely enough has been presented to show, that *if great power to do good* is what entitles persons to be called honourable, then domestics have a pre-eminent claim.

But it has been shown, that it is not only the power to do good, but the actual *use* of this power that entitles a person to honour and respect. Here, also, domestics will be found to have a claim equal to that of any other class of persons. It will be found, that there are individuals in every class of society, who do not use their power well. There are bad kings and bad governors, bad rich men and bad learned men, and sometimes there are bad ministers of the gospel. So, also, there are bad domestics. But, as a class, I believe domestics use their power for the benefit, rather than the injury of society, as much so as any other class. Most of the work, that is necessary to sustain the family state, is actually done by them, the sick are taken care of by their help, children are nursed and taken care of by them, and the comfort of a family is promoted by their services, to a degree never realized till their help is gone.

No class in the community do more in promoting the comfort, health, and prosperity of society than domestics. It thus appears, that they are an honourable and respectable class in society, not only because they have great power to do good, but because they actually use this power beneficially, to a very great extent.

Source: Catharine Beecher, *Letters to Persons Who Are Engaged In Domestic Service* (New York: Leavitt & Trow, 1842).

Treat All of These Comers with a Politeness Truly Lady-Like

When the Boston Associates decided to locate their new textile mills in Lowell, Massachusetts, in the 1820s, they dreamed of an American industrial utopia. To this end, they hired young women from New England farms—virtuous, hardworking, relatively inexpensive, and most important temporary wage earners who would return home after a season or a few years. And so, at the moment when the middle class idealized women as keepers of the domestic sphere, the Boston Associates imagined them as workers. To resolve this contradiction, mill owners celebrated the impeccable morality of their workforce and built boardinghouses to provide their female employees with domestic influences and protection while away from home. Excerpted here is one mill worker's depiction of boardinghouse life in the 1840s. She suggests that the respectable female inhabitants must improve and uplift the boardinghouse rather than the

other way around, as the home for workers is permeated not only by their own labor but by commercial relationships.

Home in a boarding-house is always different from home anywhere else; and home in a factory boarding-house, differs materially from home in any other. The difference is perceptible at the first entrance. There is a peculiarity "all its own," in the great domicil, which usually shelters us. One might readily see by its accommodations, or rather its "fixings," (we beg pardon of Dickens) for they are not always acknowledged as accommodations, by the party most directly concerned, that it cannot be exactly a home, but only a place to eat and lodge in, a sort of rendezvous, after the real home, the daily habitation, is abandoned. This is tacitly acknowledged by the cognomen of the room, which is the only one common to all boarders. This is the dining-room—or, more properly the eating-room, for breakfast and supper, as well as dinner, are demolished in its precincts. This is always amply furnished with chairs and tables, though but little of anything else, for, amidst all our deprivations, we have never been deprived of the privilege of sitting at our meals. Chairs, chairs—one, two, three, four, and so on to forty. It is really refreshing, sometimes, to go where there is only now and then a chair. This pleasure we can usually enjoy, by leaving the dining-room for our chambers, where there is not often a surplus of this furniture; but then there are always plenty of trunks, boxes, &c., which will answer for seats, and the bed is easily persuaded to stand proxy for a sofa.

But these are all trifles, compared with the perplexities to which we are subjected in other ways; and some of these might be remedied by the girls themselves. We now allude to the importunities of evening visitors, such as peddlers, candy and newspaper boys, shoe-dealers, book-sellers, &c., &c., breaking in upon the only hours of leisure we can call our own, and proffering their articles with a pertinacity which will admit no denial. That these evening salesmen are always unwelcome we will not assert, but they are too often inclined to remain where they know they are considered a nuisance. And then they often forget, if they ever knew, the rules of politeness which should regulate all transient visitors. They deal about their hints, innuendoes, and low cunning, as though a factory boarding-house was what no boarding-house should ever be.

The remedy is entirely with the girls. Treat all of these comers with a politeness truly lady-like, when they appear as gentlemen, but let your manners change to stern formality when they forget that they are in the company of respectable females.

Never encourage evening traders, unless you see some very good reason for so doing. The reason usually given is that they can trade cheaper with these men, than with the storekeepers of Lowell. There is competition enough among the shopkeepers to keep things at a reasonable price, and *good* articles are seldom purchased cheaper of a peddler. "But," say others, "it is much more convenient for us, if we can be suited at home, to have our things brought to us, than to go out for them." Even when this is true, it should be remembered that each buyer is interrupting the occupations of one, two, or three dozen girls.

Source: "Home in a Boarding-House," *Lowell Offering* 3 (1842): 69–70.

Something to Think of Besides Working away from Home and Friends Just for Money

Before being married, Lizzie A. Wilson Goodenough worked as a domestic servant for several families in Brattleborough, Vermont. Her 1865 diary records her work for the Howe and Tripp families and also describes a visit to her brother Edd Wilson. Most important, it provides a detailed record of her work, differentiating labor for her employers from that she did for herself and for her own family. Despite her friendly tone and social interactions with the families who employ her, Goodenough emphasizes the economic, more than moral, imperatives that shape her labor. Orphaned in 1860, she clearly works to support herself. Even when describing a death in the Howe family, Goodenough remains focused on changing beds and larger-than-usual amounts of washing.

1865

WEDNESDAY, JANUARY 4

we have been washing today had a very large washing to do the children have been full of mischief all day today, it has been a very pleasant day

THURSDAY, JANUARY 12
have not had much to do this forenoon have been crochetting collars this afternoon and evening have made two.

FRIDAY, JANUARY 13
have been mopping this forenoon sewing this afternoon

SATURDAY, JANUARY 14
Mrs Howe has been baking this forenoon we have been mopping and cleaning up some this forenoon.

MONDAY, JANUARY 16
we have been washing today could not put out the clothes have been knitting cotton this afternoon

TUESDAY, JANUARY 17
have put out the clothes this morning have been busy all day picking at the odd ends of work around the house and then went to sewing a little this afternoon

WEDNESDAY, JANUARY 18
have been ironing today

FRIDAY, JANUARY 20
have not been doing much today have sewed some croched some and knit a little this afternoon

FRIDAY, JANUARY 27
is very pleasant this morning but is growing cold quite fast have had quite an easy days work today have been crocheting and sewing some this afternoon

SATURDAY, JANUARY 28
is a pleasant day have been up to Brattleboro this afternoon got me a pair of boots calico dress & some other things.
    Mrs Howe paid me six dollars.
    Was fourteen degrees below zero this morning

SUNDAY, JANUARY 29

is very cold today is as cold as any day we have had but very pleasant George and his wife have been here today I have been busy nearly all day

THURSDAY, FEBRUARY 2

we have been baking mopping &c this forenoon. has been a splendid day. Arad has not been dressed today. is very low cant help himself at all I have been sewing this afternoon Sarah has been in here this afternoon

FRIDAY, FEBRUARY 3

is another beautiful day is warm and pleasant. we have been changing beds for Arads room this forenoon he is very tired now has not been up today.

MONDAY, FEBRUARY 6

am washing this morning. Arad has had another choaking spell is failing fast. finished washing had a large wash this week mopped and made my beds this afternoon Arad is worse cannot live the night out.

TUESDAY, FEBRUARY 7

Arad died this morning at half past twelve died an easy death
we have been ironing this forenoon George was down here last night

THURSDAY, FEBRUARY 9

today is for the funerall. Arad is burried with massonic honors had a verry large funerall. there were a great many of the friends here to supper.

FRIDAY, FEBRUARY 10

have been washing this forenoon had a very large washing to do Ellen Putnam is here is going to stay a few days with Celia Sarah was in here this afternoon.

SATURDAY, FEBRUARY 11

is not a verry pleasant morning. we have not had any baking today have been ironing this forenoon had a lot of fine clothes to iron had a chance to go to Lysander Howes to work today.

MONDAY, FEBRUARY 13

is still verry cold but quite pleasant this morning we have been washing this forenoon did not have so large a wash as common have been sewing on my calico dress this afternoon

TUESDAY, FEBRUARY 14

have been ironing this forenoon finished at eleven is a verry cold day today I have been sewing on my calico dress this afternoon. went in to see Sarah this afternoon took the baby with me Mrs Amos Washburne sent up word by Ellen Putnam tonight to ask me to come up and work for her.

FRIDAY, FEBRUARY 17

have got the work all done for this morning. it is a cloudy day. Mr & Mrs Howe & Celia have been up to Brattleboro this forenoon Mrs Howe got me some alpacca braid for my dress. i have been sewing this forenoon have got dinner all out of the way at half past one sewing again this afternoon. . . .

SUNDAY, MARCH 19

is pleasant today or at least the sun shines brightly but it has been a long lonesome day to me oh how i wish the time would come when the time would seem pleasant to me. something to think of besides working away from home and friends just for money. Long years have past since i had a Fathers home to go to.

MONDAY, MARCH 20

is pleasant again this morning we have been washing had a verry large washing to do this forenoon yet we finished before noon and mopped all through the sheds and all. have been knitting this afternoon. Henry Ellis came down here this afternoon Tyler Johnson was here this forenoon wanted to hire me to go and work for him this summer

TUESDAY, MARCH 21

is pleasant and verry still. we have been ironing this morning we had a large lot of clothes to iron but got through at ten. Henry went away this morning. i have been pleeting a skirt for Mellissa this afternoon.

Mr Carlton [?] begun work on the other house this morning

WEDNESDAY, MARCH 22

it rains this morning but looks a little like clearing of now i expected to go home today but shall have to wait untill tommorrow or some other convenient day have been knitting some untill it cleared of then went to mopping mopped all over the house Sarah was in here this afternoon

THURSDAY, MARCH 23

this is another dull morning as we have not got much to do this forenoon except get boiled dinner have been knitting nearly all the time since i got the work done we have had quite a knitting circle this afternoon Mrs Howe. Celia. Sarah. Mellissa & myself have all been knitting

FRIDAY, MARCH 24

got up early this morning have got the work all out of the way at eight Mr Howe is going to carry me over to Edd this morning have got through work for them got home about ten found verry bad going the horse got into the mud twice but got along safe and sound at last.

SATURDAY, MARCH 25

this is a pleasant morning the ground is still bare has not snowed at all and the ground is drying fast have been baking and mopping for Leitt she gone down home her Father is sick with the lung-fever have just got through baking bread half past three

SUNDAY, MARCH 26

is pleasant this morn Tyler Johnson was here this morning Edd has been down to Mr Stones today Leitt & I have been up to Mr Barkers this evening a little while the ground has got dried of so it is good walking anywhere

MONDAY, MARCH 27

is pleasant today George Clarke was down here to hire me this forenoon could not see going there as he said he had been hiring a girl for 175 a week told him there was no use in talking

TUESDAY, MARCH 28

was rather cloudy but has cleared of pleasant now. i am going to sew this forenoon on my white skirt

WEDNESDAY, MARCH 29

is pleasant this morning Leitt has been baking and ironing today i have been trying to sew a little this forenoon but did not sew much have had the sick headache today have been sick all the afternoon

THURSDAY, MARCH 30

have been trying to sew a little today have not sewed much my head ached so i could not see so gave it up and went to bed. slept awhile and felt better so that i got up and went to work. Sumner Clarke called here this afternoon. it has rained all day

FRIDAY, MARCH 31

is raining still looks as though we might have fair weather before long but cant tell have been sewing and knitting some today.

SATURDAY, APRIL 8

have been very busy this morning have been washing dishes making beds sweeping dusting &c am going up to the street today

Mr Howe came after me this forenoon to go and stay two or three weeks did not go to Brattleboro so much as i thought i should when i started but went to Vernon

SUNDAY, APRIL 9

this is a pleasant morning the sun shines brightly and the birds are singing as happy as can be has not any one been here today only Mr Fowlers [?] folks and ourselves. we have been out maying this afternoon found some verry pretty flowers so we had a boquet.

SUNDAY, APRIL 16

This is another sunny but rather windy morning George Howe and wife have been down here this afternoon it has been verry pleasant today [?] was in here this evening

President Lincoln was shot dead yesterday was assassinated & killed by J Wilkes Boothe an actor. . . .

SUNDAY, JULY 16

this is a dull rainy morning it now rains quite hard

still another lonesome dreaded week of tiresome housework & drudgery is begun for me. nothing better was my lot it seems than to be a slave to others wants oh would that i knew when i might be free to call my time my own and think once if i had a will of my own or not.

MONDAY, JULY 17

it has been a rainy morning but looks brighter now and i hope it will clear of so i can put out my clothes have had a verry large washing today did not get through washing untill noon have been down the street this afternoon saw Mrs Howe & was glad to hear from them got some buttons for my sack went to walk with Lizzie and Nell tonight

TUESDAY, JULY 18

this is a lovely morning i have been baking and ironing some this forenoon have got the skirts dresses aprons &c ironed have been in the circus this afternoon it was verry good but nothing extra though we enjoyed ourselves finely. have been sewing on my muslin waist this evening. . . .

SUNDAY, NOVEMBER 19

this is a dull and lonesome morning is my birthday am twenty-two today. one more long weary year dragged away from us forever mine is a hard lonely life day after day comes & brings its work. it seems that my life is made up of nothing but long long days for nothing but work work and dig for others. be it so

[Goodenough neglects her diary for several days at the end of November.]

THURSDAY, DECEMBER 7 (AT THE TRIPPS)

this is thanksgiving day. a sad & solemn one its has been to me. eleven years ago now our whole family were at home thanksgiving but oh since then sikness & death has ben there and made a wreck of a once happy home yes Father Mother one Sister & one Brother have been taken and only two remain of the once happy family

MONDAY, DECEMBER 25

have been washing today although tis christmas. did not have a verry large washing today Mr & Mrs Tripp took dinner over to Mr Hanson today, they had a christmas tree we all went over in the evening Mrs Tripp gave me a pair of scissors just what I needed

Source: Volume 1 of the diary of Lizzie A. Wilson Goodenough (1865), courtesy of the American Antiquarian Society. Spelling and grammar have been left as in the original.

Housekeeping Ain't No Joke

Louisa May Alcott's *Little Women* was a must-read for American girls during the last third of the nineteenth century, and its popularity has continued across generations of female readers. At the time of its first printing in October 1868, the story of the March sisters—Meg, Jo, Beth, and Amy—and their beloved mother, Marmee, described female coming of age in a new way. Based on Alcott's own girlhood in the 1840s, her novel combined moral teachings with depictions of boisterous play, high ideals with the latest slang, domestic harmony with economic concerns and consumer longings. When the story opens, the two elder sisters work for wages, and throughout the text, all the March girls not only desire to be good but desire goods—books, gloves, colored pencils, sheet music, fine clothes, and jewelry. In the passage here, the March girls take a vacation from their unpaid domestic labor and discover that there can be no true comfort without work.

"What shall you do all your vacation?" asked Amy, changing the subject, with tact.

"I shall lie abed late, and do nothing," replied Meg, from the depths of the rocking-chair.

"I've been routed up early all winter, and had to spend my days working for other people; so now I'm going to rest and revel to my heart's content."

"Hum!" said Jo; "that dozy way wouldn't suit me. I've laid in a heap of books, and I'm going to improve my shining hours reading on my perch in the old apple-tree, when I'm not having l——"

"Don't say 'larks!'" implored Amy, as a return snub for the "samphire" correction.

"I'll say 'nightingales,' then, with Laurie; that's proper and appropriate, since he's a warbler."

"Don't let us do any lessons, Beth, for a while, but play all the time, and rest, as the girls mean to," proposed Amy.

"Well, I will, if mother don't mind. I want to learn some new songs, and my children [dolls] need fixing up for the summer; they are dreadfully out of order, and really suffering for clothes."

"May we, mother?" asked Meg, turning to Mrs. March, who sat sewing, in what they called "Marmee's corner."

"You may try your experiment for a week, and see how you like it. I think by Saturday night you will find that all play, and no work, is as bad as all work, and no play."

"Oh, dear, no! it will be delicious, I'm sure," said Meg, complacently. . . .

. . . Next morning, Meg did not appear till ten o'clock; her solitary breakfast did not taste good, and the room seemed lonely and untidy, for Jo had not filled the vases, Beth had not dusted, and Amy's books lay scattered about. Nothing was neat and pleasant but "Marmee's corner," which looked as usual; and there she sat, to "rest and read," which meant yawn, and imagine what pretty summer dresses she would get with her salary. Jo spent the morning on the river, with Laurie, and the afternoon reading and crying over *The Wide, Wide World*, up in the apple-tree. Beth began by rummaging everything out of the big closet, where her family resided; but, getting tired before half done, she left her establishment topsy-turvy, and went to her music, rejoicing that she had no dishes to wash. Amy arranged her bower, put on her best white frock, smoothed her curls, and sat down to draw, under the honeysuckles, hoping some one would see and inquire who the young artist was. As no one appeared but an inquisitive daddy-long-legs, who examined her work with interest, she went to walk, got caught in a shower, and came home dripping.

At tea-time they compared notes, and all agreed that it had been a delightful, though unusually long day. Meg, who went shopping in the afternoon, and got a "sweet blue muslin," had discovered, after she had cut the breadths off, that it wouldn't wash, which mishap made her slightly cross. Joe had burnt the skin off her nose boating, and got a raging headache by reading too long. Beth was worried by the confusion of her closet, and the difficulty of learning three or four songs at once; and Amy deeply regretted the damage done her frock, for Katy Brown's party was to be the next day; and now, like Flora McFlimsy, she had "nothing to wear." But these were mere trifles; and they assured their mother that the experiment was working finely. She smiled, said nothing, and, with Hannah's help, did their neglected work, keeping home pleasant, and the domestic machinery running smoothly. It was astonishing what a peculiar and uncomfortable state of things was produced by the "resting and reveling" process. The days kept getting longer and longer; the weather was unusually variable, and so were tempers; an unsettled feeling possessed every one, and Satan found plenty of mischief for the idle hands to do. As the height of luxury, Meg put out some of her sewing, and then found time hang so heavily, that she fell to snipping and spoiling her clothes, in her attempts to furbish them up, à la Moffat. Jo read till her eyes gave out, and she was sick of books; got so fidgety that even good-natured Laurie had a quarrel with her, and so reduced in spirits that she desperately wished she had gone with Aunt March. Beth got on pretty well, for she was constantly forgetting that it was to be *all play, and no work*, and fell back into her old ways, now and then; but something in the air affected her, and, more than once, her tranquility was much disturbed; so much so, that, on one occasion, she actually shook poor dear Joanna, and told her she was "a fright." Amy fared worst of all, for her resources were small; and, when her sisters left her to amuse and care for herself, she soon found that accomplished and important little self a great burden. She didn't like dolls; fairy tales were childish, and one couldn't draw all the time. Tea-parties didn't amount to much, neither did picnics, unless very well conducted. "If one could have a fine house, full of nice girls, or go travelling, the summer would be delightful; but to stay at home with three selfish sisters, and a grown-up boy, was enough to try the patience of a Boaz," complained Miss Malaprop, after several days devoted to pleasure, fretting, and *ennui*.

No one would own that they were tired of the experiment; but, by Friday night, each acknowledged to herself that they were glad the week was nearly done. Hoping to impress the lesson more deeply, Mrs. March, who had a good deal of humor, resolved to finish off the trial in an appropriate manner; so she gave Hannah a holiday, and let the girls enjoy the full effect of the play system.

When they got up on Saturday morning, there was no fire in the kitchen, no breakfast in the dining-room, and no mother anywhere to be seen.

"Mercy on us! What *has* happened?" cried Jo, staring about her in dismay.

Meg ran upstairs, and soon came back again, looking relieved, but rather bewildered, and a little ashamed.

"Mother isn't sick, only very tired, and she says she is going to stay quietly in her room all day, and let us do the best we can. It's a very queer thing for her to do, she don't act a bit like herself; but she says it *has* been a hard week for her, so we mustn't grumble, but take care of ourselves."

"That's easy enough, and I like the idea; I'm aching for something to do—that is, some new amusement, you know," added Jo, quickly.

In fact it *was* an immense relief to them all to have a little work, and they took hold with a will, but soon realized the truth of Hannah's saying, "Housekeeping ain't no joke."

There was plenty of food in the larder, and, while Beth and Amy set the table, Meg and Jo got breakfast; wondering, as they did so, why servants ever talked about hard work.

"I shall take some up to mother, though she said we were not to think of her, for she'd take care of herself," said Meg, who presided, and felt quite matronly behind the teapot.

So a tray was fitted out before any one began, and taken up, with the cook's compliments. The boiled tea was very bitter, the omelette scorched, and the biscuits speckled with saleratus; but Mrs. March received her repast with thanks, and laughed heartily over it after Jo was gone.

"Poor little souls, they will have a hard time, I'm afraid; but they won't suffer, and it will do them good," she said, producing the more palatable viands with which she had provided herself, and disposing of the bad breakfast, so that their feelings might not be hurt;—a motherly little deception, for which they were grateful. . . .

"Are you satisfied with your experiment, girls, or do you want another week of it?" she asked, as Beth nestled up to her, and the rest turned toward her with brightening faces, as flowers turn toward the sun.

"I don't!" cried Jo, decidedly.

"Nor I," echoed the others.

Figures 2.2 and 2.3. Sheet music for "Song of the Shirt," 1847, and "Song of the Sewing Machine," 1869 (both courtesy of the American Antiquarian Society) depicts two versions of women's domestic work—one among the working poor and the other among the middle class. Both women are involved in the making of clothing, but only the poor woman toils for wages. Consider the contrasting domestic settings in which the two women sew.

"You think, then that it is better to have a few duties, and live a little for others, do you?" . . .

"Mother! did you go away and let everything be, just to see how we'd get on?" cried Meg, who had had suspicions all day.

"Yes; I wanted you to see how the comfort of all depends on each doing their share faithfully. While Hannah and I did your work, you got on pretty well, though I don't think you were very happy or amia-

Figure 2.4. *Scene in a Fashionable Boarding House* (Bufford's Lith., 1835; courtesy of the American Antiquarian Society) portrays life in the parlor of a middle-class boarding-house. Popular depictions of boardinghouses often contended that they were all a true home was not—commercial, public, and immoral—and yet many middle-class men and women lived in respectable boardinghouses by both necessity and choice. As this lithograph suggests, single men and women frequently lived in boardinghouses, as did married couples that could not afford a private home or wished to avoid the demands of home management. Of course, not all boardinghouses were fashionable, instead catering to working-class men and women and often providing a lesser standard of domestic comfort and respectability.

ble; so I thought, as a little lesson, I would show you what happens when every one thinks only of herself. Don't you feel that it is pleasanter to help one another, to have daily duties which make leisure sweet when it comes, and to bear or forbear, that home may be comfortable and lovely to us all?"

"We do, mother, we do!" cried the girls.

Source: Louisa May Alcott, "Experiments," in *Little Women* (1869; repr., Boston: Little, Brown, 1922).

The Most Deserving of Women Are Asked to Call This Spot of Bareness—Home

Nellie Bly was the pen name of Elizabeth Cochrane, arguably the most famous female journalist of the late nineteenth century. Writing for Joseph Pulitzer's *New York World* in the 1880s, she was determined to stay off the paper's woman's page and to cover stories of importance—especially those that focused on the conditions of poor and working women. Often described as a pioneer of "stunt journalism," Bly feigned madness in order to get herself committed to Blackwell's Island so that she could report on the treatment of the mentally ill. In the passage here, she explains why a female boardinghouse was the ideal place to begin her deception and offers insight into the living conditions that many working-class women routinely endured. Bly herself lived in a more genteel boardinghouse at the time, underscoring that many respectable women, men, and even middle-class families lived in establishments that blurred domestic and commercial relationships.

I first thought it best to go to a boarding-house, and, after securing lodging, confidentially tell the landlady, or lord, whichever it might chance to be, that I was seeking work, and, in a few days after, apparently go insane. When I reconsidered the idea, I feared it would take too long to mature. Suddenly I thought how much easier it would be to go to a boarding-home for working women. I knew, if once I made a houseful of women believe me crazy, that they would never rest until I was out of their reach and in secure quarters.

From a directory I selected the Temporary Home for Females, No. 84 Second Avenue. As I walked down the avenue, I determined that, once inside the Home, I should do the best I could to get started on my journey to Blackwell's Island and the Insane Asylum.

. . . I passed through the little paved yard to the entrance of the Home. I pulled the bell, which sounded loud enough for a church chime, and nervously awaited the opening of the door to the Home, which I intended should ere long cast me forth and out upon the charity of the police. The door was thrown back with a vengeance, and a short, yellow-haired girl of some thirteen summers stood before me.

"Is the matron in?" I asked, faintly.

"Yes, she's in; she's busy. Go to the back parlor," answered the girl, in a loud voice, without one change in her peculiarly matured face.

I followed these not overkind or polite instructions and found myself in a dark, uncomfortable back-parlor. There I awaited the arrival of my hostess. I had been seated some twenty minutes at the least, when a slender woman, clad in a plain, dark dress entered and, stopping before me, ejaculated inquiringly, "Well?"

"Are you the matron?" I asked.

"No," she replied, "the matron is sick; I am her assistant. What do you want?"

"I want to stay here for a few days, if you can accommodate me."

"Well, I have no single rooms, we are so crowded; but if you will occupy a room with another girl, I shall do that much for you."

"I shall be glad of that," I answered. "How much do you charge?" I had brought only about seventy cents along with me, knowing full well that the sooner my funds were exhausted the sooner I should be put out, and to be put out was what I was working for.

"We charge thirty cents a night," was her reply to my question, and with that I paid her for one night's lodging, and she left me on the plea of having something else to look after. Left to amuse myself as best I could, I took a survey of my surroundings.

They were not cheerful, to say the least. A wardrobe, desk, book-case, organ, and several chairs completed the furnishment of the room, into which the daylight barely came.

By the time I had become familiar with my quarters a bell, which rivaled the door-bell in its loudness, began clanging in the basement, and simultaneously women went trooping down-stairs from all parts of the house. I imagined, from the obvious signs, that dinner was served, but as no one had said anything to me I made no effort to follow in the hungry train. Yet I did wish that some one would invite me down. It always produces such a lonely, homesick feeling to know others are eating, and we haven't a chance, even if we are not hungry. I was glad when the assistant matron came up and asked me if I did not want something to eat. I replied that I did, and then I asked her what her name was. Mrs. Stanard, she said, and I immediately wrote it down in a notebook I had taken with me for the purpose of making memoranda, and in which I had written several pages of utter nonsense for inquisitive scientists.

Thus equipped I awaited developments. But my dinner—well, I followed Mrs. Stanard down the uncarpeted stairs into the basement; where a large number of women were eating. She found room for me at a table with three other women. The short-haired slavey who had opened the door now put in an appearance as waiter. Placing her arms akimbo and staring me out of countenance she said:

"Boiled mutton, boiled beef, beans, potatoes, coffee or tea?"

"Beef, potatoes, coffee and bread," I responded.

"Bread goes in," she explained, as she made her way to the kitchen, which was in the rear. It was not very long before she returned with what I had ordered on a large, badly battered tray, which she banged down before me. I began my simple meal. It was not very enticing, so while making a feint of eating I watched the others.

I have often moralized on the repulsive form charity always assumes! Here was a home for deserving women and yet what a mockery the name was. The floor was bare, and the little wooden tables were sublimely ignorant of such modern beautifiers as varnish, polish and table-covers. It is useless to talk about the cheapness of linen and its effect on civilization. Yet these honest workers, the most deserving of women, are asked to call this spot of bareness—home.

When the meal was finished each woman went to the desk in the corner, where Mrs. Stanard sat, and paid her bill. I was given a much-used, and abused, red check, by the original piece of humanity in shape of my waitress. My bill was about thirty cents.

After dinner I went up-stairs and resumed my former place in the back parlor. I was quite cold and uncomfortable, and had fully made up my mind that I could not endure that sort of business long, so the sooner

I assumed my insane points the sooner I would be released from enforced idleness. Ah! that was indeed the longest day I had ever lived. I listlessly watched the women in the front parlor, where all sat except myself.

One did nothing but read and scratch her head and occasionally call out mildly, "Georgie," without lifting her eyes from her book. "Georgie" was her over-frisky boy, who had more noise in him than any child I ever saw before. He did everything that was rude and unmannerly, I thought, and the mother never said a word unless she heard some one else yell at him. Another woman always kept going to sleep and waking herself up with her own snoring. I really felt wickedly thankful it was only herself she awakened. The majority of the women sat there doing nothing, but there were a few who made lace and knitted unceasingly. The enormous door-bell seemed to be going all the time, and so did the short-haired girl. The latter was, besides, one of those girls who sing all the time snatches of all the songs and hymns that have been composed for the last fifty years. There is such a thing as martyrdom in these days. The ringing of the bell brought more people who wanted shelter for the night. Excepting one woman, who was from the country on a day's shopping expedition, they were working women, some of them with children. . . .

When the supper-bell rang I went along with the others to the basement and partook of the evening meal, which was similar to dinner, except that there was a smaller bill of fare and more people, the women who are employed outside during the day having returned. After the evening meal we all adjourned to the parlors, where all sat, or stood, as there were not chairs enough to go round.

It was a wretchedly lonely evening, and the light which fell from the solitary gas jet in the parlor, and oil-lamp the hall, helped to envelop us in a dusky hue and dye our spirits navy blue. I felt it would not require many inundations of this atmosphere to make me a fit subject for the place I was striving to reach.

Source: Nellie Bly, *Ten Days in a Mad-House* (New York: N. L. Munro, 1887).

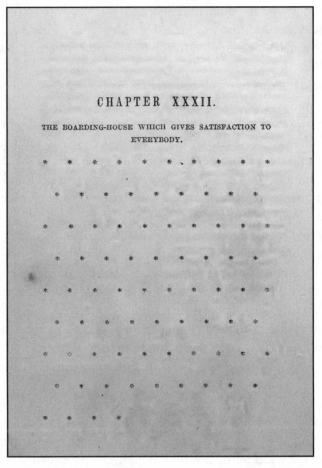

Figure 2.5. "The Boarding-House Which Gives Satisfaction to Everybody" is the final entry in Thomas Butler Gunn's humorous catalog of urban boardinghouses, *The Physiology of New York Boarding-Houses* (New York: Mason Brothers, 1857). Gunn was representative of the many young, single men who migrated to New York City in the 1830s and 1840s and made up the vast majority of the city's boarders. A journalist, Gunn turned the necessity of his living arrangements into research and dedicated his volume "to all inmates of metropolitan boarding-houses, especially single young men." Chapters considered the fate of male boarders in "The Dirty Boarding-House," "The Fashionable Boarding-House Where You Don't Get Enough to Eat," and "The Boarding-House Where There Are Marriageable Daughters," as well as in "The Chinese Boarding-House," "The Irish Immigrant Boarding-House," and "The Boarding-House Frequented by Bostonians." This image is his ultimate punch line, mocking the ability of any boardinghouse to provide comfort and homelike accommodations suited to all.

Figure 2.6. This photograph of a woman in front of a kitchen hearth, Refuge Plantation, Camden County, Georgia, c. 1880s (Library of Congress, Prints & Photographs
Division, HABS, HABS GA, 20-WOBI.V, 1–3) evokes the history of American slavery
and the domestic labor performed in the homes of southern slaveholders. Cook was
one of the few skilled jobs available to enslaved African American women. As kitchens
were often separate from plantation houses, cooks experienced a certain degree of
autonomy, while also controlling key resources. Harriet Jacobs in *Incidents in the Life of
a Slave Girl* boasts of her grandmother's skills: "Her nice crackers became so famous in
the neighborhood that many people were desirous of obtaining them. In consequence
of numerous requests of this kind, she asked permission of her mistress to bake
crackers at night, after all the household work was done" (Boston, 1861, p. 12). Jacobs's
grandmother turned her skills into wages and used her earnings to mitigate the
hardships of slavery. But Jacobs also notes that owners were the ultimate judges, and
for the less skilled cook, every meal brought the threat of punishment.

The Softest Couches . . . Are Not to Be Found in the Log
Mansion of the Slave

Solomon Northrup was born free in New York State in 1808, kidnapped
in Washington, DC, in 1841, and soon after sold at auction in New Orleans. He worked for several different masters in Louisiana until his family was able to secure his freedom. In this passage drawn from his widely

read narrative, Northup describes life in the slave quarters of a cotton plantation owned by Edwin Epps, a master he describes as "repulsive and coarse." In his account, Northup indicates not only the extent of his deprivation as a slave but also his own understanding of what a home should be. His slave cabin provided no respite from labor, no bodily comforts, and no escape from worry. The authority of the slaveholder is omnipresent, even hanging over simple acts such as going to bed or making one's own breakfast.

Finally, at a late hour, [the slaves] reach the quarters, sleepy and overcome with the long day's toil. Then a fire must be kindled in the cabin, the corn ground in the small hand-mill, and supper, and dinner for the next day in the field, prepared. All that is allowed them is corn and bacon, which is given out at the corncrib and smoke-house every Sunday morning. Each one receives, as his weekly allowance, three and a half pounds of bacon, and corn enough to make a peck of meal. That is all—no tea, coffee, sugar, and with the exception of a very scanty sprinkling now and then, no salt. I can say, from a ten years' residence with Master Epps, that no slave of his is ever likely to suffer from the gout, superinduced by excessive high living. Master Epps' hogs were fed on shelled corn—it was thrown out to his "niggers" in the ear. The former, he thought, would fatten faster by shelling, and soaking it in the water—the latter, perhaps, if treated in the same manner, might grow too fat to labor. Master Epps was a shrewd calculator, and knew how to manage his own animals, drunk or sober.

The corn mill stands in the yard beneath a shelter. It is like a common coffee mill, the hopper holding about six quarts. There was one privilege which Master Epps granted freely to every slave he had. They might grind their corn nightly, in such small quantities as their daily wants required, or they might grind the whole week's allowance at one time, on Sundays, just as they preferred. A very generous man was Master Epps!

I kept my corn in a small wooden box, the meal in a gourd; and, by the way, the gourd is one of the most convenient and necessary utensils on a plantation. Besides supplying the place of all kinds of crockery in a slave cabin, it is used for carrying water to the fields. Another, also, contains the dinner. It dispenses with the necessity of pails, dippers, basins, and such tin and wooden superfluities altogether.

When the corn is ground, and fire is made, the bacon is taken down from the nail on which it hangs, a slice cut off and thrown upon the coals to broil. The majority of slaves have no knife, much less a fork. They cut their bacon with the axe at the woodpile. The corn meal is mixed with a little water, placed in the fire, and baked. When it is "done brown," the ashes are scraped off; and being placed upon a chip, which answers for a table, the tenant of the slave hut is ready to sit down upon the ground to supper. By this time it is usually midnight. The same fear of punishment with which they approach the gin-house, possesses them again on lying down to get a snatch of rest. It is the fear of oversleeping in the morning. Such an offence would certainly be attended with not less than twenty lashes. With a prayer that he may be on his feet and wide awake at the first sound of the horn, he sinks to his slumbers nightly.

The softest couches in the world are not to be found in the log mansion of the slave. The one whereon I reclined year after year, was a plank twelve inches wide and ten feet long. My pillow was a stick of wood. The bedding was a coarse blanket, and not a rag or shred beside. Moss might be used, were it not that it directly breeds a swarm of fleas.

The cabin is constructed of logs, without floor or window. The latter is altogether unnecessary, the crevices between the logs admitting sufficient light. In stormy weather the rain drives through them, rendering it comfortless and extremely disagreeable. The rude door hangs on great wooden hinges. In one end is constructed an awkward fire-place.

An hour before day light the horn is blown. Then the slaves arouse, prepare their breakfast, fill a gourd with water, in another deposit their dinner of cold bacon and corn cake, and hurry to the field again. It is an offence invariably followed by a flogging, to be found at the quarters after daybreak. Then the fears and labors of another day begin; and until its close there is no such thing as rest. He fears he will be caught lagging through the day; he fears to approach the gin-house with his basket-load of cotton at night; he fears, when he lies down, that he will oversleep himself in the morning. Such is a true, faithful, unexaggerated picture and description of the slave's daily life, during the time of cotton-picking, on the shores of Bayou Boeuf.

Source: Solomon Northup, *Twelve Years a Slave: Narrative of Solomon Northup, a Citizen of New-York, Kidnapped in Washington City in 1841, and Rescued in 1853, from a Cotton Plantation near the Red River in Louisiana* (London: Sampson Low, Son, 1853).

An Effort to Cherish and Cultivate the Feelings and Habits of Delicacy and Morality among Our Negroes Is Forcibly Urged upon Us

While many slaves like Solomon Northup lived in simple log cabins constructed without floors or windows, other types of slave quarters did exist. Between 1820 and 1860, slaveholders debating the best methods for managing slaves engaged one another in the pages of southern agricultural journals. Housing was at the center of many of these exchanges, as slaveholders balanced construction costs against investments in healthy slaves, notions of moral uplift against commitments to racial hierarchy, and concerns about plantation aesthetics against desires for social control. These tensions are reflected in this letter to the *Southern Cultivator* from a slaveholder in 1850. Like Andrew Jackson Downing in the previous chapter, the author seeks to create "good houses" suited to the needs of their inhabitants, but in the context of slavery, details about building materials and house dimensions also reflect masters' contradictory assumptions about African Americans' capacities for domestic life.

In building houses for negroes, it is important to set them well up, (say 2½ or 3 feet from the ground to the sills) so as to be conveniently swept underneath. When thus elevated, if there should be any filth under them, the master or overseer, in passing can see it, and have it removed. The houses should be neat and comfortable; as far as circumstances will allow, it looks best to have them of uniform size and appearance; 16 by 18 feet is a convenient size for a small family. If there be many children in a family a larger house will be necessary.

Many persons, in building negro houses, in order to get clay convenient for filling the hearth, and for mortar, dig a hole under the floor. As such excavations uniformly become a common receptacle for filth, which generates disease, they should by no means be allowed. In sods where the clay will make brick, the saving of fuel, and the greater security against fire, render it a matter of economy to build brick chimneys. In all cases the chimneys should be extended fully two feet above the roof, that there may be less danger in discharging sparks. They are also less liable to smoke from currents of wind driving down the fire. This may be effectually prevented by the following simple precaution: Around the top of the chimney throw out a base of some 8 or 10 inches wide and from the outer edge of this draw in the cap at an angle of 35 or 40 degrees with the horizon until true with the flue. No matter in what direction the wind blows, on striking this inclined plain the current will glance upwards and pass the chimney, without the possibility of blowing it. On page 454 of Reports of Commissioner of Patents for 1844, will be found plates illustrative of my meaning, which Dr. Lee will please copy in the CULTIVATOR, with the necessary explanation. The wings of the angles as explained in the Reports, are however, unnecessary, as the remedy is effectual without them, though they evidently increase the draft. A coat of white-wash inside and out, every Summer, adds very much to the neat and comfortable appearance of the buildings and is also, by its cleansing and purifying effect, conducive to health. The cost is almost nothing, as one barrel of good lime will whitewash a dozen common-sized negro houses, and any negro can put it on.

If there be not natural shades sufficient to keep the houses comfortable, a row of Mulberries, or such other shades as may suit the owner's fancy, should by all means, be planted in front, and so as to protect the houses on the south and southwest.

The negroes should be required to keep their houses and yards clean; and in case of neglect should receive such punishment as will be likely to insure more cleanly habits in future.

In no case should two families be allowed to occupy the same house. The crowding a number into one house is unhealthy. It breeds contention; is destructive of delicacy of feeling, and it promotes immorality between the sexes.

In addition to their dwellings, where there are a number of negroes, they should be provided with a suitable number of properly located water closets. These may contribute an income much greater than their cost, by enabling the owner to prepare poudrette; while they serve the much more important purpose of cultivating feelings of delicacy. . . .

Most persons allow their negroes to cultivate a small crop of their own. For a number of reasons the plan is a bad one. It is next to impossible to keep them from working their crops on Sabbaths. They labor of nights when they should be at rest. There is no saving more than to give them the same amount, for like all other animals he is only capable of doing a certain amount of labor without injury. To this point he may be worked at his regular task, and any labor beyond this is an injury to both master and slave. They will pilfer to add what corn and cotton they may have made. If they sell their crop and trade for themselves they are apt to be cheated out of a good portion of their labor. They will have many things in their possession under color of purchase which we know not whether they obtained honestly. As far as possible it is best to place temptation out of their reach. We have all their time and service, and can surely afford to furnish them with such things as they ought to have. Let us spend on them in extra presents as much as their crop (if they had one) would yield. By this means we may keep them from whiskey and supply them with articles of service to a much greater extent than they would get if allowed to trade for themselves, while we avoid the objections above stated.

Believing that the strolling about of negroes for a week at a time during what are called the Christmas Holidays, is productive of much evil, the writer has set his face against the custom. Christmas is observed as a Sacred Festival. On that day as good a dinner as the plantation will afford is served for the negroes, and they all set down to a common table, but the next day we go to work. From considerations both of morality and needful rest and recreation to the negro, I much prefer giving a week in July when the crop is laid by, to giving three days at Christmas.

On small farms where there are few negroes, it may be proper to allow them to visit to a limited extent, but on large plantations there can be no want of society, and consequently no excuse for visiting except among themselves. If allowed to run about, they will rarely ever take wives at home. The men wish an excuse for absence, that under pretext of being at their wife's house, they may run about all over the neighborhood. Let it be a settled principle that men and their wives must live together. That if they cannot be suited at home they must live single, and there will be no further difficulty. If a master has a servant and no suitable one of the other sex for a companion, he had better give an extra price for one he would be willing to marry, than to have one man owning the husband and another the wife. It frequently happens where a husband and wife belong to different persons that one owner sells out and wishes to move. Neither is willing to part with his servant, or if one will consent, the other is not able to buy; consequently husband and wife must part. This is a sure evil, surely much greater than restricting to the plantation in making a selection. . . .

In the intercourse of negroes among themselves, no quarreling nor opprobrious epithets, no swearing nor obscene language, should ever be allowed. Children should be required to be respectful to those who are grown, more especially to the old, and the strong should never be allowed to impose on the weak. Men should be taught that it is disgraceful to abuse or impose on the weaker sex, and if a man should so far forget and disgrace himself as to strike a woman, the women should be made to give him the hickory stick and then ride him on a rail. The wife, however, should never be required to strike her husband, for fear of its unhappy influence over their future respect and kindness to each other.

The negroes should not be allowed to run about over the neighborhood; they should be encouraged to attend Church when it is within convenient distance. Where there are pious negroes on the plantation who are so disposed, they should be allowed and encouraged to hold prayer-meetings among themselves: and where the number is too great to be accommodated in one of the negro houses, they should have a separate building for the purpose of worship. Where it can be done, the services of a Minister should be procured for their special benefit. By having the appointments for preaching at noon, during Summer, and at night during Winter, the Preacher could consult his own convenience as to the day of the week, without in the least interfering with the duties of the farm.

A word to those who think and care but little about their own soul or the soul of the negro, and yet desire a good reputation for their children. Children are fond of the company of negroes, not only because the deference shown them makes them feel perfectly at ease, but the subjects of conversation are on a level with their capacity, while the simple tales, and the witch and ghost stories so common among negroes, excite the young imagination and enlist the feelings. If in this association the child becomes familiar with indelicate, vulgar, and lascivious manners and conversation, an impression is made upon the mind and heart, which lasts for years—perhaps for life. Could we in all cases trace these effects to their real causes, I doubt not but many young men and women of respectable parentage and bright prospects who have made shipwreck of all their earthly hopes have been led to the fatal step by the seeds of corruption, which in the days of childhood and youth were sown in their hearts by the indelicate and lascivious manners and conversation of their father's negroes. If this opinion be correct, an effort to cherish and cultivate the feelings and habits of delicacy and morality among our negroes is forcibly urged upon us by a regard for the respectability of our children, to say nothing of the prospects of both child and servant in another world and of our own responsibility when the great Master shall require an account of our stewardship.

I have given you, Mr. Editor, an outline of my own management. If any of your correspondents will point out a more excellent way, he will benefit your readers, and much oblige your friend.

Source: "Management of Negroes," *Southern Cultivator*, November 1850, 162–164.

3

Home, Civilization, and Citizenship

As the domestic ideal increasingly included those beyond the white middle class (albeit in uneven and problematic ways, as depicted in the previous chapter), it inspired unexpected claims for political rights and supported new notions of citizenship. Harriet Beecher Stowe's famous antislavery novel, *Uncle Tom's Cabin*, renders the connection between home life and rights explicit, introducing Tom in the context of his respectable domesticity. How could Americans justify the enslavement of such a moral and homely man? How could the nation countenance an institution that endangered respectable home life? Echoing Stowe, after emancipation, Reconstruction, and the rise of Jim Crow, W. E. B. Du Bois used writings and photographs to document and advocate for a new black domesticity fitted for freedom and capable of instilling the skills of citizenship. This new African American home would, as depicted in the writings of Ida B. Wells, share white, middle-class moral ideas yet be adapted to community circumstances and goals.

Indeed many groups struggled to articulate the balance between conformity to the Victorian domestic mainstream and maintenance of cultural distinctiveness. While the 1887 Dawes Severalty Act reveals the U.S. government's faith that dwelling in a private home would "civilize" Native Americans and fit them for citizenship, Susan La Flesche's account of Native American home life quietly refutes the homogenizing effects of domesticity, instead noting continuity with the past and the persistence of tradition among her people.

Recognizing the ways in which domestic order and morality had become credentials for citizenship and objects of public policy, many marginalized groups seized upon them to advance a variety of political agendas. As a result, traditional domesticity was stretched in new directions, and seemingly radical calls for reform remained tied to conservative rhetoric and values. And so labor leader William Sylvis advocates for trade unions, and Frances Willard argues for women's suffrage, each building a case on women's proper role as keepers of the moral home.

Even those who sought to challenge Victorian notions of gendered labor and paid employment often failed to think themselves free of the conventions of idealized domesticity. For example, the feminist lecturer Caroline Dall decries women's isolation in the home yet buttresses her argument for women's employment in terms of improved marital relations and a happy home life. Likewise, the legal case of Nancy Miller contends that women's domestic labor has economic value but ultimately suggests that women's financial independence within marriage will preserve domestic harmony. Again, rather than undermining domesticity, demands for new rights and economic relationships emphasized how reform would safeguard the home and better permit it to do its true moral and cultural work. What do you think of this as a strategy for change? Why did the domestic ideal prove so resilient at the end of the nineteenth century?

There Was Something about His Whole Air Self-Respecting and Dignified

Harriet Beecher Stowe's *Uncle Tom's Cabin* was first published serially in 1851 and 1852 in the *National Era*, an abolitionist journal. When the book was released in March 1852, the first printing of five thousand copies sold out in two days, and three hundred thousand copies were sold in the first year of publication. A response to the 1850 Fugitive Slave Law requiring the return of runaway slaves, Stowe's novel is essentially about the possibilities for a moral life in a nation committed to slavery. When readers encounter Tom's idealized domestic arrangements, they already know that his master, Mr. Shelby, has agreed to sell him. The fragility of domestic life is a recurrent theme as Tom is passed from one situation and owner to the next. Every family he encounters—white and black, free and enslaved—has been compromised by slavery's influence. Throughout the novel, domestic settings serve as markers and measures of characters' morality—punctuating Tom's journey from his own humble cabin to Simon Legree's mansion of "coarse neglect and discomfort."

The cabin of Uncle Tom was a small log building close adjoining to "the house," as the negro *par excellence* designates his master's dwelling. In front it had a neat garden-patch, where, every summer, strawberries, raspberries, and a variety of fruits and vegetables, flourished under careful tending. The whole front of it was covered by a large scarlet bignonia and a native multiflora rose, which, entwisting and interlacing, left scarce a vestige of the rough logs to be seen. Here, also, in summer, various brilliant annuals, such as marigolds, petunias, four-o'clocks, found an indulgent corner in which to unfold their splendors, and were the delight and pride of Aunt Chloe's heart.

Let us enter the dwelling. The evening meal at the house is over, and Aunt Chloe, who presided over its preparation as head cook, has left to inferior officers in the kitchen the business of clearing away and washing dishes, and come out into her own snug territories, to "get her ole man's supper"; therefore, doubt not that it is she you see by the fire, presiding with anxious interest over certain frizzling items in a stewpan, and anon with grave consideration lifting the cover of a bake-kettle from whence steam forth indubitable intimations of "something good." A round, black, shining face is hers, so glossy as to suggest the idea that she might have been washed over with white of eggs, like one of her own tea rusks. Her whole plump countenance beams with satisfaction and contentment from under her well-starched checked turban, bearing on it, however, if we must confess it, a little of that tinge of self-consciousness which becomes the first cook of the neighborhood, as Aunt Chloe was universally held and acknowledged to be.

A cook she certainly was, in the very bone and centre of her soul. Not a chicken or turkey or duck in the barnyard but looked grave when they saw her approaching, and seemed evidently to be reflecting on their latter end; and certain it was that she was always meditating on trussing, stuffing, and roasting, to a degree that was calculated to inspire terror in any reflecting fowl living. Her corn-cake, in all its varieties of hoe-cake, dodgers, muffins, and other species too numerous to mention, was a sublime mystery to all less practised compounders; and she would shake her fat sides with honest pride and merriment, as she would narrate the fruitless efforts that one and another of her compeers had made to attain to her elevation.

The arrival of company at the house, the arranging of dinners and suppers "in style," awoke all the energies of her soul; and no sight was more welcome to her than a pile of travelling trunks launched on the verandah, for then she foresaw fresh efforts and fresh triumphs.

Just at present, however, Aunt Chloe is looking into the bakepan; in which congenial operation we shall leave her till we finish our picture of the cottage.

In one corner of it stood a bed, covered neatly with a snowy spread; and by the side of it was a piece of carpeting, of some considerable size. On this piece of carpeting Aunt Chloe took her stand, as being decidedly in the upper walks of life; and it and the bed by which it lay, and the whole corner, in fact, were treated with distinguished consideration, and made, so far as possible, sacred from the marauding inroads and desecrations of little folks. In fact, that corner was the *drawing-room* of the establishment. In the other corner was a bed of much humbler pretensions, and evidently designed for *use*. The wall over the fireplace was adorned with some very brilliant scriptural prints, and a portrait of General Washington, drawn and colored in a manner which would certainly have astonished that hero, if ever he happened to meet with its like.

On a rough bench in the corner, a couple of woolly-headed boys, with glistening black eyes and fat shining cheeks, were busy in superintending the first walking operations of the baby, which, as is usually the case, consisted in getting up on its feet, balancing a moment, and then tumbling down,—each successive failure being violently cheered, as something decidedly clever.

A table, somewhat rheumatic in its limbs, was drawn out in front of the fire, and covered with a cloth, displaying cups and saucers of a decidedly brilliant pattern, with other symptoms of an approaching meal. At this table was seated Uncle Tom, Mr. Shelby's best hand, who, as he is to be the hero of our story, we must daguerreotype for our readers. He was a large, broad-chested, powerfully made man, of a full glossy black, and a face whose truly African features were characterized by an expression of grave and steady good sense, united with much kindliness and benevolence. There was something about his whole air self-respecting and dignified, yet united with a confiding and humble simplicity.

He was very busily intent at this moment on a slate lying before him, on which he was carefully and slowly endeavoring to accomplish a copy of some letters, in which operation he was overlooked by young Mas'r

George, a smart, bright boy of thirteen, who appeared fully to realize the dignity of his position as instructor.

"Not that way, Uncle Tom,—not that way," said he, briskly, as Uncle Tom laboriously brought up the tail of his *g* the wrong side out; "that makes a *q*, you see."

"La sakes, now, does it?" said Uncle Tom, looking with a respectful, admiring air, as his young teacher flourishingly scrawled *q*'s and *g*'s innumerable for his edification; and then, taking the pencil in his big, heavy fingers, he patiently recommenced.

"How easy white folks al'us does things!" said Aunt Chloe, pausing while she was greasing a griddle with a scrap of bacon on her fork, and regarding young Master George with pride. "The way he can write, now! and read, too! and then to come out here evenings and read his lessons to us,—it's mighty interestin'!"

"But, Aunt Chloe, I'm getting mighty hungry," said George. "Isn't that cake in the skillet almost done?"

"Mose done, Mas'r George," said Aunt Chloe, lifting the lid and peeping in,—"browning beautiful—a real lovely brown. Ah! let me alone for dat. Missis let Sally try to make some cake, t' other day, jes to *larn* her, she said. 'Oh, go way, Missis,' says I; 'it really hurts my feelin's, now, to see good vittles spiled dat ar way! Cake ris all to one side—no shape at all; no more than my shoe;—go way!"

And with this final expression of contempt for Sally's greenness, Aunt Chloe whipped the cover off the bake-kettle, and disclosed to view a neatly baked pound-cake, of which no city confectioner need to have been ashamed. This being evidently the central point of the entertainment, Aunt Chloe began now to bustle about earnestly in the supper department.

"Here you, Mose and Pete! get out de way, you niggers! Get away, Polly, honey,—mammy'll give her baby somefin, by and by. Now, Mas'r George, you jest take off dem books, and set down now with my old man, and I'll take up de sausages, and have de first griddle full of cakes on your plates in less dan no time."

"They wanted me to come to supper in the house," said George; "but I knew what was what too well for that, Aunt Chloe."

Source: Harriet Beecher Stowe, *Uncle Tom's Cabin; or, Life among the Lowly* (Boston: John P. Jewett, 1852; repr., Cambridge: Belknap Press, 1962).

Figure 3.1. Game cards from the Game of Uncle Tom's Cabin (V. S. W. Parkhurst, Providence, 1852; courtesy of the American Antiquarian Society) depict Uncle Tom, Aunt Chloe, and their two sons. Note that Uncle Tom's humble but respectable domesticity is suggested by the inclusion of his cabin. The game itself underscores the ways in which slavery disrupted the home lives of both black and white southerners. The specific rules of play are difficult to follow, but players are instructed to "ascertain what family would be most pleasing to complete." Families, enslaved and free, are united and divided throughout the play of the game.

Figure 3.2. "Happy Family," from Clinton B. Fisk, *Plain Counsel for the Freedmen* (1866; Library of Congress, Prints & Photographs Division, LC-USZ62-86365) was intended to offer newly emancipated slaves a vision of freedom: "Heretofore, you have had no opportunity to provide homes for yourselves and families. . . . But all that is now changed. . . . No one can make you move away. You need not ask permission to live and die there. You command the situation." This image clearly reflects Fisk's advice to "make your homes as pretty as possible. A little paint, a little whitewash, a few yards of paper, some gravel walks and a few flowers, make all the difference in the world in the appearance of homes." Compare this illustration with those in chapter 1 as well as the accounts of slave dwellings. How realistic was this image at the time it was published?

Everything of Beauty and Daintiness Had Disappeared with the
Rude Uprooting of the African Home

**Nearly forty years after Clinton Fisk offered his advice to freedmen,
W. E. B. Du Bois considered "the problem of housing the Negro." Published in 1901, this article uses the tools and insights of the latest sociology
to interpret the impact of slave housing on the domestic lives of African
Americans. In it, Du Bois considers the consequences of the spatial separation of slaves and masters and of house slaves and those who lived in
the "quarters." In many respects, Du Bois's analysis echoes contemporary
accounts of other Progressive reformers investigating the geographic segmentation and social stratification of turn-of-the-century cities. Slavery,
poor housing, and social isolation denied African Americans the good
habits and training needed to create proper homes. Unlike the southern
planters who hoped well-designed slave cabins would produce moral and
well-behaved slaves, Du Bois emphasizes the connections between home
and the skills required of free men and women.**

Commercial slavery, which looked upon the slave primarily as an investment, meant death to the Negro home. One of the first signs of the
changed condition of things was perhaps the "Detached Group" as I
shall designate the second type of slave homes. The "Detached Group"
was the group of slave cabins without a Big House—i.e. removed from
the direct eye of the master, either to a far part of the same plantation or
to a different plantation. The Big House has turned to brick, with imposing proportions, surrounding trees and gardens and a certain state and
elegance with which the old South was flavored. The house servants are
now either lodged in the Big House or in trim cabins near. The mass of
the slaves are down at the "quarters" by themselves, under the direct eye
of the overseer. This change was slight in appearance but of great importance; it widened the distance between the top and bottom of the social
ladder, it placed a third party between master and slave and it removed
the worst side of the slave hierarchy far from the eyes of its better self.

At first thought it might seem an advantage to remove thus the ex-
tremes of society from each other. Nineteenth century experience has,
however, taught us better. It not only deprives the helpless of their sole
source of help, but among the lowest orders themselves it strengthens

the hands of the worst element. Thieving, sexual looseness and debauchery could now be spread among the slave cabins by the act of the Negroes themselves far faster than occasional visits of the mistress could counteract the evil. The Negro home, deprived of nearly every method of self-protection, received here its deadliest hurt, from which it has not yet recovered.

From the "Detached Group" to "Absentee Landlordism" was but a step. The rich lands to the southwest, the high price of cotton, and the rapidly increasing internal slave trade, was the beginning of a system of commercial slavery in the gulf states which will ever remain a disgraceful chapter in American history. In its worst phase there was no Big House and cultivated master, only an unscrupulous, paid overseer, lawless and almost irresponsible if he only made crops large enough. The homes of the field-hands were filthy hovels where they slept. There was no family life, no meals, no marriages, no decency, only an endless round of toil and a wild debauch at Christmas time. In the forests of Louisiana, the bottoms of Mississippi, and the Sea Islands of Georgia, where the Negro slave sank lowest in oppression and helplessness, the Negro home practically disappeared, and the house was simply rude, inadequate shelter.

But whither went the Big House, when so entirely separated from the slave quarters? It moved to town and with it moved the house-servants. These privileged slaves were trained and refined from contact with the masters; they were often allowed to accumulate a *peculium*; they were in some cases freed and gained considerable property, holding it in some friendly white man's name. Their home life improved and although it was far from ideal, yet it was probably as good as that of the Northern workingman, with some manifest differences; sexual looseness was the weakest point, arising from subordination to the whites and the lessons learned therefrom by the servants themselves. They lived often in small one- or two-room homes behind the masters' mansions, reached by alleys—a method which has since left the peculiar alley problem in Southern cities. Some of the slaves and the freedmen lived in a Negro quarter by themselves, although the distinctive Negro quarter of towns is largely post-bellum.

Thus we have in slavery times, among other tendencies and many exceptions, three fairly distinct types of Negro homes: the patriarchal type, found at its best in Virginia, where the housing of the field hands might be compared with that of the poorer of the Northern working-men; the separate group and absentee type where the slaves had practically no homes and no family life; and the town group where the few house-servants were fairly well housed. In discussing slavery and incidents connected with it these varying circumstances are continually lost sight of. Nowhere are they portrayed with more truth and sanity than in "Uncle Tom's Cabin," and yet to this day there are unbalanced minds that, having known personally only the Shelbys or the St. Clairs, refuse absolutely to believe in the reality of Legree.

The house of the slave, which I have sought to show in its various relationships and degrees of squalor, had certain general characteristics which we must notice carefully. First, there was the lack of comfort; the African knew nothing of the little niceties and comforts of the civilized home—everything of beauty and daintiness had disappeared with the rude uprooting of the African home, and little had been learned to replace them. Thus, even to this day, there is a curious bareness and roughness in the ordinary Negro home, the remains of an uncouthness which in slavery times made the home anything but a pleasant lovable place. There were, for instance, few chairs with backs, no sheets on the beds, no books, no newspapers, no closets or out-houses, no bed-rooms, no table-cloths and very few dishes, no carpets and usually no floors, no windows, no pictures, no clocks, no lights at night save that of the fire-place, little or nothing save bare rough shelter.

Secondly, and closely connected with the first, was the lack of hygienic customs: every nation has its habits and customs, handed down from elders, which have enabled the race to survive. But the continuity of Negro family tradition had been broken and the traditions of the white environment never learned; then too the rules and exactions of the plantation favored unhealthy habits; there ensued a disgusting lack of personal cleanliness, bad habits of eating and sleeping, habits of breathing bad air, of wearing inadequate clothing—all such changes and abuses in everyday life for which the world's grandchildren must eventually pay.

Thirdly, there was in the slave home necessarily almost an entire lack of thrift, or the ordinary incentives to thrift. The food and fuel were certain and extra faithfulness or saving could make little or no difference. On the other hand, cunning and thieving could secure many a

Figures 3.3 and 3.4. These photographs of an African American man giving a piano lesson to a young African American woman, 1899 or 1900, and of the home of C. C. Dodson, Knoxville, Tennessee, c. 1899 (Library of Congress, Prints and Photographs Division, LC-DIG-ppmsca-08779 and LC-USZ62-49479, respectively) were part of the Georgia Negro Exhibit compiled by W. E. B. Du Bois for the 1900 Paris Exposition. Included in a larger exhibit documenting the history and present circumstances of African Americans, the photographs were intended to capture the progress made since emancipation. Despite Du Bois's concerns about slavery's impact on black domesticity, these images suggest a high level of refinement among the black elite. The exposition judges awarded Du Bois a gold medal for his contribution.

forbidden knick-knack, far more than honest cultivation of the little garden spot which each family often had. The thriftiest slave could only look forward to slavery for himself and children.

Fourthly, there was the absence of the father—that is, the lack of authority in the slave father to govern or protect his family. His wife could be made his master's concubine, his daughter could be outraged, his son whipped, or he himself sold away without his being able to protest or lift a preventing finger. Naturally, his authority in his own house was simply such as could rest upon brute force alone, and he easily sank to a position of male guest in the house, without respect or responsibility.

Fifthly, and correlated to the last, was the absence of the mother. The slave mother could spend little or no time at home. She was either a field-hand or a house-servant, and her children had little care or attention. There was consequently in the family no feeling of unity or permanence; it was a temporary, almost fortuitous agglomeration of atoms—it was not an organism, and it had neither force nor pride.

Such was the home and the family which slavery bequeathed to freedom.

Source: W. E. B. Du Bois, "The Problem of Housing the Negro: The Home of the Slave," *Southern Workman* 30 (1901): 486–495.

Separate and Apart from Any Tribe of Indians Therein

Sponsored by Representative Henry Dawes of Massachusetts in 1887, the General Allotment Act (known also as the Dawes Severalty Act) was intended to encourage the breakup of tribal lands in order to "civilize" Indians and ease their assimilation into the U.S. cultural mainstream. Each head of a family would receive 160 acres of land (or 320 acres of grazing land), which could not be sold for twenty-five years. At that time, the Indians would receive full title to the land and become American citizens. Many white reformers called the legislation the "Indian Emancipation Act." Committed to their faith in the transformative power of homeownership, they failed to foresee the hardships of farming and the threat of predatory white settlers for whom homes and land were commodities as much as tools of civilization. Between 1887 and the act's repeal in 1934, ninety million acres of Indian land were lost to non-Indian ownership.

An Act to provide for the allotment of lands in severalty to Indians on the various reservations, and to extend the protection of the laws of the United States and the Territories over the Indians, and for other purposes.

Be it enacted by the Senate and House of Representatives of the United States of America in Congress assembled, That in all cases where any tribe or band of Indians has been, or shall hereafter be, located upon any reservation created for their use, either by treaty stipulation or by virtue of an act of Congress or executive order setting apart the same for their use, the President of the United States be, and he hereby is, authorized, whenever in his opinion any reservation or any part thereof of such Indians is advantageous for agricultural and grazing purposes, to cause said reservation, or any part thereof, to be surveyed, or resurveyed if necessary, and to allot the lands in said reservation in severalty to any Indian located thereon in quantities as follows:

To each head of a family, one-quarter of a section;

To each single person over eighteen years of age, one-eighth of a section;

To each orphan child under eighteen years of age, one-eighth of a section; and

To each other single person under eighteen years now living, or who may be born prior to the date of the order of the President directing an allotment of the lands embraced in any reservation, one-sixteenth of a section: Provided, That in case there is not sufficient land in any of said reservations to allot lands to each individual of the classes above named in quantities as above provided, the lands embraced in such reservation or reservations shall be allotted to each individual of each of said classes pro rata in accordance with the provisions of this act: And provided further, That where the treaty or act of Congress setting apart such reservation provides for the allotment of lands in severalty in quantities in excess of those herein provided, the President, in making allotments upon such reservation, shall allot the lands to each individual Indian belonging thereon in quantity as specified in such treaty or act: And provided further, That when the lands allotted are only valuable for grazing purposes, an additional allotment of such grazing lands, in quantities as above provided, shall be made to each individual.

Sec. 2. That all allotments set apart under the provisions of this act shall be selected by the Indians, heads of families selecting for their minor children, and the agents shall select for each orphan child, and in such manner as to embrace the improvements of the Indians making the selection. Where the improvements of two or more Indians have been made on the same legal subdivision of land, unless they shall otherwise agree, a provisional line may be run dividing said lands between them, and the amount to which each is entitled shall be equalized in the assignment of the remainder of the land to which they are entitled under this act: Provided, That if any one entitled to an allotment shall fail to make a selection within four years after the President shall direct that allotments may be made on a particular reservation, the Secretary of the Interior may direct the agent of such tribe or band, if such there be, and if there be no agent, then a special agent appointed for that purpose, to make a selection for such Indian, which election shall be allotted as in cases where selections are made by the Indians, and patents shall issue in like manner.

Sec. 3. That the allotments provided for in this act shall be made by special agents appointed by the President for such purpose, and the agents in charge of the respective reservations on which the allotments are directed to be made, under such rules and regulations as the Secretary of the Interior may from time to time prescribe, and shall be certified by such agents to the Commissioner of Indian Affairs, in duplicate, one copy to be retained in the Indian Office and the order to be transmitted to the Secretary of the Interior for his action, and to be deposited in the General Land Office.

Sec. 4. That where any Indian not residing upon a reservation, or for whose tribe no reservation has been provided by treaty, act of Congress, or executive order, shall make settlement upon any surveyed or unsurveyed lands of the United States not otherwise appropriated, he or she shall be entitled, upon application to the local land-office for the district in which the lands are located, to have the same allotted to him or her, and to his or her children, in quantities and manner as provided in this act for Indians residing upon reservations; and when such settlement is made upon unsurveyed lands, the grant to such Indians shall be adjusted upon the survey of the lands so as to conform thereto; and patents shall be issued to them for such lands in the manner and with the restrictions as herein provided. And the fees to which the officers of such local land-office would have been entitled had such lands been entered under the general laws for the disposition of the public lands shall be paid to them, from any moneys in the Treasury of the United States not otherwise appropriated, upon a statement of an account in their behalf for such fees by the Commissioner of the General Land Office, and a certification of such account to the Secretary of the Treasury by the Secretary of the Interior.

Sec. 5. That upon the approval of the allotments provided for in this act by the Secretary of the Interior, he shall cause patents to issue therefor in the name of the allottees, which patents shall be of the legal effect, and declare that the United States does and will hold the land thus allotted, for the period of twenty-five years, in trust for the sole use and benefit of the Indian to whom such allotment shall have been made, or, in case of his decease, of his heirs according to the laws of the State or Territory where such land is located, and that at the expiration of said period the United States will convey the same by patent to said Indian, or his heirs as aforesaid, in fee, discharged of said trust and free of all charge or incumbrance whatsoever: Provided, That the President of the United States may in any case in his discretion extend the period. And if any conveyance shall be made of the lands set apart and allotted as herein provided, or any contract made touching the same, before the expiration of the time above mentioned, such conveyance or contract shall be absolutely null and void: Provided, That the law of descent and partition in force in the State or Territory where such lands are situate shall apply thereto after patents therefor have been executed and delivered, except as herein otherwise provided; and the laws of the State of Kansas regulating the descent and partition of real estate shall, so far as practicable, apply to all lands in the Indian Territory which may be allotted in severalty under the provisions of this act: And provided further, That at any time after lands have been allotted to all the Indians of any tribe as herein provided, or sooner if in the opinion of the President it shall be for the best interests of said tribe, it shall be lawful for the Secretary of the Interior to negotiate with such Indian tribe for the purchase and release by said tribe, in conformity with the treaty or statute under which such reservation is held, of such portions of its reservation not allotted as such tribe shall, from time to time, consent to sell, on such terms and conditions as shall be considered just and equitable between the United

States and said tribe of Indians, which purchase shall not be complete until ratified by Congress, and the form and manner of executing such release shall also be prescribed by Congress: Provided however, That all lands adapted to agriculture, with or without irrigation so sold or released to the United States by any Indian tribe shall be held by the United States for the sole purpose of securing homes to actual settlers and shall be disposed of by the United States to actual and bona fide settlers only in tracts not exceeding one hundred and sixty acres to any one person, on such terms as Congress shall prescribe, subject to grants which Congress may make in aid of education: And provided further, That no patents shall issue therefor except to the person so taking the same as and for a homestead, or his heirs, and after the expiration of five years occupancy thereof as such homestead; and any conveyance of said lands so taken as a homestead, or any contract touching the same, or lien thereon, created prior to the date of such patent, shall be null and void. And the sums agreed to be paid by the United States as purchase money for any portion of any such reservation shall be held in the Treasury of the United States for the sole use of the tribe or tribes of Indians; to whom such reservations belonged; and the same, with interest thereon at three per cent per annum, shall be at all times subject to appropriation by Congress for the education and civilization of such tribe or tribes of Indians or the members thereof. The patents aforesaid shall be recorded in the General Land Office, and afterward delivered, free of charge, to the allottee entitled thereto. And if any religious society or other organization is now occupying any of the public lands to which this act is applicable, for religious or educational work among the Indians, the Secretary of the Interior is hereby authorized to confirm such occupation to such society or organization, in quantity not exceeding one hundred and sixty acres in any one tract, so long as the same shall be so occupied, on such terms as he shall deem just; but nothing herein contained shall change or alter any claim of such society for religious or educational purposes heretofore granted by law. And hereafter in the employment of Indian police, or any other employees in the public service among any of the Indian tribes or bands affected by this act, and where Indians can perform the duties required, those Indians who have availed themselves of the provisions of this act and become citizens of the United States shall be preferred.

Figure 3.5. A model Indian cottage at Hampton Institute in Virginia from Alice C. Fletcher, *Historical Sketch of the Omaha Tribe of Indians* (Washington, DC: Judd & Detweiler, 1885) illustrates the ideal of domesticity that the Dawes Act was intended to foster. Fletcher's ethnological study documented the tribe's traditional practices of farming and holding property. Over time, the Omaha incorporated "the advantages of civilization," building frame and log houses and adopting modern agricultural tools. Some left Nebraska to study at schools such as Hampton Institute, where model cottages "accustomed them to the refinements of life." Fletcher's work helped persuade Congress to allot the Omaha's lands in severalty to the tribe, and Fletcher herself oversaw the process from 1882 to 1884. A supporter of the Dawes Act, she was appointed a special allotting agent by the United States in 1887.

Sec. 6. That upon the completion of said allotments and the patenting of the lands to said allottees, each and every member of the respective bands or tribes of Indians to whom allotments have been made shall have the benefit of and be subject to the laws, both civil and criminal, of the State or Territory in which they may reside; and no Territory shall pass or enforce any law denying any such Indian within its jurisdiction the equal protection of the law. And every Indian born within the territorial limits of the United States to whom allotments shall have been made under the provisions of this act, or under any law or treaty, and every Indian born within the territorial limits of the United States who has voluntarily taken up, within said limits, his residence separate and apart from any tribe of Indians therein, and has adopted the habits of civilized life, is hereby declared to be a citizen of the United States, and is entitled to all the rights, privileges, and immunities of such citizens, whether said Indian has been or not, by birth or otherwise, a member of any tribe of Indians within the territorial limits of the United States without in any manner impairing or otherwise affecting the right of any such Indian to tribal or other property. . . .

Approved, February 8, 1887.

Source: Dawes Severalty Act of 1887, *United States Statutes at Large* (49th Cong., 2nd sess., chap. 119, pp. 388–391).

Living in a Frame House and Learning Very Fast How to Transact Business like White People

Supporters of the Dawes Severalty Act shared the Victorian belief that the right household arrangements would foster proper values and the reformers' faith that improved domestic circumstances could instill good habits and create American citizens. This article by Susan La Flesche suggests the complexities and contradictions of the "civilizing process" from one who experienced them firsthand. La Flesche was born on the Omaha reservation in 1865 and eventually attended Hampton Institute before earning a medical degree from the Woman's Medical College of Pennsylvania at Philadelphia. The first Native American woman to earn a medical degree, she worked as a physician among the Omaha. Here she celebrates the progress made by her people while trying to differentiate changes in external domestic arrangements from an alteration in the nature of "home life."

The home life of the Indian of to-day is essentially the same as the home life of the Indian of thirty years ago. Any progress he may have made is due to the change of environment, produced by the coming of white people, and the consequent passing away of old customs.

The daily routine of home life is the same, the aforesaid change produced by environment being shown by the fact that in place of the tepee the Indian once occupied, he now lives in a frame house and can boast of a well, a stable, a few fruit trees and a vegetable garden. The fact that in place of hunting wild game over the prairies, he now farms and raises good crops of corn, wheat, and oats makes but little difference in the internal workings of the home.

Long ago the Indian had a removable house suited to his requirements, a tepee or tent which was made of buckskin or canvas stretched over a pyramid formed by means of poles tied together at the top with buckskin, a house easy to carry around with him in his nomadic journeyings.

When the tribe found a place where they could settle down and live eight months in the year they built mud lodges as their permanent residences. These are dome-shaped, the frame work consisting of poles, willow branches and rushes, and from base to apex it is covered with sod several inches thick. They have wide entrance ways, several feet long and high enough to permit a tall person to stand upright. They are like tunnels leading into the lodge which is circular in form. Light and air enter by means of a large circular opening in the top of the dome, this also serving as a means of exit for the smoke. The lodge is well ventilated— warm in winter and cool in summer. Several families live in them at a time, and the only two or three now left on this reservation are used for holding councils, public gatherings and dances, as they can accommodate over a hundred people.

How often as children we used to climb upon these lodges and pick the sunflowers and grasses growing on them. Near sunset the old men would sit up on these lodges where they could pursue their meditations undisturbed and alone, and I remember looking at them reverently as I played around with the other children, for I regarded them with a great deal of awe, for to me they seemed so wise.

Trodden by hundreds of feet the earthen floor is almost as hard as stone, and coming in from the hot dusty road how gratefully cool it felt to our little bare feet as we played in and out, riding our make-believe horses made of sun flower stalks. In the centre is a little hollow where the fire is built and all the cooking is done. Around this place we used to gather to listen to thrilling stories of battles with the dreaded Sioux, buffalo hunts and *ghost stories*. When it came to the last I used to look up fearfully at the opening above, for fear I should see a dog looking down, for it is a superstition among the Indians that if a dog looks down through this opening into the lodge some one of the company is sure to die soon. If such a thing happened the dog was killed immediately. It was always a relief to see the blue sky and stars looking down.

After a while the Indians built log houses of only one room the roof covered with turf.

Now, on this reservation we have almost every family living in a neat frame house, one story or one story and a half high, wainscoted, plastered or papered inside; very clean and neatly painted outside. The premises are clear of rubbish.

These houses are built by the Indians with their own money, but the desire to own such houses was started several years ago when the "Connecticut Home-Building Fund" started the Home-Building Department of the Women's National Indian Association. The seed then sown has borne fruit here and elsewhere. Whether you enter with me into a tent, a mud-lodge or log house, or one of these neat frame houses you would see the same home-life going on in every one of them.

There is little variation, one day of the week being almost the same as another.

The family usually arise early—in the summer about sunrise, but in winter the breakfast is usually considerably delayed, for they follow suntime. In most cases the hostess arises and builds the fire, gets the water and cooks the simple meal. Very few have had bread, but it is now getting to be the general rule in many families to make light bread. They have biscuits made with soda or baking powder, and sometimes "fried cakes," light brown in color and very appetizing. Coffee, sometimes fresh beef, for, in this country where there are thousands of head of cattle it is hard to get beef; sometimes fruit, dried, and in the summer potatoes and beans. You can see that their diet is very simple. The food is divided and put on plates, the coffee poured out into cups and then the food is handed around to each individual. Usually after the meal is over the dishes are put away in a little cupboard. If it is summer the husband and men in the family go out to their work and the wife cleans up the house and begins to get the noon-meal. It is the same at breakfast. They do not do very much sewing for their clothes are simply and quickly made. The houses on the reservation are far apart and the women cannot very well pass away the time by gossip with the neighbors, as some of our white friends have the *privilege* of doing. What a deprivation is this! Let us all be thankful for our privileges.

The evening meal is simple, and the time between that and the retiring hour is spent in talking over the events of the day or in telling news.

We have no telegraph lines or telephones, but news has a wonderfully quick way of travelling from one house to another. Rumors on a reservation are the same as rumors anywhere else. When they reach the end of their journey they have received quite an addition, and a wise person will credit only one third of the story as truth.

There are no books, pictures or recreations save the dances, and no games except cards which are used for gambling. A narrow life in some respects. The Indians are passionately fond of their children, having no books, pictures or recreations in their home life they lavish all attention on their children. There are some cases where the step-father or step-mother, as the case may be, makes no difference whatever between their children and the step-children. They *show* their affection for their children also.

Some ask the absurd question, "Do the Indians really love their wives?" The Indians are *human beings* just as the white people are, and there are Indian men who are just as careful, watchful and affectionate to their wives as any one would wish to see anywhere. They do not make an outward show of their affection, but I know from personal observation that they are truly devoted to each other. One day I had to pull a young woman's tooth, and as the husband was a strong muscular man I was in hopes he would support her head for me. He sent for his brother to do it and when he saw me take the forceps up he beat a hasty retreat. I heard him walking up and down in the other room, and when they told him I was through he appeared with such a happy relieved look on his face and thanked me so earnestly. I could not help but be glad for him that she was through with her suffering. There are many instances like this that I know of. Of course, there are some cases entirely different, and where there is no happiness. But so we find it wherever we go in the world.

Indian women no longer stand in the background. Few work in the fields or do heavy work. Where it used to be the lot of the women to provide the wood, now the men get it in almost all cases. Even in so small a thing as walking or riding where the woman had to walk behind or ride in the back of the wagon, now she walks beside her husband, and in vehicles you see the woman riding beside her husband on the seat.

The old customs are fast disappearing and in place of the Indian of twenty years ago, who lived in a tent and supported himself by hunting wild game, we have an independent man who is earning his bread by his own toil, living in a frame house and learning very fast how to transact business like white people. The wife standing beside her husband shows only his true advancement, and the home is happier for this progress.

Source: Susan La Flesche, "The Home-Life of the Indian," *Indian's Friend* 4, no. 10 (1892): 39–40.

They Are, I Know, the Sweet and Pleasant Sunshine of Our Homes

As president of the Woman's Christian Temperance Union from 1879 until 1898, Frances Willard made the connections between domestic life, civilization, and citizenship explicit, drawing even more conservative temperance supporters to call for women's suffrage. In this speech, Willard invokes both the civilizing influence of women's domestic natures and their vulnerability when confined to homes afflicted by drink. Giving women the ballot would expand domestic uplift into the public world of politics while enabling women to bring the power of law to bear on the saloon and home. In other words, the vote would enable the best of the private and public spheres to cross the domestic threshold for the improvement of both realms. Reflecting this blending, Willard's speech uses the tools of womanly moral influence (family stories and biblical references) in service of her reform agenda and political goals.

Think of it! There is a class in every one of our communities—in many of them far the most numerous class—which (I speak not vauntingly; I but name it as a fact) has not in all the centuries of wine, beer, and brandy-drinking developed, as a class, an appetite for alcohol, but whose instincts, on the contrary, set so strongly against intoxicants that if the liquor traffic were dependent on their patronage alone, it would collapse this night as though all the nitro-glycerine of Hell Gate reef had exploded under it.

There is a class whose instinct of self-preservation must forever be opposed to a stimulant which nerves, with dangerous strength, arms already so much stronger than their own, and so maddens the brain God meant to guide those arms, that they strike down the wives men love, and the little children for whom, when sober, they would die. The wife, largely dependent for the support of herself and little ones upon the brain which strong drink paralyzes, the arm it masters, and the skill it renders futile, will in the nature of the case, prove herself unfriendly to the actual or potential source of so much misery. But besides this primal instinct of self-preservation, we have, in the same class of which I speak, another far more high and sacred—I mean the instinct of a mother's love, a wife's devotion, a sister's faithfulness, a daughter's loyalty. And now I ask you to consider earnestly the fact that none of these blessed rays of light and power from woman's heart, are as yet brought to bear upon the rum-shop at the focus of power. They are, I know, the sweet and pleasant sunshine of our homes; they are the beams which light the larger home of social life and send their gentle radiance out even into the great and busy world. But I know, and as the knowledge has grown clearer, my heart was thrilled with gratitude and hope too deep for words, that in a republic all these now divergent beams of light can, through the magic lens, that powerful sun-glass which we name the ballot, be made to converge upon the rum-shop in a blaze of light that shall reveal its full abominations, and a white flame of heat, which, like a pitiless moxa, shall burn this cancerous excrescence from America's fair form. Yes, for there is nothing in the universe so sure, so strong, as love; and love shall do all this—love of maid for sweetheart, wife for husband, or a sister for her brother, of a mother for her son. And I call upon you who are here to-day, good men and brave—you who have welcomed us to other fields in the great fight of the angel against the dragon in society—I call upon you thus to match force with force, to set over against the liquor-dealer's avarice our instinct of self-preservation; and to match the drinker's love of liquor with our love of him! When you can centre all this power in that small bit of paper which falls

> "As silently as snow-flakes fall upon the sod,
> But executes a freeman's will as lightnings do the will of God,"

the rum power will be as much doomed as was the slave power when you gave the ballot to the slaves.

In our argument it has been claimed that by the changeless instincts of her nature and through the most sacred relationships of which that nature has been rendered capable, God has indicated woman, who is the born conservator of home, to be the Nemesis of home's arch enemy, King Alcohol. And further, that in a republic, this power of hers may be most effectively exercised by giving her a voice in the decision by which the rum-shop door shall be opened or closed beside her home. . . .

Nothing worse can ever happen to women at the polls than has been endured by the hour on the part of conservative women of the churches in this land, as they, in scores of towns, have plead with rough, half-drunken men to vote temperance tickets they have handed them, and which, with vastly more of propriety and fitness they might have dropped into the box themselves. They could have done this in a moment, and returned to their homes, instead of spending the whole day in the often futile endeavor to beg from men like these the vote which would preserve their homes from the whisky serpent's breath for one uncertain year. I spent last May in Ohio, traveling constantly, and seeking on every side to learn the views of the noble women of the Crusade. They put their opinions in words like these: "We believe that as God led us into this work by way of the saloons,

HE WILL LEAD US OUT BY WAY OF
THE BALLOT.

We have never prayed more earnestly over the one than we will over the other. One was the Wilderness, the other is the Promised Land." . . .

Longer ago than I shall tell, my father returned one night to the far-off Wisconsin home where I was reared; and, sitting by my mother's chair, with a child's attentive ear, I listened to their words. He told us of the news that day had brought about Neal Dow and the great fight for prohibition down in Maine, and then he said: "I wonder if poor, rum-cursed Wisconsin will ever get a law like that?" And mother rocked a while in silence in the dear old chair I love, and then she gently said:

"YES, JOSIAH, THERE'LL BE SUCH A LAW
ALL OVER THE LAND SOME DAY,
WHEN WOMEN VOTE."

My father had never heard her say so much before. He was a great conservative; so he looked tremendously astonished, and replied, in his keen, sarcastic voice: "And pray how will you arrange it so that women shall vote?" Mother's chair went to and fro a little faster for a minute, and then, looking not into his face, but into the flickering flames of the grate, she slowly answered: "Well, I say to you, as the apostle Paul said to his jailor, 'You have put us into prison, we being Romans, and you must come and take us out.'"

That was a seed-thought in a girl's brain and heart. Years passed on, in which nothing more was said upon this dangerous theme. My brother grew to manhood, and soon after he was twenty-one years old he went with his father to vote. Standing by the window, a girl of sixteen years, a girl of simple, homely fancies, not at all strong-minded, and altogether ignorant of the world, I looked out as they drove away, my father and my brother, and as I looked I felt a strange ache in my heart, and tears sprang to my eyes. Turning to my sister Mary, who stood beside me, I saw that the dear little innocent seemed wonderfully sober, too. I said: "Don't you wish we could go with them when we are old enough? Don't we love our country just as well as they do?" and her little frightened voice piped out: "Yes, of course we ought. Don't I know that? But you mustn't tell a soul— not mother, even; we should be called strong-minded."

In all the years since then I have kept these things, and many others like them, and pondered them in my heart. . . .

I thought that women ought to have the ballot as I paid the hard-earned taxes upon my mother's cottage home—but I never said as much—somehow the motive did not command my heart. For my own sake, I had not courage, but I have for thy sake, dear native land, for thy necessity is as much greater than mine as thy transcend[e]nt hope is greater than the personal interest of thy humble child. For love of you, heart-broken wives, whose tremulous lips have blessed me; for love of you, sweet mothers, who, in the cradle's shadow, kneel this night beside your infant sons, and you, sorrowful little children, who listen at this hour, with faces strangely old, for him whose footsteps frighten you; for love of you have I thus spoken.

Source: Frances E. Willard, "My First Home Protection Address," in *Woman and Temperance; or, The Work and Workers of the Woman's Christian Temperance Union* (Hartford, CT: James Betts, 1883). The speech itself was first delivered in 1876.

The Real Want Was Proper Home and Moral Training

In this early essay, journalist and antilynching reformer Ida B. Wells imagines looking back on the career of a middle-class African American teacher. Wells herself worked as a teacher in the 1880s, and it is likely that this essay reflects her own experiences and frustrations. Like Du Bois, Wells here notes the lack of "proper" homes among her African American students and links domestic improvements to racial progress. Realizing that formal education alone is inadequate to the task of racial uplift, the teacher turns her classroom into a setting for conveying moral lessons that would ideally be learned at home. Later, she visits the homes of her students to instruct their parents in the practices and values of a respectable and Christian home. How do the actions of Wells's teacher compare with those of the friendly visitors mentioned in chapter 2? Does the context of racial uplift make a difference in how you view them?

Twenty years ago a young girl went from one of the many colleges of our Southland to teach among her people. While she taught for a livelihood she performed her duty conscientiously with a desire to carry the light of education to those who dwelt in darkness, by faithfully instructing her charge[s] in their text-books and grounding them firmly in the rudiments. She was born, reared and educated in the South, consequently the sentiments regarding, and the treatment of, the Negro were not unknown to her. Justice compelled her to acknowledge sadly that his moral and temporal status had not kept pace with the intellectual, and while reluctantly admitting this fact that was so often so exultantly and contemptuously cited against him she wondered if there were no remedy for a state of things that she knew was not irremediable. Since it had been amply proven that education alone would not be the salvation of the race, that his religion generally, was wholly emotional and had no bearing on his everyday life she thought that if the many ministers of the gospel, public and professional men of the race would exert their influence specifically—by precept and example—that they might do much to erase the stigma from the name. She never thought of the opportunities she possessed to mould high moral characters by—as the Episcopalians do their religion—instilling elevated thoughts, race pride and ambition with their daily lessons. One day a gentleman visited the school and mentioned a promising youth, 18 years old, who had attended that school, as being sentenced to the penitentiary the day before for three years for stealing a suit of clothes; he concluded his recital by sorrowfully saying: "That's all our boys go to school for, they get enough education to send them to the penitentiary and the girls do worse." It flashed on her while he was talking that the real want was proper home and moral training combined with mental, that would avert a too frequent repetition of this sad case and that the duty of Negro teachers was to supplement this lack, as none had greater opportunities. There came over her, such a desire to make the case in point an impressive lesson that school-work was suspended while she related the story and for half an hour earnestly exhorted them to cultivate honest, moral habits, to lay a foundation for a noble character that would convince the world that worth and not color made the man. From that time forth, whenever a case in point came up, she would tell them to illustrate that the way of the transgressor is hard; also that every such case only helped to confirm the discreditable opinion already entertained for the Negro. These casual earnest talks made a deep impression, her pupils became thoughtful and earnest, a deeper meaning was given to study; school-life began to be viewed in a new light; as a means to an end; they learned, through her, that there was a work out in the world waiting for them to come and take hold, and these lessons sunk deep in their minds.

Their quiet deportment and manly independence as they grew older was noticeable. This teacher who had just awakened to a true sense of her mission did not stop here; she visited the homes, those where squalor and moral uncleannes[s] walked hand in hand with poverty, as well as the better ones and talked earnestly with the parents on these themes, of laboring to be self-respecting so they might be respected; of a practical Christianity; of setting a pure example in cleanliness and morals before their children. Before, she viewed their sins with loathing and disgust; now she was animated by a lofty purpose and earnest aim and the Son of Righteousness sustained her. She spent her life in the school-room and one visiting the communities to-day in which she labored will say when observing the intelligent happy homes and families, the advanced state of moral and temporal elevation of her one time pupils— that she has not lived in vain, that the world is infinitely better for her having in one corner of the earth endeavored to make it bloom with wheat, useful grain or beautiful flowers instead of allowing cruel thorns, or rank and poisonous thistles to flourish unmolested.

Some may ask, why we have been thus premature in recording a history of twenty years hence. The answer is short and simple that the many teachers of the race may not be content simply to earn a salary, but may also use their opportunity and influence. Finally gentle reader that you and I "may go and do likewise."

Source: Ida B. Wells, "A Story of 1900," *Fisk Herald*, April 1886.

To Fearlessly Assert Their Claims to an Equality Which Is Not Measured by Dollars and Cents

When Catharine Maria Sedgwick imagined the domestic life of the "rich poor man" in 1837 (see chapter 2), she described a respectable working-class home that mimicked the morality of its middle-class counterpart. Although a site of labor, the working-class home was also a place to seek comfort and learn moral lessons. Here the labor leader William Sylvis rejects such romantic portrayals of "the poor man's home," instead emphasizing that poverty makes it impossible for the working man to enjoy the pleasures of domesticity, even transforming parenthood into a "calamity." Without sentimentality, Sylvis shows that the homes of rich and poor are divided by their ability to consume and connected by labor, as poor women take on the domestic tasks of elite wives. Only trade unionism and a manly wage will elevate the working-class home by freeing the working man's wife from paid and unpaid labor and supporting some domestic comforts.

Poets and essayists have sung and written a great deal about the beauty and simplicity of the poor man's home, and theorists have employed the aid of art to prove that contentment and poverty are inseparable; but "The Cotter's Saturday Night," "The Village Blacksmith," "The Flat-Boat," etc., as *illustrations* are far more welcome to the rich man's parlor than would be the living *realities* which they represent. The whitewashed cottage, the clean-swept hearth, the creeping vines, the fresh-budding flowers, and "the moss-covered bucket," afford themes for highly-colored pictures of humble life, which never fail to captivate romantic misses and sentimental young men, whose ideas of "love in a cottage" form a part of their youthful dreams. Those who enjoy wealth and luxury too often derive their impressions from the artist's pencil or the fine-spun theories of magazine writers, and settle down in the belief that the poor are exempt from many cares incident to riches, and that it's "all moonshine" to prate of the distress and privations of the toiling poor. This outside view of poverty is very apt to satisfy the conscience, and shut out from the heart those feelings of charity which make us "feel each other's woes."

But there *is* an inside view of poverty which the true Christian and philanthropist will sometimes pause to gaze upon. The smile of cheerful greeting, as wealth passes the door of poverty, is not always an index to sunshine within. The canker gnaws none the less when pride places the "best foot foremost," and many a weary and worn soul struggles hardest to keep up appearances in the darkest hour of adversity. If the poor man is blessed with a thrifty wife who turns his weekly pittance to the best advantage, his condition, and that of the family, are proportionately benefited; but what can the affluent know of the pinch and stint, the self-denial and privation practised to "make both ends meet"? What one throws away as mere offal, the other dishes up in various ways to tempt the palate; for nothing must be wasted in the poor man's home. One selects the rib or juicy sirloin, the other must be satisfied with the neck and other cheap pieces; one can have his pick, while the other must be content with the refuse of the market. The toiler must put up with nourishless soups and frequent meatless meals. Deteriorated tea and coffee must suffice, when it can be afforded at all; and, as to clothing, a change of inferior domestic fabrics is all that he can aspire to.

This is the difference between rich and poor, under the best management; but it as often occurs with one as the other, that want of experience, indolence, or incompatibility of temper, proves the curse of the household. Such a condition of things is, indeed, a calamity to the poor. The former can provide against this misfortune by hiring help—but not the latter. With them it sometimes happens that the husband is idle, intemperate, or improvident, and, on the other hand, the wife may be thriftless, slovenly, and wasteful. She may be broken down by excessive labor, or crushed by the despondency of her hopeless condition. Under such circumstances, there is a life-battle with want and suffering, uncheered by one ray of hope—with no prospect of deliverance. No word of encouragement is given—no helping hand is extended. They are shunned because they *are* poor, and proscribed because they show it. Is it any wonder that despair drives many such to vice and crime? for there is nothing before them but hunger and want in the meridian of life, or the almshouse in old age.

But, in the brightest phase of poverty, look at the incident "pull backs" in the shape of lost time, sickness, medicine, doctors' bills, etc.—perhaps a periodical increase of the family, adding other mouths to be fed, other backs to be clothed. What the rich would consider a blessing, is often a calamity to the poor, in multiplying household care. Let that rich lady, lounging on her cushioned ottoman, perusing the last novel, with her children consigned to servants in the nursery, take a peep at the poor man's home. She will find the mother laboring at the wash-tub, a baby crying in the rude cradle, another, a little older, tied in a chair, and the next crying for bread, perhaps. That mother may be weak and feeble, working beyond her strength. It may be that she is getting through with the week's wash of the novel-reading millionaire, and depending upon the hard-earned pittance for necessary comforts. And what if the husband and father should be sick—the body prostrated by racking pain, and the mind frenzied with apprehensions of a starving family? Who shall describe his agony—who can comprehend his misery?

This, reader, is the other side of the picture which has never been looked upon by poets and sensation writers, who cater for the public. But these painters of fancy scenes in poverty are too sensitive to gaze upon the reality; and, besides, it would not comport with their mission, to "draw from nature" or to paint "the living truth." It would grate too harshly upon the public ear, which needs a sweeter melody; and shock eyes which require all that is unlovely to be veiled from sight. They place the garb of romance around suffering and poverty, and deck the poor man's home in flowers, while they plant thorns in his pathway, and render him helpless for self-elevation.

There is a hidden purpose, however, in all this flattery bestowed upon humble life. It is designed to make poor men contented with their lot, and to blind them to the necessity of making proper exertions to extricate themselves from the slough of despond into which the odious distinctions of society have plunged them. It would be the height of imprudence—the extreme of presumption—on the part of a class whose condition in life is painted in such gaudy colors, to express dissatisfaction, or to make an effort to place themselves higher in the social scale. So contented—what need is there for combinations, trade-unions, strikes, etc.? These scene-painters of the poor have satisfied wealth that it has no duty to perform—that there are no claims upon the rich—and that the preposterous pretensions of the poor are entitled to no consideration. Hence, any attempt on the part of workingmen to ameliorate their condition is met with opposition at the outset, and they are looked upon as a "never-satisfied" class.

But, happily for the cause of labor, its oppressed victims have awakened from their long sleep of lethargy, and begin to fearlessly assert their claims to an equality which is not measured by dollars and cents. They have mounted the car of progress, and are determined to ride until they reach the goal of a new manhood, if they have to seize the ribbons and drive the drivers. Caste, distinctions, prejudice, proscription, must clear the track, or be run down, for they have taken off the brakes. "Upward and onward!" is shouted along the whole line; and the time will soon come, we hope, when the poor man's home may merit some of the fulsome praise bestowed upon it.

Source: William H. Sylvis, "The Poor Man's Home," in *The Life, Speeches, Labors and Essays of William H. Sylvis* (Philadelphia: Claxton, Remsen & Haffelfinger, 1872).

Occupied with Real Service to Men and Each Other, How Happily Would They Meet at Night

The reformer and feminist Caroline Dall also looked to paid employment as a means to bring home life into greater alignment with the Victorian domestic ideal. In this excerpt, she argues that women's paid labor outside the home would enhance domestic harmony, foster shared interest in family life, and redress poverty among the working class. Envisioning work as a source of satisfaction and ambition, here she argues that women of all classes must be given the right to work outside the home. Only the employment of middle-class women will undermine the stigma associated with women's work and increase the value of working-class women's labor. How does Dall depict women's labor, and why does she see it as a right rather than a necessity or a burden? Compare her analysis to that of

Sylvis. Whose argument do you think would have greater appeal among nineteenth-century working-class women?

In my first lecture, I showed you that women were starving, and that vice is a better paymaster than labor. I showed you the awful falsity of the cry, "Do not let women work: we will work for them. They are too tender, too delicate, to bide the rough usage of the world." I showed you that they were not only working hard, but had been working at hard and unwholesome work, not merely in this century, but in all centuries since the world began. I showed you how man himself has turned them back, when they have entered a well-paid career. Practically the command of society to the uneducated class is, "Marry, stitch, die, or do worse."

Plenty of employments are open to them; but all are underpaid. They will never be better paid till women of rank begin to work for money, and so create respect for woman's labor; and women of rank will never do this till American men feel what all American men profess,—a proper respect for Labor, as God's own demand upon every human soul,—and so teach American women to feel it. How often have I heard that every woman willing to work may find employment! The terrible reverses of 1837 taught many men in this country that they were "out of luck:" how absurd, then, this statement with regard to women! One reason why so many young women are attracted to the Catholic Church is, that the Catholic Church is a good economist, and does not tolerate an idle member. In Catholic countries,—nay, in Protestant,—the gray hood of the Sister of Charity is as sacred as a crown.

When I think how happy human life might be, if men and women worked freely together, I lose patience. Such marriages as I can dream of,—where, household duties thriftily managed and speedily discharged, the wife assumes some honorable trust, or finds a noble task for her delicate hands; while the husband follows his under separate auspices! Occupied with real service to men and each other, how happily would they meet at night to discuss hours they had lived apart to help each other's work by each other's wit, and to draw vital refreshment from the caresses of their children! It is your distrust, O men! That prevents your having such homes as poets fancy. You will not help women to form them. The sturdy pine pushes through the tightest soil, and will grow, though nothing more genial than November sky bid it welcome; but tender anemones—wind flowers, as we call them—must be coaxed through the loose loam sifted from thousands of autumn leaves, and tremble to the faintest air. Yet are anemones fairer than pine, and their lovely blossoming a fit reward for Nature's pains. Follow Nature, and offer the encouragement which those you love best daily need. Do it for your own sakes; for proper employment will diffuse serenity over the anxious faces you are too apt to see. Do not fancy that the conventions of society can ever prevail over the will, it may be the freak, of Nature. That stepdame is absolute. She set Hercules spinning, and sent Joan of Arc to Orleans. She taught Mrs. John Stewart Mill political economy, and Monsieur Malignon netting and lace-work. She enables women to bear immense burdens, heat, cold, and frost; she sets them in the thick of the battle even; while in South Carolina, and in the heart of Africa, or among the Indians of the Rocky Mountains, old men croon over forsaken babes till the milk flows in their withered breasts.

Women want to work for all the reasons that men want it. When they see this, and begin to do it faithfully, you will respect their work, and pay them for it. We are all taught that we are the children of God; only Mohammedans deny their women that rank: yet we are left without duties, as if such a thing were possible,—left without work that offers any adequate *end* as a stimulus to diligence or ambition; and, until "Work" becomes man's cry of inspiration, woman will never train herself to do her work well.

It was Margaret Fuller, I think, who wrote of the Polish heroine, the Countess Emily Plater, "*She* is the figure I want for my frontispiece. Short was her career. Like the Maid of Orleans, she only lived long enough to *verify her credentials*, and then passed from a scene on which she was probably a premature apparition." Ah! that is what all women should do,—verify their credentials! "Say what you please," said a young girl to her lover, as they passed out of a Woman's Convention; "a woman that *can* speak like Lucretia Mott, *ought* to speak." And men themselves cannot escape from this conviction. The duty of women, therefore, is to inspire it by doing whatever they undertake worthily and well; patient in waiting for opportunities, prompt to seize, conscientious to profit by them.

Source: Caroline H. Dall, "*Woman's Right to Labor*"; or, *Low Wages and Hard Work: In Three Lectures, Delivered in Boston, November, 1859* (Boston: Walker, Wise, 1860).

Peace and Harmony Were to Prevail in the Future—All for Two Hundred Dollars a Year

The 1889 case of Nancy Miller before the Iowa State Supreme Court offers another interpretation of the relationship between domesticity, labor, and the rights of citizenship. As recounted in the *Woman's Standard*, Iowa's suffrage newspaper, Nancy Miller entered into a labor contract with her husband in order to preserve domestic harmony. When her husband refused to pay her agreed-on wage, she sued and lost. Even though her husband had acknowledged the monetary value of her labor, he was under no legal obligation to honor the contract. While married women's property acts (1850s) had given wives legal control over wages earned outside the home, the court found that the domestic labor Nancy preformed was already owed to her husband on the basis of their marriage contract. Such legal interpretations buttressed the cultural assumptions that erased women's contributions to the family economy and kept their labor "pastoralized."

For the benefit of the future historian of the woman's movement, I want to call attention to the Nancy Miller case. The case, which was tried before or decided by the Supreme Court of Iowa, is thus stated by a Chicago daily paper:

"This case was that of Nancy Miller versus her husband for breach of contract. The two had had quarrels as husband and wife often do. To prevent their recurrence, they agreed that if Mrs. Miller would look closely after all the wants of the family, he would pay her $200 yearly. Past rows were to be forgotten, and peace and harmony were to prevail in the future—all for two hundred dollars a year, payable monthly, in advance. Mrs. Miller did her part, but her husband failed to pay, and she sued for the money. The court held that the contract was void because against public policy, and that it imposed no duties not in the marriage contract."

If Mr. Miller had made this contract with a male business partner and had refused to fulfill his part when his partner had faithfully complied with the terms of the compact, would there have been any hesitation in the mind of the judge who heard the case, as to Miller's obligations to pay? None at all.

One of the questions which must be faced and solved in the interests of pure justice in the future, is that of the pecuniary independence of wives. It sounds very sweet and sentimental and vicariously altruistic to declare that love is the coin woman likes best to be paid in; but, though that is true, it is also true that when other human beings are pecuniarily benefited by her willing service, justice demands that she be paid a certain percentage of that benefit.

We are not given the particulars of this case, but it can be fairly assumed that this was but one of thousands never brought before the courts, where the husband, with plenty of money at command, yet stinted the money allowance of his wife, while demanding of her services for which, had she been his hired servant, the two hundred dollars per year, promised but not paid her, would have been but a small part of the wage legally her due.

If marriage were in reality the equal partnership in money matters and in all else which it is sometimes represented to be, then the Iowa judge's decision would not be so unjust. But nowhere is it such equal partnership in law. While there are hundreds of husbands whose own natural sense of justice causes them to give their wives unquestioned disposal of the family funds, yet in these cases it is still a gift and not a legal right; while there are, on the contrary, thousands of husbands who, taking advantage of the sanction of law, and the laxity of public opinion on this subject, commit cruel injustice to their wives, such injustice that if they did it to any other than the woman they have sworn to "cherish and protect," their names would become a by-word and a disgrace among their fellow men.

Source: "The Unpaid Laborer," *Woman's Standard* 4, no. 1 (September 1889): 1.

4

The American Home on the Move in the Age of Expansion

Among the more remarkable qualities of the nineteenth-century home ideal was its ability to move not only metaphorically across lines of class or race but often quite literally as American domestic goods (and by extension domestic values) spread across the continent and globe. Indeed the word "domestic" implies both the home and the nation, and at the end of the nineteenth century, the two meanings were often collapsed. In new settings and uncertain circumstances, Americans looked to domesticity as a stabilizing force and as evidence of their own civility and advancing civilization.

On the western frontier, for example, attention to domestic details enabled white settlers to offer their families some physical comfort while also maintaining ties to communities and family they had left behind. As depicted in W. A. Marin's account, this was frequently achieved through considerable labor and with varying degrees of gentility, as migrants struggled with limited resources and harsh conditions. Living in sod houses or traveling in fast-moving railroad cars, Americans of varied economic means adapted the trappings of refined domesticity in order to feel "at home." It was no matter that the adaptations involved compromises, approximations, and even misunderstandings; the shared vocabulary of domestic refinement and genteel consumption created a sense of cultural cohesion in the face of unprecedented geographic and social mobility. To many nineteenth-century Americans, it made perfect sense that William Dean Howells and Stephen Crane both imagined a domesticated train car as the setting to launch two very different couples into married life.

As domesticity symbolized a uniquely American civilization in the West, it was also being transformed by increased immigration and the United States' growing presence in world politics and commerce. In a self-consciously international context, domestic spaces, goods, and values permitted an exploration of what it meant to be American. For immigrants such as Mary Antin, a tenement home was filled with new experiences—living behind a brick façade, sitting in a rocking chair, eating mass-produced canned goods—that signaled the formation of a new identity. Likewise, *Ladies' Home Journal* and other magazines offered middle-class readers advice about domestic goods and decorating styles from overseas, providing a safe way to test the boundaries of their own American identities in private.

Increasingly one need not travel the world to be cosmopolitan, as domestic goods and styles came to stand for their places of origin. At the 1893 Columbian Exposition, Americans and visitors from around the world walked through displays of domestic spaces intended to rank nations and peoples on a scale of civilization from primitive cliff dwellers to the finest palaces of Europe. Such exhibits, like Theodore Roosevelt's condemnation of "foreign marriages," sought to define the United States' unique position among the civilized nations of the world as both refined and rugged. Certainly Caroline Shunk took a similar understanding of American domesticity with her as she set up housekeeping in the Philippines in support of her nation's imperial ambitions.

We Had an Organ, the Only One in the Neighborhood

In 1893, Frederick Jackson Turner delivered his famous paper, "The Significance of the Frontier in American History," at the World's Columbian Exposition in Chicago. In it, he considered how the repeated settlement of "free land" had created a uniquely American character, as settlers encountered primitive conditions, were stripped of their civilized ways, and sought again to conquer the wilderness. But as depicted in W. A. Marin's reminiscences of his childhood in western Minnesota in the 1880s, settlers often carried the materials and values of civilized domesticity with them. Marin catalogs his family's domestic luxuries with great care while suggesting the incongruence between these items and his sod dwelling. Even on the frontier, he notes the domestic refinement (or its absence) among his neighbors and celebrates his parents' efforts to improve their home. Of what does he seem especially proud?

We were living on a claim in Fairfax Township about ten miles southeast of Crookston in 1880, when a neighbor, Ole Anderson, whose farm was a mile east of us, became disgusted with the country and decided to go back to Fillmore County. My father bought his homestead rights and all his cattle—a herd of about thirty head—and relinquished the rights of his own filing to his brother, Uncle Sam, who with a numerous family was coming from Michigan; so we moved late that fall to our new location. Ole Anderson fixed up his old wagon into a prairie schooner, in which he placed his few household goods and his family and took the back trek to Fillmore County. Thus we were established in a typical frontier homestead, and it proved to be a comparatively permanent residence as we lived there two winters and one summer.

The original Anderson house was a one-story, two-room, frame shack, with a gable roof of the lowest pitch possible. The sides were sodded up to the eaves. Heavy sod from the prairie breaking was one of the principal building materials of the time. The sod was cut about a foot wide, a foot and a half to two feet long, and three or four inches thick. It was laid like brick or stone usually on the outside of a frame shack, with openings for doors and windows, though some of the houses of the poorer settlers were made entirely of sod. A well-built sod shanty or stable is a black, fortress-like bit of architecture. The veneering usually consisted of one layer of sod, but the walls of some of the sod barns were three and four feet thick. Rain, sun, and wind combined with growing weeds, burrowing field mice, and rotting grass to reduce the sod buildings to a pile of dirt in a few years. Houses veneered with sod were warm in winter. Father built a story-and-a-half addition to the Anderson house, leaving the old part as an ell. He covered the addition with black tar paper, fastening the paper to the outside walls with lath. He then lined the inside with building paper so that we had a warm comfortable house.

We found that the frost would sometimes gather on our windows half an inch thick so that we could not see out and the light could hardly filter in. During warm periods the frost would melt and run over the floors, and sometimes the freezing and thawing would cause the ice to be several inches thick on the lower parts of the windows. So father put on double windows. This is the first time I remember seeing storm windows in Minnesota. I think it was an original idea with him, but now it is customary throughout the state.

Anderson had started the building of a straw stable, a structure peculiar to the prairies of the Northwest. Such a stable is built of posts that are forked or crotched in the upper end; heavy poles are placed horizontally in the crotches so as to form a framework, and lighter poles are placed across these to hold up the roof. Following the harvest the grain is threshed near this framework and the straw from the carrier is used to supply a heavy cover for it. Frequently a thatch of heavy long prairie grass is placed over the straw to make the roof shed the rain. The drawback to this kind of barn is that it has no windows or ventilation. It is warm, but dark and insanitary for animals, and when the rain gets in through the roof or the drainage is not good, the ground inside becomes a quagmire. In a few years the roof rots so that it is no longer serviceable and the straw settles, leaving an opening between the roof and the sides. It is necessary either to put more straw over this framework, or, what is better still, to remove the framework and rebuild. For the horses we built a one-story frame stable.

Our home was probably furnished much better than that of the average prairie pioneer. We had an organ, the only one in the neighborhood, and some of the old walnut furniture that we had saved from the hotel fire, including tall walnut beds and dressers and chairs of the U. S. Grant period. Of course there was a whatnot, and we had a rather fine old cherry center table on which reposed a pressed leather family album. Two beds stood side by side at the end of the room that formed the entire downstairs of the main part of the house. These beds were built up almost like small haystacks. First there was a high straw tick. On top of this were a feather tick and innumerable patchwork quilts. In the winter time the house became so cold at night that it was necessary to have plenty of covering. We also had rocking chairs, cane-seated dining-room chairs, and a sofa covered with large figured Brussels. A rag carpet covered the floor and on it were placed at intervals homemade rag rugs. The pictures on the wall were chromos of the style of 1870 that might now be attractive to the amateur curio-seeker who believes that such specimens are valuable antiques. One was a picture of Valley Forge. Enlarged crayon pictures of grandfather, grandmother, father, mother, and other relatives, so commonly seen in the eighties, were conspicuous by their absence in our home. A large wood heater occupied the center of the room, which was neat, clean, and comfortable, and was the center of family life. I cannot remember that we ever had in our home the sacred precincts of a parlor—musty, dank, and severe, closed to everyone but the occasional guest—for we lived each day as best we could using the entire house. We did not live in the kitchen as was usual with most pioneers.

The kitchen was in the old part of the house and also served as the dining room. Another room in this part was used as a shed or storehouse in winter and as a kitchen in summer. In one corner of the main kitchen stood a large iron cook stove at the back of which was a reservoir for heating water and for melting ice and snow. Wooden homemade cupboards stood against the walls, and in the center of the room was a walnut extension dining table covered with marbled white oilcloth when not in use and with a red and white table cloth or, on occasions, a white one, at meal time. Heavy wooden chairs, painted brown with yellow stripes, were set around the edge of the room. The floor was made of wide, white pine boards, and it was kept scrupulously white and clean in spite of the grease splashed from fried pork and dirt brought in by the men of the family on their shoepacks and overshoes. For lighting we used kerosene lamps most of the time, but had candles also. The majority of the farmers made much use of candles, employing kerosene only for lanterns.

Instead of a stairway leading to the upper story, a hatch was cut in the floor and cleats were nailed to the studding for a ladder. Mother, father, and my sisters slept downstairs, and I slept upstairs with Uncle Jim, the hired man, and any other male who might be a guest. As I was inclined to walk in my sleep, my mother, fearful that I might fall through the hatchway, had a cover made for it, and she religiously saw that it was in place every night when I went to bed. The upstairs contained beds, trunks, and miscellaneous clothing and furniture, and it was more like an attic than anything else. It was heated by a drum attached to a stovepipe. In the early eighties a brick chimney was a rarity in Fairfax Township.

Many of the early settlers did not have the pretentious home, comparatively speaking, that we had. A large majority of the newcomers were young married couples with small children, so that a one-room shanty was all they required. A single room of small dimensions served as kitchen, bedroom, and parlor all in one. All the furniture, with the exception of the stove and a few chairs, was homemade. A pine table, benches, beds, a truck or two, a couple of chairs, and a wooden cupboard comprised practically all the furniture. Sometimes a good-sized family lived in one of these small one-room shanties. Two beds, foot to foot, stood across one end of the room. Under the beds were stored during the day the bedding for two others beds to be made up on the floor, and in this way six, eight, or ten persons slept in one small room. Sometimes there was a small attic, probably just high enough at the peak so that the average man could stand upright in it, where the boys and men slept. When I have visited some of the small homes occupied by large families, I have marveled how everyone was accommodated with sleeping quarters. At threshing time the extra men slept in the straw pile, barn, haystacks, or granary.

A single man keeping "bachelor's hall" in a claim shanty enjoyed another variety of "home life," if the manner in which the average bachelor lived could be called living at all. He had a bed or bunk in the corner, with blankets, quilts, and buffalo robes—no sheets, no pillows, or pillow cases. Here he probably slept every night with most of his clothes on, and he seldom made up the bed. His one room was probably ten by twelve feet, the floor being made of rough, wide, and warped pine boards with large cracks. It was swept only occasionally and it was never scrubbed until it became enameled with a black coating of gumbo mud and spattered pork grease. The one small dirty window let in a dim light, so that it always appeared to be twilight in the shanty except at night, when a small kerosene lamp, lantern, or candle made one vagrant spot of light in the darkness. The cooking was done on a small rusty cook stove, the tin stovepipe of which went directly through the roof. Against the wall was built a small pine table, on which reposed from day to day the owner's tin dishes, knives, forks, and coffeepot. A few shelves built against the wall for a cupboard and a couple of pine benches completed the equipment. Outside the door were a bench and a tin washdish, with a grimy flour sack for a towel, and near at hand an old kerosene barrel containing water brought from the nearest buffalo wallow. The housekeeping particulars of such an establishment would not be at all edifying.

Source: W. A. Marin, "Sod Houses and Prairie Schooners," *Minnesota History Magazine* 12 (1931): 135–156. Reprinted with the permission of the Minnesota Historical Society.

Figures 4.1 and 4.2. Solomon D. Butcher's photographs *The David Hilton Family near Weissert, Custer County*, Nebraska, 1887, and *Family and Horses in Front of a Farmhouse in Northwest Custer County*, Nebraska, 1880s (both courtesy of the Nebraska State Historical Society), capture the material conditions and values of frontier domesticity. Butcher migrated to Custer County in 1880 but quickly realized he was not cut out for life as a homesteader. Instead he documented the pioneer experiences of others, eventually taking over one thousand photographs of sod houses on the Great Plains. Many of his subjects were eager to show off their homes, farms, and domestic items to family back east; note the pump organ and Bible displayed in these examples. Mrs. Hilton, however, asked that her sod house not be included in her family photograph.

A Precious Souvenir, a Sacred Memory, a Beautiful Dream

Industrialist George Pullman designed his luxurious railroad cars not only to attract customers but also to shape their behavior. Pullman cars were routinely outfitted with fine woods, rich upholstery, and elegant rugs to encourage passengers to associate railroad cars with the conduct, comfort, and safety of a well-appointed home. In "The Parlor-Car," William Dean Howells depicts an engaged couple in the midst of an argument. Reconciled after averting a train wreck, they consider the domestic qualities of their railroad car. The female traveler is so taken by the car's domestic amenities that she wishes to purchase it; it is the ideal setting for future marital happiness. Of course, the play is a farce, and while suggesting that train travel has approximated the feel and comfort of home, Howells also implies the silliness of likening these two very different spaces.

Miss Galbraith, starting away again, and looking about the car: "Allen, I have an idea! Do you suppose Mr. Pullman could be induced to sell this car?"

Mr. Richards: "Why?"

Miss Galbraith: "Why, because I think it's perfectly lovely, and I should like to live in it always. It could be fitted up for a sort of summer-house, don't you know, and we could have it in the garden, and you could smoke in it."

Mr. Richards: "Admirable! It would look just like a travelling photographic saloon. No, Lucy, we won't buy it; we will simply keep it as a precious souvenir, a sacred memory, a beautiful dream,—and let it go on fulfilling its destiny all the same."

Porter, entering, and gathering up *Miss Galbraith's* things: "Be at Schenectady in half a minute, miss. Won't have much time."

Miss Galbraith, rising, and adjusting her dress, and then looking about the car, while she passes her hand through her lover's arm: "Oh, I do hate to leave it. Farewell, you dear, kind, good, lovely car! May you never have another accident!" She kisses her hand to the car, upon which they both look back as they slowly leave it.

Mr. Richards, kissing his hand in the like manner: "Good-by, sweet chariot! May you never carry any but bridal couples!"

Miss Galbraith: "Or engaged ones!"

Mr. Richards: "Or husbands going home to their wives!"

Miss Galbraith: "Or wives hastening to their husbands."

Mr. Richards: "Or young ladies who have waited one train over, so as to be with the young men they hate."

Miss Galbraith: "Or young men who are so indifferent that they pretend to be asleep when the young ladies come in!" They pause at the door and look back again. "'And must I leave thee, Paradise?'" They both kiss their hands to the car again, and, their faces being very close together, they impulsively kiss each other. Then Miss Galbraith throws back her head, and solemnly confronts him. "Only think, Allen! If this car hadn't broken its engagement, we might never have mended ours."

Source: William D. Howells, "The Parlor-Car," in *The Sleeping-Car and Other Farces* (Boston: Houghton Mifflin, 1876).

It's Fine, Ain't It?

If the engaged couple in Howell's "The Parlor-Car" found familiar domestic surroundings aboard the railroads, other travelers were introduced into an unfamiliar world of luxury and domestic consumption. By paying as little as twenty-five cents extra to ride in a Pullman car, men and women of lesser means might experience refined domesticity that they could not achieve at home. In this excerpt from "The Bride Comes to Yellow Sky," Stephen Crane uses the opulence of the railcar to convey the ways in which a honeymoon trip promised geographic and social mobility, even if only temporarily. How might such experiences have shaped the way that Americans understood class difference at the end of the nineteenth century? Has the meaning of domestic decoration changed since Andrew Jackson Downing designed "good houses" (see chapter 1)?

The great Pullman was whirling onward with such dignity of motion that a glance from the window seemed simply to prove that the plains of Texas were pouring eastward. Vast flats of green grass, dull-hued spaces of mesquite and cactus, little groups of frame houses, woods of light and tender trees, all were sweeping into the east, sweeping over the horizon, a precipice.

A newly married pair had boarded this coach at San Antonio. The man's face was reddened from many days in the wind and sun, and a direct result of his new black clothes was that his brick-colored hands were constantly performing in a most conscious fashion. From time to time he looked down respectfully at his attire. He sat with a hand on each knee, like a man waiting in a barber's shop. The glances he devoted to other passengers were furtive and shy.

The bride was not pretty, nor was she very young. She wore a dress of blue cashmere, with small reservations of velvet here and there and with steel buttons abounding. She continually twisted her head to regard her puff sleeves, very stiff, straight, and high. They embarrassed her. It was quite apparent that she had cooked, and that she expected to cook dutifully. The blushes caused by the careless scrutiny of some passengers as she had entered the car were strange to see upon this plain, under-class countenance, which was drawn in placid, almost emotionless lines.

They were evidently very happy. "Ever been in a parlor-car before?" he asked, smiling with delight.

"No," she answered, "I never was. It's fine, ain't it?"

"Great! And then after a while we'll go forward to the diner and get a big layout. Finest meal in the world. Charge a dollar."

"Oh, do they?" cried the bride. "Charge a dollar? Why that's too much—for us—ain't it, Jack?"

"Not this trip, anyhow," he answered bravely. "We're going to go the whole thing."

Later he explained to her about the trains. "You see, it's a thousand miles from one end of Texas to the other, and this train runs right across it and never stops but four times." He had the pride of an owner. He pointed out to her the dazzling fittings of the coach, and in truth her eyes opened wider as she contemplated the sea-green figured velvet, the shining brass, silver, and glass, the wood that gleamed as darkly brilliant as the surface of a pool of oil. At one end a bronze figure sturdily held a support for a separated chamber, and at convenient places on the ceiling were frescoes in olive and silver.

To the minds of the pair, their surroundings reflected the glory of their marriage that morning in San Antonio. This was the environment of their new estate, and the man's face in particular beamed with an elation that made him appear ridiculous to the negro porter.

Source: Stephen Crane, "The Bride Comes to Yellow Sky," *McClure's Magazine*, February 1898.

Figures 4.3 and 4.4. The interiors of a Pullman parlor car and an immigrant sleeper (both from "Railway Passenger Travel," *Scribner's Magazine*, September 1888) offered two very different visions of domesticated rail travel. The first image shows the respectable and opulent amenities available to those who were able to pay for them. The second records the accommodations in which immigrants crossed the continent. Traveling in unadorned boxcars with wooden berths and shared stoves, passengers provided their own bedding and cooked their own meals. Such distinctions undercut claims that American rail travel was uniquely egalitarian.

We Were All Impressed with Our New Home and Its Furniture

Mary Antin emigrated from Belarus to Boston in 1894, and in 1912, at the age of thirty, she published her autobiography, *The Promised Land*. In many ways, Antin's life embodied the immigrants' version of the American dream—a life shaped by new opportunities, especially access to education. In this passage, she recounts her first encounter with the trappings of American life. She invites her readers to reimagine the urban "slum" through the eyes of a nine-year-old girl and to appreciate the wonder contained in a sparsely furnished room. Her account underscores all that was unfamiliar and reveals her eagerness to embrace domestic goods as symbols of her new country.

Anybody who knows Boston knows that the West and North Ends are the wrong ends of that city. They form the tenement district, or, in the newer phrase, the slums of Boston. Anybody who is acquainted with the slums of any American metropolis knows that that is the quarter where poor immigrants foregather, to live, for the most part, as unkempt, half-washed, toiling, unaspiring foreigners; pitiful in the eyes of social missionaries, the despair of boards of health, the hope of ward politicians, the touchstone of American democracy. The well-versed metropolitan knows the slums as a sort of house of detention for poor aliens, where they live on probation till they can show a certificate of good citizenship.

He may know all this and yet not guess how Wall Street, in the West End, appears in the eyes of a little immigrant from Polotzk. What would the sophisticated sight-seer say about my Union Place, off Wall Street, where my new home waited for me? He would say that it is no place at all, but a short box of an alley. Two rows of three-story tenements are its sides, a stingy strip of sky is its lid, a littered pavement is the floor, and a narrow mouth its exit.

But I saw a very different picture on my introduction to Union Place. I saw two imposing rows of brick buildings, loftier than any dwelling I had ever lived in. Brick was even on the ground for me to tread on, instead of common earth or boards. Many friendly windows stood open, filled with uncovered heads of women and children. I thought the people were interested in us, which was very neighborly. I looked up to the topmost row of windows, and my eyes were filled with the May blue of an American sky!

In our days of affluence in Russia we had been accustomed to upholstered parlors, embroidered linen, silver spoons and candlesticks, goblets of gold, kitchen shelves shining with copper and brass. We had feather beds heaped halfway to the ceiling; we had clothes presses dusky with velvet and silk and fine woollen. The three small rooms into which my father now ushered us, up one flight of stairs, contained only the necessary beds, with lean mattresses; a few wooden chairs; a table or two; a mysterious iron structure, which later turned out to be a stove; a couple of unornamented kerosene lamps; and a scanty array of cooking-utensils and crockery. And yet we were all impressed with our new home and its furniture. It was not only because we had just passed through our seven lean years, cooking in earthen vessels, eating black bread on holidays and wearing cotton; it was chiefly because these wooden chairs and tin pans were American chairs and pans that they shone glorious in our eyes. And if there was anything lacking for comfort or decoration we expected it to be presently supplied—at least, we children did. Perhaps my mother alone, of us newcomers, appreciated the shabbiness of the little apartment, and realized that for her there was as yet no laying down of the burden of poverty.

Our initiation into American ways began with the first step on the new soil. My father found occasion to instruct or correct us even on the way from the pier to Wall Street, which journey we made crowded together in a rickety cab. He told us not to lean out of the windows, not to point, and explained the word "greenhorn." We did not want to be "greenhorns," and gave the strictest attention to my father's instructions. I do not know when my parents found opportunity to review together the history of Polotzk in the three years past, for we children had no patience with the subject; my mother's narrative was constantly interrupted by irrelevant questions, interjections, and explanations.

The first meal was an object lesson of much variety. My father produced several kinds of food, ready to eat, without any cooking, from little tin cans that had printing all over them. He attempted to introduce us to a queer, slippery kind of fruit, which he called "banana," but had to give it up for the time being. After the meal, he had better luck with a curious piece of furniture on runners, which he called "rocking-chair." There were five of us newcomers, and we found five different ways of getting into the American machine of perpetual motion, and as many ways of getting out of it. One born and bred to the use of a rocking-chair cannot imagine how ludicrous people can make themselves when attempting to use it for the first time. We laughed immoderately over our various experiments with the novelty, which was a wholesome way of letting off steam after the unusual excitement of the day.

In our flat we did not think of such a thing as storing the coal in the bathtub. There was no bathtub. So in the evening of the first day my father conducted us to the public baths. As we moved along in a little procession, I was delighted with the illumination of the streets. So many lamps, and they burned until morning, my father said, and so people did not need to carry lanterns. In America, then, everything was free, as we had heard in Russia. Light was free; the streets were as bright as a synagogue on a holy day. Music was free; we had been serenaded, to our gaping delight, by a brass band of many pieces, soon after our installation on Union Place.

Source: Mary Antin, *The Promised Land* (Boston: Houghton Mifflin, 1912).

Between the Hunter's Cabin and Marie Antoinette's Bed-Chamber in the French Section There Was a Wide Divergence

On May 1, 1893, the World's Columbian Exposition opened in Chicago. Planned in honor of the four hundredth anniversary of Christopher Columbus's landing in America, the fair included forty-six countries and over two hundred buildings. Visitors who strolled through the neoclassical White City and the ethnological exhibits of the Midway Plaisance were educated and entertained as they took in the highest achievements of civilization and contemplated the latest scientific insights into "primitive" societies. The images that follow are from a series of souvenir albums printed to commemorate the fair and are accompanied by their original captions. Together they suggest how domestic practices and spaces provided a recognizable vocabulary for comparing nations and peoples—a subtle yet explicit language for expressing national pride and racist beliefs.

Figure 4.5. THE CLIFF-DWELLERS.—Near the Anthropological Building, in the southern part of the park, was the striking reproduction which is portrayed in the engraving. It represented Battle Rock Mountain, in the Mac Eimo Valley of Colorado. It had the appearance of rock and earth, though built of timbers, iron, staff, stone and boards, and paint was used to simulate nature. The entrance was into a cavern, made to give the effects of a canyon, and in niches, high up, were the miniature houses of the ancient men who once peopled the mesas and table lands of the southwestern territories. These houses were built one-sixth of the real size, but portions of the real houses were also displayed, in order to give a clear and truthful impression to the visitor. In another room was a museum of relics, showing remains of the cliff-dwellers and their implements, weapons and pottery. The reader is to know that, ages ago, a people, for reasons unknown, sought niches in the cliffs, now hundreds of feet above the rivers, and there, in places almost inaccessible, built their houses and villages. Ledges of rock were shown in a fallen state, with houses crushed beneath, and houses again built above them. Tortuous paths led up the cliffs and through to the outer air, whence the visitor might ascend to the summit, as seen in the engraving. A fee of twenty-five cents was charged to enter this instructive exhibit, which was one of the worthiest entertainments of the Exposition.

Figure 4.6. A BEDROOM OF MARIE ANTOINETTE.—One may easily judge that house-decoration has made no progress for many centuries; otherwise it would be impossible to re-introduce the styles of Henry VIII., Louis XIV., XV. and XVI. The scene on this page represents a reproduction of Queen Marie Antoinette's bedroom at the Little Trianon, in Versailles, which was shown in the French section of the Manufactures Building by MM. Alavoine, leading manufacturers of Paris. All of this work on textiles was done by hand in silk, and the skill and patience displayed by the French workman must evoke astonishment. Even to the picture on the wall, all is the product of needlework. From this luxurious room, thick carpeted, perfumed, and beautified with every ingenuity, the French Queen, dragged by fishwomen, who called her "the baker's wife," "the Austrian she-wolf," was transferred to the Tuilleries, and later translated to the prison of the Temple, where the head of her dearest friend, the Princess de Lamballe, was shown on a pike at the window. Then, after the beheadal of her husband, the king, she left her two children, a widow, to undergo mock trial before Judge Fouquier-Tinville, to be sentenced, and to mend her tattered garments with needle at the prison of the Conciergerie, in order to go decently to the scaffold in a republican cart. We look upon this one of her many palace-rooms and contemplate her dizzy and dreadful fall.

Figure 4.7. CEYLON TEA ROOM, WOMAN'S BUILDING.—The large company of
Singhalese which arrived in Chicago in the winter-time, early in 1893, set resolutely at
work under Mr. Grinlinton and prepared not only its main building or court in the
region of France and Germany, on the lake shore, but set up tea-booths in the
Agricultural, Manufactures, and Woman's Buildings. Their hope was to further
introduce their spices, ebony and tea to the Western Republic, and British interests
were behind them. There was the frugal hope, however, that the tea-saloons would be
profitable, and there is little doubt that this hope was realized. The scene before us
represents the most elegant of these places of refreshment. It was built at the southern
end of the main floor of the Woman's Building, and at the foreground, inside the ropes,
excels in the display of luxurious and beautiful furnishings. The difference between
this inclosure and that to which the general public was invited for the purpose of
purchasing tea may be easily detected. A parlor of delicate and wonderful carvings and
embroideries is on one side, a restaurant on the other. The hangings of the entire room,
the parlor, the scent of sandal-wood, the carved ceilings, well-lit with electricity, and,
above all, the gentle demeanor of the Singhalese, endeared the resort to tea-lovers, and
probably won many of them over to the use of the new brand.

Figure 4.8. NEW JERSEY'S BUILDING.—This structure was situated on the northern circle of State houses, at a corner where a north and south avenue ran to the New York Building. Nothing could be more surprising than the contrast between the exterior and interior. Plain and unostentatious from the street, the house startled the visitor from its entrance with the luxury and elegance of its furnishings, and the stateliness of its occupants. Colored servants to take the guest's card or lead him to the registry, silken ribbons across doorways and stair-cases, to remind him that he was not of the elect, pianos, chairs, tables and sideboards of rosewood, with carpets of deepest velvet, and hangings of richest silk, spoke of the wealth, pride, and exclusive spirit of the little State. The house itself reproduced the appearance of Washington's headquarters at Morristown, in the Revolutionary War, and was the work of Charles A. Gifford, architect, of Newark. It was three stories high, and 81 by 31 feet in area; the cost was $18,000. A room was shown that was called Washington's bed-chamber and dining-room, and a wine buffet was set with fine cut glassware, well in keeping with the general interior display. There were rooms for the use of the women commissioners, rooms for the commission, parlors, a large hall, with broad fire-place, and a whole story for the care-takers. The material was brought largely from New Jersey by James W. Lanning, of Trenton, the contractor.

Figure 4.9. THE HUNTER'S CABIN.—At the south end of Wooded Island was a log house with clay floor and stick chimney which was built by Theodore Roosevelt, of New York, a lover of huntsman's sports, as a museum and memorial in honor of Daniel Boone and Davy Crockett. A rope divided the large room of the building into a public and a private compartment. On chilly days a fire blazed in the broad fireplace, and in that regard the interior exactly resembled the houses of pioneers in timbered regions forty years ago. Otherwise the furnishings were more comfortable than those enjoyed in northern Indiana when Pierce and Buchanan were in the White House. The skins of wild animals covered the floor, and beds and settees were made of stretched skins. A double-bunk afforded two wide and easy couches. A stool was made out of a section of log, and primitive cooking apparatus and tin dishes and candles gave a realistic appearance to the domicile. To complete this picture, a hunter in long hair and wide-brimmed felt hat made his home in the cabin and answered the questions of many visitors, for there was a charm about the premises, pioneers loving to recall the vanished days, and younger inquirers seeming pleased to see before them the picture so often drawn in the tales of their grandsires and this chapter of their romances. Between the Hunter's Cabin and Marie Antoinette's bed-chamber in the French section there was a wide divergence.

Source: The Dream City: A Portfolio of Photographic Views of the World's Columbian Exposition (St. Louis: N. D. Thompson, 1893–1894).

These Home-Made Divans Become Real Luxuries

As the United States celebrated its growing presence in the global market-place, many women embraced what the historian Kristin Hoganson has called "cosmopolitan domesticity." By adopting decorative styles and domestic goods from other nations and regions, women literally displayed their understanding of the world beyond the U.S. Like the exhibits at the Columbian Exposition, these displays reflected national and racial assumptions. For example, while many women looked to Europe for inspiration, home decorators also incorporated styles and goods from "the East," often failing to differentiate between Chinese and Japanese or Turkish and Moorish aesthetics. "Cozy corners" were a popular and economical way to participate in this Orientalist trend, permitting women to convert a small part of a room into an Eastern oasis. Decorating books and magazines such as _Ladies' Home Journal_ provided examples and instructions.

I wonder how many women know how to contrive a pretty corner for a large parlor. Take a long, narrow mirror, framed as cheaply as possible, and fasten it firmly against the wall corner-wise, with a corner shelf above it; then have India drapery silk, plain figured, or the Oriental muslin imitation (the former is about seventy-five cents a yard—fifty cents if plain—and the latter fifteen cents), and festoon it across the top, tacking it to the edge of the shelf. On each side catch it here and there in a knot through which a tiny Japanese fan may be thrust, if you have not tired of this style of decoration. Continue the drapery across the bottom, and in front of the mirror stand a small table holding a palm, in a handsome bit of pottery, a figure or a pretty photograph. On the top shelf have a large Japanese jar or a bright piece of bric-a-brac of some kind.

Another "cozy corner" is made by running a curtain pole diagonally across, and from it hang Oriental muslin, India silk, serge, and tapestry curtains, looping one high and far back, with a brass chain; spread a rug in front of the curtains, and behind them put a small divan, which I will tell you how to make, and you will find that this corner is about the first part of the room to be occupied. A corner bracket above the curtains, holding a tall vase or jar, is an improvement.

In regard to the divan: First, have a carpenter—or one of the men about the house, if he belongs to the "handy" tribe—make a strong

Figure 4.10. This trade card, reading "I'll put a girdle (of Willimantic Thread) around the Earth in forty minutes" (1880s; author's collection), conveys the interplay between domestic goods and global ambitions at the end of the nineteenth century. Increasingly, American manufactured products could be found around the world and suggested a gentler mode of foreign expansion. Commercial expansion was often represented by women and children on advertising cards. Here a cherub does the job.

framework about forty-two inches long, twenty inches wide and fourteen inches high, and put rollers on each corner; this should be of pressed pine and need not be painted. Now make a comfortable mattress for it of husks or the filling called excelsior, first putting slats across the top of the frame, and covering with ticking. Over this have a plain-colored upholstery serge, or figured cretonne cover, and a ruffle around the four sides of the same, reaching to the floor. Two large square pillows covered with the cretonne, are then finished all around with heavy cord or ruffle and placed against the wall at either end. If the divan is put flat against the wall, the pillows stand up at the back. These home-made divans become real luxuries when furnished with a wire spring of the size made for cots, under a wool mattress, though in such a case the frame must be made lower.

If possible, always have long curtains inside, as they furnish a room, almost. Even the printed scrim ones, at seventeen cents a yard, look cozy when hung. They are really artistic in deep ecru shades, with spider webs in brown, and a border one each side of brown flowers. If poles are beyond your means, put them up with a drawing-string run in at the top, forming an erect ruffle two inches wide. Let them hang loosely, or tie back with ribbon. "Where there is a will there is a way," and even ten dollars will do wonders in giving a room a cozy, home-like appearance.

Source: "Cozy Corners for Parlors," *Ladies' Home Journal*, July 1890.

The President Did Not Have Any Particular Marriage in Mind

Between 1870 and 1914, over 450 American women married European aristocrats, with eighty-five marriages between American women and British peers. Public awareness of these marriages was amplified by generous coverage in magazines and newspapers that portrayed American brides as both victims and upstarts and used their marriages as occasions and metaphors to consider the place of the United States in the international order. President Theodore Roosevelt, like so many of his contemporaries, shared a belief in the larger significance of international marriages to the domestic life and politics of the nation. What are his concerns, and why might he have believed it appropriate to share them with Congress?

Roosevelt Censures Foreign Marriages: Believes American Girl Cannot Fulfill Her Duty by Wedding a Dissipated Nobleman; Would Forbid, If He Could; President Had Richard Croker in Mind as the Type of "Millionaire Who Is the Least Enviable"

By John Callan O'Laughlin

WASHINGTON, May 2.—"But his counterpart in evil is to be found in that particular kind of a multi-millionaire who is almost the least enviable, and is certainly the least admirable, of all our citizens; a man whose son is a fool and his daughter a foreign Princess."

This is President Roosevelt's opinion of the marriage of American girls with members of the nobility of Europe, as expressed in the message which was read in the two Houses of Congress several days ago. Probably, of all the President said, the above expression caused the most comment at the Capitol and in social circles in Washington. At the outset, it may be said positively that the President did not have any particular marriage in mind when he wrote the above sentence.

He meant to put the stamp of disapproval upon all contracts of this kind. Not that he does not understand that occasionally such unions turn out happily, and the man and woman and the world generally are benefited. But the rule has been that the bridegroom has led a dissolute life and the girl, translated to a lower atmosphere than that in which she has lived at home, becomes either cynical or vitiated.

If the President could have his way marriage between American girls and foreign noblemen would be forbidden. He recognizes, however, that there is no more chance of an effective prohibition than there is, to quote the experience of King Canute, to prevent the tide from rising. But if there were a way to accomplish this result there is not the slightest doubt that in the present frame of mind of the Chief Executive he would urge that it be taken.

BILL TO IMPOSE TAX UPON DOWRIES

To discourage the alliance of American girls with titled Europeans Representative Sabath of Chicago recently introduced a bill providing for the imposition of a tax upon the dowries given in such cases. The bill was referred to the Ways and Means Committee of the House, where it has lain without signs of life. It is the view of the lawyers of Congress that the bill is unconstitutional. Mr. Sabath, however, insists that it is constitutional, and he believes if it were placed upon the statu[t]e books, it would work a double benefit. It would tend to prevent foreign marriages, and if such marriages occurred then the Treasury of the United States would receive at least a small portion of the money made in America, which a European nobleman is put in a position to dissipate.

It is realized by the President, as it is realized by members of Congress, that the sentiment against these marriages is growing in intensity. Examining the history of such unions in recent years, as the President has done, it will be found that they have terminated under circumstances in many cases disgraceful and in others, to say the least, unhappily. In view of the experience of the past the President believes that the wise thing for American girls to do is to marry American men; and it is understood he makes no exception to this general rule, though he appreciates that at times a foreigner, who has done manly things like the

Duke d'Abruzzi, comes to the United States as a suitor for the hand of one of our young women.

DUTIES OF AMERICAN WOMEN

The President repeatedly has expressed views as to the duties of American women. He has said that exactly as the first duty of a normal man is the duty of being the homemaker, so the first duty of a normal woman is to be the homekeeper; and exactly as no other learning is as important for the average man as the learning which will teach him how to make his livelihood, so no other learning is as important for the average woman as the learning which will make her a good housewife and mother.

The President has not the slightest sympathy with those hysterical and foolish creatures who wish women to attain to easy lives by shirking their duties, and he has as hearty a contempt for the woman who shirks her duty of bearing and rearing the children, of doing her full housewife's work, as he has for the man who is an idler, who shirks his duty of earning a living for himself and for his household, or who is selfish or brutal toward his wife and children.

The President feels that an obligation rests upon the American girl to do her part in adding to the general welfare and prosperity of the country, and this cannot be done by her marriage to a foreign nobleman, whose one idea is to get hold of her money and to use it either in defraying huge debts or to spend it in riotous living.

MILLIONAIRES WHO ARE A MENACE

In the same paragraph in which he denounced European marriages the President included among the men of means who are a menace to the community those "whose nominal pleasures are, at best, of a tasteless and extravagant luxury, and whose real delight, whose real lifework, is the accumulation and use of power in its most sordid and least elevating form." In the former class Mr. Roosevelt included the millionaires who ostentatiously display their wealth, and in one case particularly, which is well known, the host gave a dinner where each plate cost a thousand dollars. The President regarded this as a wicked and wanton misuse of money.

Richard Croker is the type the President had in mind in connection with "the accumulation and use of power in its most sordid and least elevating form." The President is not at all surprised that the King of

England refused to meet Croker after the latter's horse had won the Derby, thus breaking a custom and creating a precedent, which he thinks ought to work for social betterment.

The children of persons of this type necessarily are handicapped in making their way in life. They are compelled to carry on their shoulders the burden of their father's reputation. The President regards this as grossly unfair, and for this reason, as well as for the greater one of the effect of the conduct of such persons upon the community in which he exercises his power, he has included Croker and the men like him among the class of "undesirables."

Source: "Roosevelt Censures Foreign Marriages," *New York Times*, May 3, 1908.

The Hardest Problem in Home-Making I Have Ever Tried to Solve

In 1898, when Spain ceded the Philippines to the United States after the Spanish-American War, many Americans debated the wisdom of annexation. They weighed doubts about Filipino self-rule and desires for access to Asian markets against racist concerns about Filipinos as future Americans and beliefs that, given U.S. history, the country should not become a colonial power. Then in 1899, Filipino nationalists established the independent Philippine Republic, and U.S. forces fought for control of the islands. The Philippine-American War waged from 1899 to 1902, and the Philippines became an American colonial territory until 1935. The brutality of this conflict is absent from Caroline Shunk's account of her life as an army colonel's wife. Instead she depicts colonial authority in terms of expanding American domestic order. How are Filipinos incorporated into her vision of proper home life? What connections does she draw to race relations in the U.S.?

En Route

SAN FRANCISCO, FEBRUARY, 1909

Our trunks have gone, and the Colonel is down at the boat on duty, while I am sitting, like Marius amid the ruins, surrounded by Japanese baskets and satchels. Nothing else is left in our rooms. We are engaged in laying a substantial pavement of goodly intentions; not to worry, to enjoy everything except leprosy or smallpox, and to get the most out of our trip and our station in the Philippines.

The Colonel commands the troops, and has all of the "fifty-seven varieties." The boat can carry two thousand people, but not that many will be aboard. There are twenty-five regular officers, a few Army ladies, and many civil employees—clerks, nurses, school-teachers, and two young girls going over to marry American men in the islands. In all, there are one hundred and twenty first-class passengers, about the same number of second-class, a hundred and fifty sailors, and the same number of recruits. Rank or length of service is observed in every detail aboard a troop-ship. State-rooms, places at table, use of bath-rooms, etc., are allotted to the highest in rank, the eldest in service, and so on down the list. We come second, which, from my long "following of the guidon," I think no more than fair.

I must tell you of three passengers who are going across the Pacific with us, who bid fair to be interesting. Last night I encountered an old-time darky mammy, sitting in the hotel lobby beside a pile of luggage. She wore a black dress and white apron and a white cap was visible under her mourning bonnet. I felt sure that she was maid to some Army woman. Sure enough, in the writing-room a pretty, white-haired old lady, also clad in deep mourning, sat at one of the desks. It was Mme. X——, the mother of Major X——, who is to be stationed at our camp. She is going to the Philippines with her son, and Lucindy, her maid for many years, and "raised in Kentucky, bress Gawd!" is going with her. The Major goes about with his tiny old mother tucked under his arm, and Lucindy following in the "middle distance." It is a pretty picture.

We yearn for a Lucindy. She is an excellent cook, her mistress says, and irons the Major's white linen uniforms to perfection. What a treasure in sepia! . . .

Settling a Home in the Tropics . . .

CAMP STOTSENBURG, LUZON, PHILIPPINE ISLANDS,
MARCH, 1909

We have moved into our new home, and I am trying to make living in some degree of comfort possible. It is the hardest problem in home-making I have ever tried to solve. Even living in an Army tent the weeks we had to spend crossing the Dakotas in the spring of 1894 was less difficult. In many ways I prefer the tent and to "move on" every day. . . .

This house makes me nearer heart-sick than any of the places called by courtesy "houses" that our Uncle Sam has given us. It is a square, one-story building of rough lumber, built on high wooden posts, each post set loosely in a cement square to sway with the earthquakes and also to keep the house cooler for the occupants. Incidentally, the white ants eat the posts and let the house down occasionally. I could easily run under our shack without stooping, if I dared brave the ants, lizards, rats, and house-snakes that there abide, not to mention cockroaches and black spiders as large as the saucer of an after-dinner coffee-cup. The steep roof slopes to form the porch-top and from that is hung native matting, called *suale* (pronounced "swalley"). This keeps the porch shady, and, with the thick vines from the porch to the roof, it makes a pleasant out-door living-room. I like the porch; I feel safer out there, where I can see the approach of all humans, beasts, and bugs, than in the dark house, with its rafters covered with all sorts of creepy things. Many of the porches are arranged and furnished charmingly with gay-colored straw mats, low willow chairs, stunning Chinese lanterns, and air plants (a kind of orchid) hanging from the edge of the roof. Card-parties are given on these verandas, and many families dine there in the evening. It is the only comfortable spot I can find in our shack. If it were only screened and bug-proof! . . .

Some of the houses are prettily furnished, as a number of the ladies were brave enough to defy advice and bring their nice home-like furniture and housekeeping things with them. Their handsome draperies, silver, and cut-glass seem doubly comfortable and joyous here on the other side of the world. . . .

Housekeeping in the Tropics . . .

CAMP STOTSENBURG, LUZON, PHILIPPINE ISLANDS,
MAY, 1909 . . .

The Filipinos are not dirty people—quite the contrary; they are the most bathed, washed, and ironed creatures you can imagine, and sally forth from wretched-looking little *nipa* huts spick and span and immaculately clean. The children are yellow-white and have abnormally large stomachs. They die by hundreds, a generous diet of crabs, green bananas, and sugar cakes not being conducive to long life.

One can spend hours trying to explain to native servants the problems of the daily routine in the household, which is complicated, compared with their own simple life. A wall of bamboo, twelve by twelve feet, a steeply pointed roof of poles and palm leaves, a floor of bamboo poles set on high wooden posts; one room, with a box of earth at one end, a fire in the middle, some brown pottery cooking utensils, grass mats on the floor to sleep on—such is the Filipino's "home, sweet home." To the natives, moving is almost as simple as it must have been in the Garden of Eden—a mere matter of gathering up the pots and pans and whistling to the dogs. The children carry the mats, the beloved carabao is driven to the new home—and it is done. . . .

Christmas in the Tropics . . .

CAMP STOTSENBURG, LUZON, PHILIPPINE ISLANDS,
DECEMBER, 1909

It is hard to realize that yesterday was really Christmas. We followed home customs as far as we could, but the tropic variations on the time-honored festivities emphasized poignantly the strangeness of this alien land. It was hot, too—a burning, blazing day.

We had a strenuous week getting a Christmas-tree and presents for all the ninety-five children on this reservation without regard to race, color, or "previous condition of servitude." Everyone had a finger in the pie. The officers gave the money, and the arrangements were made by a committee of five ladies, two of whom went to Manila to buy the presents, while the two chaplains took a detachment of soldiers and drove many miles before they found a tree which would answer the purpose. They secured a graceful bamboo that filled one end of the school-room, and the soldiers decorated it with green vines and plants. Flags and lanterns added the note of color. A fat, jolly lieutenant was Santa Claus, clad in the major-doctor's red eiderdown bath-robe, high yellow cavalry boots and spurs, cap and gauntlets, with a wig and beard of cotton. He was a brilliant, martial Santa Claus—and an exceedingly warm one. The children loved him and had a merry time.

Source: Caroline S. Shunk, An Army Woman in the Philippines: Extracts from Letters of an Army Officer's Wife, Describing Her Personal Experiences in the Philippine Islands (Kansas City, MO: Franklin Hudson, 1914).

5

At Home in the Late Nineteenth-Century City

The domestic ideal that emerged in the 1820s rested on distinctions between marketplace and home, male and female, public and private. These divisions were never as absolute as imagined, and the lines between them were repeatedly ignored, blurred, or compromised. And yet, at the end of the nineteenth century, changes in American urban life seemed to threaten these distinctions anew, testing the resilience and adaptability of domesticity in the modern industrial city. As cities grew in size and population, spatial and social segmentation imparted a sense of unknowability. Rich and poor no longer shared the same neighborhoods, and the experiences of living beside a diverse collection of strangers raised concerns about routine social encounters and urban morality more broadly.

Nonetheless, some people appreciated that the fates of all city dwellers were bound together despite the growing separation and isolation. Frederick Law Olmstead's vision for public parks and Jane Addams's account of founding Hull-House offer two examples of how domestic sentiments, activities, and even goods were reimagined in service of community and social cohesion. The two spaces—one grand and one intimate—are described as surrogate public homes designed to counteract the squalor, crowding, and absence of family feeling in working-class and poor households. The writings of Jacob Riis and Stephen Crane represent a different approach to bridging the same social and spatial distinctions, by exposing middle-class readers to unsentimental accounts of urban poverty and inadequate housing.

It is possible that better-off urbanites recognized in these writings more dire versions of shared problems. In the late nineteenth-century city, the poor were not the only ones struggling to find affordable housing capable of providing some measure of respectability and privacy. Eliza Chester's thoughts on housing for unmarried women and the *New*

York Times's account of the failed Woman's Hotel convey the social and economic challenges faced by those who lived outside traditional family arrangements. Likewise, middle-class married couples often could not afford the ideal of the single-family home and, like the Marches in William Dean Howells's *A Hazard of New Fortunes*, learned to live in "flats." Two articles from the *New York Times* suggest how contemporaries eased the transition to apartment living and differentiated these new multifamily dwellings from tenements.

Even some of the most elite city dwellers felt that their domestic privacy was on the decline. In *The Decoration of Houses*, Edith Wharton expresses such a concern alongside a pointed critique of Victorian home décor and its emphasis on "showy effects." A similar focus on goods and display is mocked in the writings of *Life* magazine; here the joke is on the wealthy, who have turned marriage into an exclusively economic relationship and houses into sites of conspicuous consumption. Ironically, these elite urban homes are depicted as possessing qualities usually reserved for the improper homes of the poor: pervaded by marketplace concerns, overly public, and lacking proper affection.

Public Provision for Recreation of This Class, Essentially Domestic and Secluded

In 1858, Frederick Law Olmstead and Calvert Vaux won the competition to design Central Park, marking Olmstead's formal entry into the field of landscape architecture. Touring the New England countryside as a child, he developed an appreciation of nature's power to elicit emotions, shape conduct, and influence values. These insights informed his later work designing urban parks, parkways, residential suburbs, and public and private grounds. Like his mentor Andrew Jackson Downing, Olmstead believed that the pastoral landscape and beauty were antidotes to urban living. In this passage, he discusses his plans for Brooklyn's Prospect Park, emphasizing the ways in which public green spaces and wholesome recreation might remedy the failings of urban homes and redress the social fragmentation of city life. He imagines the great urban park as a space apart, an extension of the private sphere. In what ways does this vision mimic the Victorian domestic ideal?

I have next to see what opportunities are wanted to induce people to engage in what I have termed *neighborly* receptive recreations, under conditions which shall be highly counteractive to the prevailing bias to degeneration and demoralization in large towns. To make clearer what I mean, I need an illustration which I find in a familiar domestic gathering, where the prattle of the children mingles with the easy conversation of the more sedate, the bodily requirements satisfied with good cheer, fresh air, agreeable light, moderate temperature, snug shelter, and furniture and decorations adapted to please the eye, without calling for profound admiration on the one hand, or tending to fatigue or disgust on the other. The circumstances are all favorable to a pleasurable wakefulness of the mind without stimulating exertion; and the close relation of family life, the association of children, of mothers, of lovers, or those who may be lovers, stimulate and keep alive the more tender sympathies, and give play to faculties such as may be dormant in business or on the promenade; while at the same time the cares of providing in detail for all the wants of the family, guidance, instruction, and reproof, and the dutiful reception of guidance, instruction, and reproof, are, as matters of conscious exertion, as far as possible laid aside.

There is an instinctive inclination to this social, neighborly, unexertive form of recreation among all of us. In one way or another it is sure to be constantly operating upon those millions on millions of men and women who are to pass their lives within a few miles of where we now stand. To what extent it shall operate so as to develop health and virtue, will, on many occasions, be simply a question of opportunity and inducement. And this question is one for the determination of which for a thousand years we here to-day are largely responsible.

Think what the ordinary state of things to many is at this beginning of the town. The public is reading just now a little book in which some of your streets of which you are not proud are described. Go into one of those red cross streets any fine evening next summer, and ask how it is with their residents? Oftentimes you will see half a dozen sitting together on the door-steps, or, all in a row, on the curb-stones, with their feet in the gutter, driven out of doors by the closeness within; mothers among them anxiously regarding their children who are dodging about at their play, among the noisy wheels on the pavement.

Again, consider how often you see young men in knots of perhaps half a dozen in lounging attitudes rudely obstructing the sidewalks, chiefly led in their little conversation by the suggestions given to their minds by what or whom they may see passing in the street, men, women, or children, whom they do not know, and for whom they have no respect or sympathy. There is nothing among them or about them which is adapted to bring into play a spark of admiration, of delicacy, manliness, or tenderness. You see them presently descend in search of physical comfort to a brilliantly lighted basement, where they find others of their sort, see, hear, smell, drink, and eat all manner of vile things.

Whether on the curb-stones or in the dram-shops, these young men are all under the influence of the same impulse which some satisfy about the tea-table with neighbors and wives and mothers and children, and all things clean and wholesome, softening and refining.

If the great city to arise here is to be laid out little by little, and chiefly to suit the views of land-owners, acting only individually, and thinking only of how what they do is to affect the value in the next week or the next year of the few lots that each may hold at the time, the opportunities of so obeying this inclination as at the same time to give the lungs a bath of pure sunny air, to give the mind a suggestion of rest from the devouring eagerness and intellectual strife of town life, will always be few to any, to many will amount to nothing.

But is it possible to make public provision for recreation of this class, essentially domestic and secluded as it is?

It is a question which can, of course, be conclusively answered only from experience. And from experience in some slight degree I shall answer it. There is one large American town, in which it may happen that a man of any class shall say to his wife, when he is going out in the morning: "My dear, when the children come home from school, put some bread and butter and salad in a basket, and go to the spring under the chestnut-tree where we found the Johnsons last week. I will join you there as soon as I can get away from the office. We will walk to the dairyman's cottage and get some tea, and some fresh milk for the children, and take our supper by the brook-side;" and this shall be no joke, but the most refreshing earnest.

There will be room enough in the Brooklyn Park, when it is finished, for several thousand little family and neighborly parties to bivouac at frequent intervals through the summer, without discommoding one another, or interfering with any other purpose, to say nothing of those who can be drawn out to make a day of it, as many thousand were last year. And although the arrangements for the purpose were yet very incomplete, and but little ground was *at all* prepared for such use, besides these small parties, consisting of one or two families, there came also, in companies of from thirty to a hundred and fifty, somewhere near twenty thousand children with their parents, Sunday-school teachers, or other guides and friends, who spent the best part of a day under the trees and on the turf, in recreations of which the predominating element was of this neighborly receptive class. Often they would bring a fiddle, flute, and harp, or other music. Tables, seats, shade, turf, swings, cool spring-water, and a pleasing rural prospect, stretching off half a mile or more each way, unbroken by a carriage road or the slightest evidence of the vicinity of the town, were supplied them without charge, and bread and milk and ice-cream at moderate fixed charges. In all my life I have never seen such joyous collections of people. I have, in fact, more than once observed tears of gratitude in the eyes of poor women, as they watched their children thus enjoying themselves.

The whole cost of such neighborly festivals, even when they include excursions by rail from the distant parts of the town, does not exceed for each person, on an average, a quarter of a dollar; and when the arrangements are complete, I see no reason why thousands should not come every day where hundreds come now to use them; and if so, who can measure the value, generation after generation, of such provisions for recreation to the over-wrought, much-confined people of the great town that is to be?

For this purpose neither of the forms of ground we have heretofore considered are at all suitable. We want a ground to which people may easily go after their day's work is done, and where they may stroll for an hour, seeing, hearing, and feeling nothing of the bustle and jar of the streets, where they shall, in effect, find the city put far away from them. We want the greatest possible contrast with the streets and the shops and the rooms of the town which will be consistent with convenience and the preservation of good order and neatness. We want, especially, the greatest possible contrast with the restraining and confining conditions of the town, those conditions which compel us to walk circumspectly, watchfully, jealously, which compel us to look closely upon others without sympathy. Practically, what we most want is a simple, broad, open space of clean greensward, with sufficient play of surface and a sufficient number of trees about it to supply a variety of light and shade. This we want as a central feature. We want depth of wood enough about it not only for comfort in hot weather, but to completely shut out the city from our landscapes.

The word *park*, in town nomenclature, should, I think, be reserved for grounds of the character and purpose thus described.

Source: Frederick Law Olmsted, *Public Parks and the Enlargement of Towns: Read before the American Social Science Association at the Lowell Institute, Boston, Feb. 25, 1870* (Cambridge, MA: American Social Science Association / Riverside, 1870).

The Fine Old House Responded Kindly to Repairs

Jane Addams published her autobiography, *Twenty Years at Hull-House*, in 1910. It is telling that she folded her life story into an account of the settlement house that she and Ellen Gates Starr founded in 1889. Although Addams lived a public life as a social reformer and peace activist, much of her settlement work—establishing kindergartens and playgrounds, guaranteeing garbage removal, advocating for pure food—carried the imprint of women's traditional domestic responsibilities. Referred to as "municipal housekeeping," such activities underscored the permeable boundary between home and city, emphasizing that good housekeeping demanded women's engagement in civic life. By imagining the city as one large household, reformers such as Addams simultaneously upheld and subverted women's association with the home. This account of setting up housekeeping in the settlement reveals the subtle play between traditional domestic values and the transformative nature of her reform work.

Another Sunday afternoon in early spring, on the way to a Bohemian mission in the carriage of one of its founders, we passed a fine old house standing well back from the street, surrounded on three sides by a broad piazza which was supported by wooden pillars of exceptionally pure Corinthian design and proportion. I was so attracted by the house that I set forth to visit it the very next day, but though I searched for it then and for several days after, I could not find it, and at length I most reluctantly gave up the search.

Three weeks later, with the advice of several of the oldest residents of Chicago, including the ex-mayor of the city, Colonel Mason, who had from the first been a warm friend to our plans, we decided upon a location somewhere near the junction of Blue Island Avenue, Halsted Street, and Harrison Street. I was surprised and overjoyed on the very first day of our search for quarters to come upon the hospitable old house, the quest for which I had so recently abandoned. The house was of course rented, the lower part of it used for offices and storerooms in connection with a factory that stood back of it. However, after some difficulties were overcome, it proved to be possible to sublet the second floor and what had been the large drawing-room on the first floor.

The house had passed through many changes since it had been built in 1856 for the homestead of one of Chicago's pioneer citizens, Mr. Charles J. Hull, and although battered by the vicissitudes, was essentially sound. Before it had been occupied by a factory, it had sheltered a second-hand furniture store, and at one time the Little Sisters of the Poor had used it for a home for the aged. It had a half-skeptical reputation for a haunted attic, so far respected by the tenants living on the second floor that they always kept a large pitcher full of water on the attic stairs. Their explanation of this custom was so incoherent that I was sure it was a survival of the belief that a ghost could not cross running water, but perhaps that interpretation was only my eagerness for finding folklore.

The fine old house responded kindly to repairs, its wide hall and open fireplaces always insuring it a gracious aspect. Its generous owner, Miss Helen Culver, in the following spring gave us a free leasehold of the entire house. Her kindness has continued through the years until the group of thirteen buildings, which at present comprises our equipment, is built largely upon land Miss Culver has put at the service of the Settlement which bears Mr. Hull's name. In those days the house stood between an undertaking establishment and a saloon. "Knight, Death, and the Devil," the three were called by a Chicago wit, and yet any mock heroics which might be implied by comparing the Settlement to a knight quickly dropped away under the genuine kindness and hearty welcome extended us by the families living up and down the street.

We furnished the house as we would have furnished it were it in another part of the city, with the photographs and other impedimenta we had collected in Europe, and with a few bits of family mahogany. While all the new furniture which was bought was enduring in quality, we were careful to keep it in character with the fine old residence. Probably no young matron ever placed her own things in her own home with more pleasure than that with which we first furnished Hull-House. We believed that the Settlement may logically bring to its aid all those adjuncts which the cultivated man regards as good and suggestive of the best life of the past.

On the 18th of September, 1889, Miss Starr and I moved into it, with Miss Mary Keyser, who began by performing housework, but who quickly developed into a very important factor in the life of the vicinity as well as in that of the household, and whose death five years later was most sincerely mourned by hundreds of our neighbors. In our enthusiasm over "settling," the first night we forgot not only to lock but to close a side door opening on Polk Street, and were much pleased in the morning to find that we possessed a fine illustration of the honesty and kindliness of our new neighbors.

Source: Jane Addams, *Twenty Years at Hull-House* (New York: Macmillan, 1910).

They Are the Hot-Beds of the Epidemics That Carry Death to Rich and Poor Alike

When Jacob Riis's *How the Other Half Lives* was published in 1890, it challenged both the isolation of the urban poor and the complacency of better-off urbanites. Many in the middle and upper classes were shocked by the detailed descriptions of tenement life and moved by his focus on mothers and children. Like Olmstead, Riis argued that what happened in the tenements did not remain there but flowed through the whole city— taxing public and private institutions and diminishing the safety and morals of all. He made his case by appealing to established beliefs that a proper home must be private and separate from market forces. In this excerpt, he contends that landlords' selfish drive for profits has guaranteed that the tenements meet neither criterion. And so, in Riis's analysis, the failed homes of the poor are not evidence of their low morals and criminality but are instead the cause.

Long ago it was said that "one half of the world does not know how the other half lives." That was true then. It did not know because it did not care. The half that was on top cared little for the struggles, and less for the fate of those who were underneath, so long as it was able to hold them there and keep its own seat. There came a time when the discomfort and crowding below were so great, and the consequent upheavals so violent, that it was no longer an easy thing to do, and then the upper half fell to inquiring what was the matter. Information on the subject has been accumulating rapidly since, and the whole world has had its hands full answering for its old ignorance.

In New York, the youngest of the world's great cities, that time came later than elsewhere, because the crowding had not been so great. There were those who believed that it would never come; but their hopes were vain. Greed and reckless selfishness wrought like results here as in the cities of older lands. "When the great riot occurred in 1863," so reads the testimony of the Secretary of the Prison Association of New York before a legislative committee appointed to investigate causes of the increase of crime in the State twenty-five years ago, "every hiding-place and nursery of crime discovered itself by immediate and active participation in the operations of the mob. Those very places and domiciles, and all that are like them, are to-day nurseries of crime, and of the vices and disorderly courses which lead to crime. By far the largest part—eighty per cent. at least—of crimes against property and against the person are perpetrated by individuals who have either lost connection with home life, or never had any, or whose *homes had ceased to be sufficiently separate, decent, and desirable to afford what are regarded as ordinary wholesome influences of home and family* . . . . The younger criminals seem to come almost exclusively from the worst tenement house districts, that is, when traced back to the very places where they had their homes in the city here." Of one thing New York made sure at that early stage of the inquiry: the boundary line of the Other Half lies through the tenements.

It is ten years and over, now, since that line divided New York's population evenly. To-day three-fourths of its people live in the tenements, and the nineteenth century drift of the population to the cities is sending ever-increasing multitudes to crowd them. The fifteen thousand tenant houses that were the despair of the sanitarian in the past generation have swelled into thirty-seven thousand, and more than twelve hundred thousand persons call them home. The one way out he saw—rapid transit to the suburbs—has brought no relief. We know now that there is no way out; that the "system" that was the evil offspring of public neglect and private greed has come to stay, a storm-centre forever of our civilization. Nothing is left but to make the best of a bad bargain.

What the tenements are and how they grew to what they are, we shall see hereafter. The story is dark enough, drawn from the plain public records, to send a chill to any heart. If it shall appear that the sufferings and the sins of the "other half," and the evil they breed, are but as a just punishment upon the community that gave it no other choice, it will be because that is the truth. The boundary line lies there because, while the forces for good on one side vastly outweigh the bad—it were not well otherwise—in the tenements all the influences make for evil; because they are the hot-beds of the epidemics that carry death to rich and poor alike; the nurseries of pauperism and crime that fill our jails and police courts; that throw off a scum of forty thousand human wrecks to the island asylums and workhouses year by year; that turned out in the last eight years a round half million beggars to prey upon our charities; that maintain a standing army of ten thousand tramps with all that that implies; because, above all, they touch the family life with deadly moral contagion. This is their worst crime, inseparable from the system. That we have to own it the child of our own wrong does not excuse it, even though it gives it claim upon our utmost patience and tenderest charity.

What are you going to do about it? is the question of to-day. It was asked once of our city in taunting defiance by a band of political cut-throats, the legitimate outgrowth of life on the tenement-house level.[1] Law and order found the answer then and prevailed. With our enormously swelling population held in this galling bondage, will that answer always be given? It will depend on how fully the situation that prompted the challenge is grasped. Forty per cent. of the distress among the poor, said a recent official report, is due to drunkenness. But the first legislative committee ever appointed to probe this sore went deeper down and uncovered its roots. The "conclusion forced itself upon it that certain conditions and associations of human life and habitation are the prolific parents of corresponding habits and morals," and it recommended "the prevention of drunkenness by providing for every man a clean and comfortable home." Years after, a sanitary inquiry brought to light the fact that "more than one-half of the tenements with two-thirds of their population were held by owners who made the keeping of them a business, *generally a speculation.* The owner was seeking a certain percentage on his outlay, and that percentage very rarely fell below fifteen per cent., and frequently exceeded thirty.[2] The complaint was universal among the tenants that they were entirely uncared for, and that the only answer to their requests to have the place put in order by repairs and necessary improvements was that they must pay their rent or leave. The agent's instructions were simple but emphatic: 'Collect the rent in advance, or, failing, eject the occupants.'" Upon such a stock grew this upas-tree. Small wonder the fruit is bitter. The remedy that shall be an effective answer to the coming appeal for justice must proceed from the public conscience. Neither legislation nor charity can cover the ground. The greed of capital that wrought the evil must itself undo it, as far as it

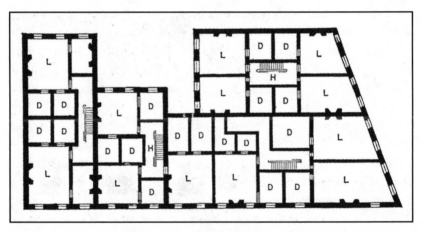

Figure 5.1. This floor plan of an 1863 tenement was included in Riis's *How the Other Half Lives* to emphasize the extreme crowding and unhygienic living conditions endured by the poor. The plan shows a single floor intended to house twelve families with living rooms measuring ten by twelve feet and bedrooms six and a half by seven feet. The "D" indicates that the room is dark without access to fresh air, the "L" stands for light, and the "H" marks hallways. Despite laws intended to improve tenement conditions, Riis observed, "It no longer excites even passing attention, when the sanitary police report counting 101 adults and 91 children in a Crosby Street house."

Figure 5.2. A photograph of outhouses, laundry, and backs of tenements (1904; Milstein Division of United States History, Local History, and Genealogy, New York Public Library, Astor, Lenox and Tilden Foundations) documents the public nature of domestic life in the tenements as well as the limited space between buildings. Twenty to twenty-five families might live in a single tenement building of five or six stories and share the facilities in the yard. While the hanging laundry conveys a feeling of confined space, it also underscores the domestic work done to maintain standards of cleanliness in spite of the surroundings.

can now be undone. Homes must be built for the working masses by those who employ their labor; but tenements must cease to be "good property" in the old, heartless sense. "Philanthropy and five per cent." is the penance exacted.

If this is true from a purely economic point of view, what then of the outlook from the Christian standpoint? Not long ago a great meeting was held in this city, of all denominations of religious faith, to discuss the question how to lay hold of these teeming masses in the tenements with Christian influences, to which they are now too often strangers. Might not the conference have found in the warning of one Brooklyn builder, who has invested his capital on this plan and made it pay more than a money interest, a hint worth heeding: "How shall the love of God be understood by those who have been nurtured in sight only of the greed of man?"

Notes

1. Footnote in original reads, "The Tweed Band of municipal robbers."
2. Riis included the following in a footnote: "Forty per cent. was declared by witnesses before a Senate Committee to be a fair average interest on tenement property. Instances were given of its being one hundred per cent. and over."

Source: Jacob Riis, *How the Other Half Lives: Studies among the Tenements of New York* (New York: Scribner, 1890).

Her Cursing Trebles Brought Heads from All Doors

Maggie, a Girl of the Streets **is often celebrated as the first work of American naturalism. In it, Stephen Crane tells the story of Maggie Johnson, who "blossomed in a mud puddle" but is doomed by poverty, violence, and the limited choices of her urban environment. In this passage, her brother, Jimmie, returns to their tenement home and meets their mother, who is drunk and raging in the hallway. The scene is in no way pivotal to the plot of Maggie's descent into prostitution and suicide, but it does convey a sense of the overwhelming, chaotic, and claustrophobic nature of tenement-house life.**

The woman floundered about in the lower hall of the tenement house and finally stumbled up the stairs. On an upper hall a door was opened and a collection of heads peered curiously out, watching her. With a wrathful snort the woman confronted the door, but it was slammed hastily in her face and the key was turned.

She stood for a few minutes, delivering a frenzied challenge at the panels.

"Come out in deh hall, Mary Murphy, damn yeh, if yehs want a row. Come ahn, yeh overgrown terrier, come ahn."

She began to kick the door with her great feet. She shrilly defied the universe to appear and do battle. Her cursing trebles brought heads from all doors save the one she threatened. Her eyes glared in every direction. The air was full of her tossing fists.

"Come ahn, deh hull damn gang of yehs, come ahn," she roared at the spectators. An oath or two, cat-calls, jeers and bits of facetious advice were given in reply. Missiles clattered about her feet.

"What deh hell's deh matter wid yeh?" said a voice in the gathered gloom, and Jimmie came forward. He carried a tin dinner-pail in his hand and under his arm a brown truckman's apron done in a bundle. "What deh hell's wrong?" he demanded.

"Come out, all of yehs, come out," his mother was howling. "Come ahn an' I'll stamp yer damn brains under me feet."

"Shet yer face, an' come home, yeh damned old fool," roared Jimmie at her. She strided up to him and twirled her fingers in his face. Her eyes were darting flames of unreasoning rage and her frame trembled with eagerness for a fight.

"T'hell wid yehs! An' who deh hell are yehs? I ain't givin' a snap of me fingers fer yehs," she bawled at him. She turned her huge back in tremendous disdain and climbed the stairs to the next floor.

Jimmie followed, cursing blackly. At the top of the flight he seized his mother's arm and started to drag her toward the door of their room.

"Come home, damn yeh," he gritted between his teeth.

"Take yer hands off me! Take yer hands off me," shrieked his mother.

She raised her arm and whirled her great fist at her son's face. Jimmie dodged his head and the blow struck him in the back of the neck. "Damn yeh," gritted he again. He threw out his left hand and writhed his fingers about her middle arm. The mother and the son began to sway and struggle like gladiators.

"Whoop!" said the Rum Alley tenement house. The hall filled with interested spectators.

"Hi, ol' lady, dat was a dandy!"

"T'ree to one on deh red!"

"Ah, stop yer damn scrappin'!"

The door of the Johnson home opened and Maggie looked out. Jimmie made a supreme cursing effort and hurled his mother into the room. He quickly followed and closed the door. The Rum Alley tenement swore disappointedly and retired.

Source: Stephen Crane, *Maggie, a Girl of the Streets* (New York, 1893).

A Club Where Woman Will Live with as Much Freedom as in a Hotel

The rise of the industrial city increased not only the demand for female workers but their cultural visibility as well. Since single women first flocked to the Lowell mills, urban women living outside of traditional family arrangements had been cause for concern. Simultaneously viewed as vulnerable and threatening, they struggled to make a living and to find decent housing that conformed to expectations of respectability. In this passage, Eliza Chester considers the prospects for unmarried urban women and lays out some of the available housing options including women's clubs, cooperative homes, and settlement houses. In what ways do the types of housing proposed uphold and transform the earlier understandings of women and domesticity?

I shall make no attempt to mention all the women's clubs, or even all the leading ones of so much as a single city like Boston; I have only called attention to the kind of work which naturally falls into the hands of women of leisure and education when they combine with each other. The majority of women in these clubs are married; and in most instances it is better for a single woman to co-operate with married women than with those of her own estate. But there are many signs that the next fifty years will see a great increase in another kind of club, which will benefit the unmarried women almost exclusively,—that is, a club where woman will live with as much freedom as in a hotel. There is something repellent in this prospect, to all who are able to grasp the real idea of a home, as a place where the affections are nourished, rather than as a collection of beautifully furnished rooms; and if such clubs should prove so satisfying that women should come to prefer them to homes, there would be reason for dismay; but for the women who cannot have homes, such institutions are an urgent want, both socially and economically.

The Young Women's Christian Association, for example, does incalculable good, by furnishing girls with a refined, well-ordered home, at a very low price. Better still, the girls find suitable companionship, both in study and recreation. They are given as much freedom as can be safely given to a very large number of undisciplined girls in a strange city.

But for women above thirty, a co-operative home where they would be entirely free is such a desideratum that such schemes are sure to be tried soon on a large scale, as they have already been on a small one. The great trouble appears to be to find enough women who are congenial, who will consent to combine and observe necessary conditions. Rich women will probably always prefer their own homes, and that is certainly to be hoped. Self-supporting women do not now command enough money to admit of their taking a large enough house, in a good street, to make the experiment a success. Half the women who would be willing to co-operate insist upon finding a location in some aristocratic quarter, and the other half are obliged to refuse because they cannot afford a large rent. Of course, it would pay in the end, if twenty or thirty women could be served from one kitchen, where all kinds of food were bought at wholesale, and cooked by the Atkinson apparatus, in the scientific, healthful, and appetizing methods of the New England Kitchen. But the wage-earning women cannot try such a venture. They have not much money in advance, and it is hard for twenty or thirty women to combine satisfactorily in any new scheme where it is necessary for each to risk almost all her savings. But the landlord who builds neat and tasteful apartment houses, with suites of two or three small rooms suited to women, with a private restaurant in the basement, as well managed as the New England Kitchen, in a respectable quarter of any New England city, and who will be content with a moderate percentage on his outlay, will find he has not builded in vain. Such a house might easily become a colony of little homes,—one woman bringing her mother, another her friend, and another a little niece or two to vary the monotony of spinsters. It would not even be necessary to insist that only single women should be admitted. If food could be served in the separate apartments (and nothing could be easier than to send down an order through a speaking-tube, which might be filled by the agency of a dumb-waiter), the privacy of each apartment would be so complete that any quiet family who found such rooms satisfactory would not be out of place in the house. But it would not do to raise the rent by a large outlay on stucco-work and frescoing. Of course such a building ought to be planned by the women themselves, who have learned their own needs practically; but what woman of experience has money enough for the venture, and what architect or builder would think of calling in such aid?

The whole cost of heat, light, food, and service in such an establishment in Boston need not be more than $200 for each person. The rent would vary with the locality, and the number of rooms; but it would be quite possible for a co-operative association to let a flat of four or five rooms in a moderately good street, to two women, for another $200 each. Now, though $400 would be a large sum for most single women to pay for a home, it is considerably less than many are obliged to pay for board in any place suited to the work they have to do. Of course smaller apartments in some very modest street ought to be had at a far less cost.

In connection with college settlements, the question how far it is possible for women of small means to live a life of refinement in the city is now being very seriously discussed, with a view to co-operation among such women.

A scheme of a somewhat different nature has been undertaken in New York. I quote from the "Business Woman's Journal": "A wealthy New York woman has had built on Rivington Street a comfortable, commodious, fire-proof structure, to be used as a lodging-house for women. For fifteen cents, a clean bed in a comfortable dormitory can be obtained, with the use of a small cupboard. For thirty cents a room with one window may be had, and in an adjoining restaurant meals can be obtained at very moderate prices. There are conveniences for washing and ironing in the building, and a sitting-room where the women may sit and read and sew."

Source: Eliza Chester, "Co-operation," in *The Unmarried Woman* (New York: Dodd, Mead, 1892).

A Woman's Kingdom

Alexander Turney Stewart was a dry-goods merchant who helped introduce the department store to American consumers. The buildings for his New York emporia, the "Marble Palace" and later the "Iron Palace," set new standards for their scale and opulence. In 1869, as Stewart was constructing a private mansion on Fifth Avenue, he sought to realize his idea of a woman's hotel to house working women. John Kellum, the architect of Stewart's mansion and most recent store, designed the building, which was intended to provide fifteen hundred working women with a respectable and moral home. Construction took almost a decade, and Stewart did not live to see it completed. Stewart's widow opened the hotel in April 1878, and less than two months later, the *New York Times* announced its closing in the article excerpted here.

Mr. Stewart conceived the plan of the Woman's Hotel about 15 years before his death. The more he thought of the project the more firmly he became convinced that it could not fail of being a grand success. He consulted with his friends about it, and could find no one among them who would take any stock in his pet theory. Every one he talked to discouraged the idea, but opposition only strengthened his own opinions on the matter. He set to work to perfect a grand plan, which the hotel, as it stood when opened two months ago, accurately embodied. The building was begun in January, 1869, and took nine years to construct. It cost to build, finish, and furnish just $3,700,000. It was to be the largest hotel in the world, perfectly fire-proof, and to be furnished in a style of comfort and luxury unprecedented. The lobbies and hallways were to be adorned with sculptures and paintings by the best masters, and the library was to be equal to a public library, and to contain every publication which any woman could desire to read. The courtyard in the centre of the structure was to be as inviting as the science of horticulture could make such a place. In order to afford exercise during unpleasant weather, every floor was to contain 600 feet of promenade in the shape of continuous hallways, beautifully furnished, and made as attractive as possible. Such great care was to be taken in every detail to make the establishment thoroughly a woman's abode that every chair on the marble floors was to be booted with rubber so that there could be no "screeching" to pain sensitive nerves. Mr. Stewart used to go to the building every day, and as he saw it advance he became correspondingly happier. He used to say: "That hotel will make 1,000 working women happy and independent. If it succeeds, the example will be imitated. It will be a woman's kingdom, where those of them that wish to be alone can be so. It will prove whether or not the sexes can live apart, and whether or not it will be better for them to do so, whether or not they will choose to." Judge Hilton, as Mr. Stewart's business manager, never believed in the enterprise. He often attempted to dissuade Mr. Stewart from the undertaking, but without success. Mr. Stewart, by his will, provided amply for the furnishing of the hotel and for its running expenses until it should either succeed or fail. Mrs. Stewart was at last convinced of the hopelessness of the enterprise and of its utter impracticability.

A Failure as a Woman's Hotel

Judge Hilton said: "The Woman's Hotel is a failure as a woman's hotel. There is no doubt of it. Mrs. Stewart has come to that conclusion, and the experiment will be at once discontinued. As manager of the estate, it devolves upon me to save the estate from being burdened by any additional expense by turning the hotel to some profitable use. It will, therefore, be opened as a commercial hotel on or about June 5. . . . Mr. Stewart's wishes and will have been carried out to the last letter. He intended [the hotel] for the very class of women whom we find will not patronize it. . . . There is no structure like it in the world, none so beautiful, safe, or comfortable; none wherein women could have enjoyed the material comforts of life to such advantage. Every room is different from every other; the furniture and fixtures were all designed and made especially for the Woman's Hotel. The library was vast, the works of art unsurpassed, and there were over $300,000 worth of oil paintings by the best masters, on the wall. The richest wom[e]n in this country have not better parlors or bedrooms, and no place in the world can produce better cooking or service. But it is a failure. I'll tell you why. It is very simple and very natural. I believe that you cannot get women to accept any help based on the condition of separation from the other sex, you can't run a hotel for women successfully, and keep away the men. Women will not be kept from the other sex. I am convinced that they cannot be tempted away by any comforts and luxuries to stay or live away from the other sex. You can run a hotel for men exclusively—but for women, you can't. I believe that the majority of women not over 50 years of age entertain some hopes of a union, and a great many over that age do; and you cannot do anything for them if you make the condition impair their chances in the least. The failure of the Woman's Hotel will be a world-wide example for philanthropists. It is a terrible disappointment to all interested. I am not greatly surprised at the failure. But I have done my full duty in the face of a conviction of inevitable failure. The scheme has been misunderstood. Some have thought the hotel was to be a working girls' home. It was for the very class we tried to get which wouldn't

Figure 5.3. This illustration of the Woman's Hotel from *Harper's Weekly*, April 13, 1878, showcases the hotel's range of amenities and facilities including the office, parlors, bedrooms, bathrooms, and dining room, as well as laundry, boiler room, and driven wells. The décor and inner works of the hotel were all intended to provide luxurious and respectable accommodations to working women. Located on Fourth Avenue between Thirty-Second and Thirty-Third Streets, the hotel was constructed on sixteen lots. It was initially met with public praise and congratulations, with an estimated twenty thousand guests attending its opening on April 2.

come. Mr. Stewart expressly provided that the place should be for ladies who earned their own living. What other class could have appreciated such a place, with porcelain from Pilivuyt, glass-ware from Bacarat, plate-glass from St. Gobain, and Prof. Edward Schelscher for cook! But the ladies could not be coaxed to the hotel, simply because they wouldn't sacrifice male company. They would rather stay at the boarding-houses, and put up with small bedrooms, poor fare, and skimp furniture, and have their gentlemen than take the luxuries of Stewart without them. It is natural, and you can't blame them. Of course, Mr. Stewart's idea about excluding men from the Woman's Hotel was most correct. They could not be admitted without subjecting the house to gossip and eventually to scandal. . . . But with all our efforts we could not get 50 boarders. . . . Why, out of the handful of boarders we have, there are at least 15 that should not be in the hotel. They don't earn their living, and are there merely out of economy. . . . How they got in I don't know. But there they are. With all our advertising and explanations and notices there are 15 out of the 50 already in the hotel whom we have been doing our best to keep out. A hotel exclusively for women on an extensive scale is an impossibility.["]

Source: "Not Only for the Women: A White Elephant to Be Made Profitable," *New York Times*, May 26, 1878.

They Have No Room Where the Family Can All Come Together and Feel the Sweetness of Being a Family

As rising urban populations increased the demand for land and drove up prices, middle-class city dwellers gradually adapted to a new type of housing, apartment houses. Referred to as "French flats," because of their popularity in Paris, apartments challenged American notions of domestic privacy and family life. (After all, the first multiple dwellings had been the tenement houses.) William Dean Howells offers a sense of middle-class concerns in this exchange between Mr. and Mrs. Basil March from *A Hazard of New Fortunes*. In the bibliographical preface to the 1909 edition, Howells recalled, "There is nothing in the book with which I amused myself more than the house-hunting of the Marches . . . ; and if the contemporary reader should turn for instruction to the pages in which their experience is detailed I assure him that he may trust their fidelity and accuracy in the article of New York housing as it was early in the last decade of the last century."

"Doesn't it make you feel rather small and otherwise unworthy when you see the kind of street these fellow-beings of yours live in, and then think how particular you are about locality and the number of bell-pulls? I don't see even ratchets and speaking-tubes at these doors." He craned his neck out of the window for a better look, and the children of discomfort cheered him, out of sheer good feeling and high spirits. "I didn't know I was so popular. Perhaps it's a recognition of my humane sentiments."

"Oh, it's very easy to have humane sentiments, and to satirize ourselves for wanting eight rooms and a bath in a good neighborhood, when we see how these wretched creatures live," said his wife. "But if we shared all we have with them, and then settled down among them, what good would it do?"

"Not the least in the world. It might help us for the moment, but it wouldn't keep the wolf from their doors for a week; and then they would go on just as before, only they wouldn't be on such good terms with the wolf. The only way for them is to keep up an unbroken intimacy with the wolf; then they can manage him somehow. I don't know how, and I'm afraid I don't want to. Wouldn't you like to have this fellow drive us round among the halls of pride somewhere for a little while? Fifth Avenue or Madison, up-town?"

"No; we've no time to waste. I've got a place near Third Avenue, on a nice cross street, and I want him to take us there." It proved that she had several addresses near together, and it seemed best to dismiss their coupe and do the rest of their afternoon's work on foot. It came to nothing; she was not humbled in the least by what she had seen in the tenement-house street; she yielded no point in her ideal of a flat, and the flats persistently refused to lend themselves to it. She lost all patience with them.

"Oh, I don't say the flats are in the right of it," said her husband, when she denounced their stupid inadequacy to the purposes of a Christian home. "But I'm not so sure that we are, either. I've been thinking about that home business ever since my sensibilities were dragged—in a coupe—through that tenement-house street. Of course, no child born and brought up in such a place as that could have any conception of home. But that's because those poor people can't give character to their habitations. They have to take what they can get. But people like us—that is, of our means—do give character to the average flat. It's made to meet their tastes, or their supposed tastes; and so it's made for social show, not for family life at all. Think of a baby in a flat! It's a contradiction in terms; the flat is the negation of motherhood. The flat means society life; that is, the pretence of social life. It's made to give artificial people a society basis on a little money—too much money, of course, for what they get. So the cost of the building is put into marble halls and idiotic decoration of all kinds. I don't object to the conveniences, but none of these flats has a living-room. They have drawing-rooms to foster social pretence, and they have dining-rooms and bedrooms; but they have no room where the family can all come together and feel the sweetness of being a family. The bedrooms are black-holes mostly, with a sinful waste of space in each. If it were not for the marble halls, and the decorations, and the foolishly expensive finish, the houses could be built round a court, and the flats could be shaped something like a Pompeiian house, with small sleeping-closets—only lit from the outside—and the rest of the floor thrown into two or three large cheerful halls, where all the family life could go on, and society could be transacted unpretentiously. Why, those tenements are better and humaner than those flats! There the whole family lives in the kitchen, and has its consciousness of being; but the flat abolishes the family consciousness. It's confinement without coziness; it's cluttered without being snug. You couldn't keep a self-respecting cat in a flat; you couldn't go down cellar to get cider. No! the Anglo-Saxon home, as we know it in the Anglo-Saxon house, is simply impossible in the Franco-American flat, not because it's humble, but because it's false."

"Well, then," said Mrs. March, "let's look at houses."

He had been denouncing the flat in the abstract, and he had not expected this concrete result. But he said, "We will look at houses, then."

Source: William Dean Howells, *A Hazard of New Fortunes* (New York: Harper, 1890).

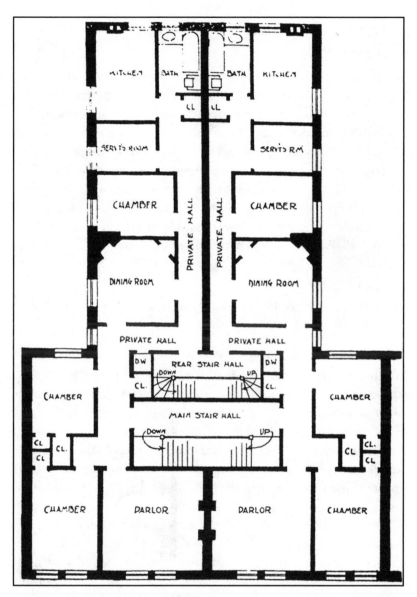

Figure 5.4. A floor plan from the Stuyvesant, one of New York City's first apartment buildings constructed for the middle class, reveals the challenges of arranging rooms for privacy. Designed by the architect Richard Morris Hunt, the building was constructed in 1869–1870. Note how more public spaces such as the parlor and dining room are located near private bedrooms. Americans considered this arrangement promiscuous and associated it with the French style of living.

We Need Hardly Comment on the Peculiar Attractions They Will Possess

The 1880s saw a marked rise in apartment house construction. Buildings like the Dakota on New York's Central Park West were designed to appeal to the upper middle class. This description underscores the self-conscious respectability and modernity of apartment house living. Private spaces are clearly delineated, with separate public spaces for ladies. Despite the building's large size, four separate entrances reduce contact with neighbors, and servants' stairs and elevators hide both domestic labor and laborers. Significantly this description also emphasizes the building's setting near the park, with views of natural landmarks and plenty of fresh air and light. The contrast with the tenements is not explicit, but is surely implied.

The Dakota: A Description of One of the Most Perfect Apartment Houses in the World

FROM THE DAILY GRAPHIC, WEDNESDAY, SEPT. 10

Probably not one stranger out of fifty who ride over the elevated roads or on either of the rivers does not ask the name of the stately building which stands west of Central Park, between Seventy-second and Seventy-third streets. If there is such a person the chances are that he is blind or nearsighted. The name of the building is the Dakota Apartment House, and it is the largest, most substantial, and most conveniently arranged apartment house of the sort in this country. It stands on the crest of the West Side Plateau, on the highest portion of land in the city, and overlooks the entire island and the surrounding country. From the east one has a bird's-eye view of Central Park. The reservoir castle and the picturesque lake, the museums, and the mall are all shown at a glance. From this point also can be seen Long Island Sound in the distance, and the hills of Brooklyn. From the north one looks down on High Bridge and the tall reservoir tower, which looks as slender as a needle. From the west can be seen the Palisades, the Orange Mountains, and the broad Hudson, which narrows into a silver thread as the double row of hills close together far away in the distance. Looking south one sees the tall towers of the Brooklyn Bridge, Governor's Island, and far beyond the green hills of Staten Island and the blue waters of the Lower Bay. Every prominent landmark in the landscape can be discerned from this location, and the great buildings of the lower city are as prominently marked as if the sightseer were floating over the island in a balloon. At this elevation every breeze which moves across Manhattan from any direction is felt. This is a feature which needs no emphasis to make attractive such stifling days as these.

The building is of the Renaissance style of architecture, built of buff brick, with carved Nova Scotia freestone trimmings and terra cotta ornamentation. Although there is a profusion of ornament in the shape of bay and octagon windows, niches, balconies, and balustrades, with spandrels and panels in beautiful terra cotta work and heavy carved cornices, the size and massive construction of the edifice prevent any appearance of superfluity. The building is about 200 feet square and 10 stories high, the two upper stories being in the handsome mansard roof which, with its peaks and gables, surmounted by ornate copper work cresting and finials, and relieved by dormer and oriel windows, gives the entire structure an air of lightness and elegance. The construction is of the most massive character, and the aim of the owners has been to produce a building monumental in solidity and perfectly fireproof. The brick and mason work is of unusual weight, the walls being in some places four feet thick, and the partitions and flooring have iron beams and framing, filled in with concrete and fireproof material.

On the Seventy-third street side there is a handsome doorway, and on the Seventy-second street front a fine arched carriage entrance, with groined roof and elegant stone carving. Both entrances lead into the inner court, from which four separate passages afford access to the interior of the building. From the ground floor four fine bronze staircases, the metal work beautifully wrought and the walls wainscoted in rare marbles and choice hard woods, and four luxuriously fitted elevators, of the latest and safest construction, afford means of reaching the upper floors. The ladies' sitting room, adjoining the staircase in the southeast corner, will be decorated by the Misses Greatorex, a guarantee that the work upon it will be artistic and unconventional. There are four iron staircases and four elevators inclosed in massive brick walls and extending from the cellar to the kitchens and servants' quarters in the upper stories, separate from the rest of the house, which can be used for domestic purposes, carrying furniture, merchandise, &c. There are electric bells to each elevator, and a complete system of electric communication throughout the house.

The building is in four great divisions, which inclose a courtyard as large as half a dozen ordinary buildings. This gives every room in the house light, sunshine, and ventilation. Under this courtyard is the basement, into which lead broad entrances for the use of tradesmen's teams. Here are situated the most interesting portions of the building, or at least the most novel ones. The floor is of asphaltum, as dry and hard as rock. This basement, also, has a courtyard as large as the one above, and lighted by two huge latticed man holes, which look like a couple of green flower beds in the stone flooring. Off of this yard are the storerooms of the house, in which the management will store the furniture and trunks of the tenants free of charge. A porter is assigned to this duty alone. The rooms are all marble floored, lighted and heated, and accessible at all hours of the day or night. The rooms of the servants are also on this floor. These consist of separate dining and toilet rooms for the male and female servants and a male reading and smoking room. These are not for the personal servants of the tenants, but for the general help of the management, which will not number far from 150 persons. The laundry, kitchen, pantry, and bake shops, and private storerooms are here also, for the owners combine a hotel with the apartment house, and furnish eating facilities for all the tenants of the building who prefer it on the table d'hôte plan. Opening from the lower court, and extending under the open ground in the rear of the building, a large vault, 150 feet long, 60 feet wide, and 18 feet deep, is now being excavated. When finished it will contain the steam boilers, steam engines, &c., for hoisting, pumping, &c., and the dynamos for supplying electric illumination in the Dakota and adjoining 27 houses. The vault will be roofed with iron beams and brick filling arches and made flush with the land in the rear of the building, 225 feet deep, which will be laid out as a garden. The boilers, with the furnaces, machinery, &c., will thus be located outside the walls of the building safely remote.

The first floor contains the dining rooms, which are finished in a perfect manner. In this case these words really mean something. The floors are of marble and inlaid. The base of the walls is of English quartered oak, carved by hand. The upper portions are finished in bronze bas-relief work, and the ceilings are also quartered oak, beautifully carved. The effect is that of an old English baronial hall, with the dingy massiveness brightened and freshened without losing any of its richness. The effect is heightened by a large Scotch brownstone engraved fireplace, which ornaments the centre of the room. The business office has oral communication with every portion of the house, and the wants of the tenants can be attended to as quickly as can be done by human ingenuity and a perfectly arranged service.

In addition to the four main staircases mentioned before, which are finished in bronze and marble, there are four iron staircases for servants, four passenger elevators, and four servants' elevators.

The Dakota will be divided into about 65 different suites of apartments, each containing from four to twenty separate rooms, so that accommodations can be furnished either for bachelors or for large families. There is an air of grandeur and elegance not only about the halls and stairways but also about the separate apartments that cannot probably be found in any other house of this kind in the country. The parlors in some instances are 25 by 40 feet, with other rooms in proportion, and there are in many cases private halls to the suites, furnished with fine bronze mantels, tiled hearths, and ornamental open fireplaces. The parlors, libraries, reception and dining rooms are all cabinet trimmed, paneled, and wainscoted in mahogany, oak, and other attractive and durable woods, and are furnished with carved buffets and mantels, mirrors, tiled hearths and open grate fireplaces, and parqueted floors. The kitchens are spacious, and provided with ranges, with ventilating hoods, all with Minton tiled facing and marble wainscoting. There are porcelain washtubs, large storerooms and closets, and butlers' pantries, equipped in the most complete manner, and each suite has its private bathrooms and closets, fitted with the most approved scientific sanitary appliances.

The plumbing and hygienic arrangements are fully equal to anything of the kind in this country. On the top story are six tanks, holding 5,000 gallons of water each, and supplied by steam pumps having a daily capacity of 2,000,000 gallons, and about 200 miles of pipe have been used in effecting its circulation. Not only in the sanitary appliances, but in every other department, there is a completeness that is surprising. The precautions taken to secure proper ventilation and a pure atmosphere, to insure safety to occupants in cases of fire or panic, and to extinguish fire are perfect. When opened the comfort and convenience of the guests will be further insured by the accommodations of the dining rooms, laundry, and barber's shop, run on the most improved plan, in connection with the building. It is the perfection of the apartment style of living, and guarantees to the tenants comforts which would require unlimited wealth to procure in a private residence. The wisest precautions have been taken to insure freedom from the ordinary cares of the household to the fortunate tenants. For instance, the coal and kindling wood are purchased by the manager in large quantities and sold to the tenants, who take in exchange for their money tickets which are presented at the office, and the fuel is carried to their rooms in convenient quantities, thereby saving the user from any of the necessary troubles in buying and storage. This may seem like a small matter, but it is only one of the hundred plans taken by the owners to secure the comfort of the tenants.

It is almost needless to state that the building is as nearly fireproof as any which can be erected. There are continuous passageways extending through the four divisions on the roof: ninth, eighth, and first stories. On the tenth floor there is provision for a play room and gymnasium for the children, well lighted and ventilated and commanding a grand view of the city and surroundings, while on the ninth floor there will be extra servants' rooms, private laundries and drying rooms, dormitories for transient male and female servants and attachés of the building, and lavatories, toilet rooms, and bathrooms for their use.

The work on both the Dakota and the neighboring apartment house and private dwellings owned by the estate has been done not only in the most careful manner, but with a view to permanence and convenience, and to symmetry as well as beauty of appearance. The greatest skill and experience and the best materials large means could command have been employed, and the manner in which the work in each department has been done reflects the greatest credit on those intrusted with it, especially upon the architect, Mr. H. J. Hardenbergh, who has supervised the work from its commencement to its now rapidly approaching completion.

Both the Dakota, the private residences, and the smaller apartment house are now ready for occupation, and we need hardly comment on the peculiar attractions they will possess for those who have experienced a desire for an eligible residence on the west side. The natural and artificial attributes of the position are all in favor of the buildings, which for comfort, ample space, salubrity, convenience, and accessibility cannot be excelled, and a glance at our description will suffice to show that everything skill could furnish, ingenuity and experience suggest has been supplied. The managers of the Clark estate, the owners of the property, are well known for their fairness and liberality to tenants, and every care will be taken to insure comfort and wellbeing. The rents are moderate when compared with the accommodations furnished, and those desiring to secure either dwellings or apartments can examine plans, &c., and make arrangements at the office of the estate, at No. 25 West Twenty-third-street, New-York.

Source: "The Dakota: A Description of One of the Most Perfect Apartment Houses in the World," New York Times, October 22, 1884.

If They Only Would Abandon Their Prejudices and Take to the Roof

This short article suggests some of the ways that city living pushed the middle class to rethink the boundary between private and public. Just decades earlier, many people had expressed concerns about apartment living. Now the search for fresh air and open space drove respectable New Yorkers to take the very private act of sleeping public, spending summer nights on the roofs of houses and office buildings. This article carefully differentiates this practice from that of poorer folks in the tenements, and yet it is difficult to ignore the similarities. How does this mingling of private activities in public spaces compare with Olmstead's vision for public parks?

Roof Sleeping Now Popular in New York: Custom Discarded by Tenement Dwellers Taken Up by Well-to-Do; Special Beds Employed; Devices with Canvas Tops to Keep Off the Dew Used— East Siders Use Fire Escapes

The heat-wave from which this city has suffered for the last ten days, has caused the inhabitants, irrespective of class, to seek all sorts of expedients to obtain fresh air. Life in many of the expensive apartment houses has been all but unendurable despite the relief brought by electric fans and other Summer luxuries within reach of the well-to-do. In the tenements, of course, with their cramped rooms and narrow air shafts, the suffering has been proportionately greater.

One of the strange circumstances brought to light by the present hot weather is that a midsummer custom, discarded by the tenement dwellers, has been taken up with enthusiasm by many persons who live in more comfortable surroundings.

TAKE UP TENEMENT PLAN

When a heat-wave struck New York a dozen years ago the tenement dwellers, with one accord, took up their beds and climbed to the roof to spend the night under the stars. To be forced to sleep on the roof they considered a hardship. That was twelve years ago, and this Summer finds not New York's tenement population upon the roof, but many of its writers, sociologists, charity workers, and even a number of its well-to-do business men, spending the hot nights in the open air.

Unlike the tenement folk, however, these stargazers do not regard the nightly pilgrimage as a hardship. On the contrary, they are quite jubilant over the fact that they have been clever enough to find a successful and simple solution to the problem of making Summer life here in the city comfortable. As for the tenement dwellers, they use the roofs no more. Since the vigorous campaign for fire-escapes upon tenement buildings, a substitute more satisfactory than the housetops is offered in the numerous platforms and balconies within easy reach of the windows, thus avoiding the trouble of carrying a mattress to the roof. The fact that thus cramming the outside stairways with mattresses and bedding defeats the first purpose of the fire-escape, does not prevent their use as open-air bedrooms.

One of the most enthusiastic of the new roof sleepers is Frederick D. Greene, the Assistant General Agent of the Charity Organization Society. Mr. Greene contracted the habit in Turkey, where he served as a mission worker for many years. The Armenians there, he asserts, are in every respect physically superior to those who have lived in America any considerable length of time, in spite of the oppressive treatment which the Armenians continually receive at the hands of the Turks. The secret of their physical well-being in their own country, Mr. Greene thinks, is the universal custom which prevails there of sleeping in the open air on the flat-tiled roofs. As far as climate is concerned, that is perfectly practical for New York City, not only for the Summer, but for all the year round as well, as the cold in the mountainous regions of Asia Minor is quite as severe as anything which we have in New York.

ROOFS POORLY ADAPTED FOR SLEEPING

The real difficulty, the charity agent says, is the fact that the city roofs are not well adapted for this variation from the customs of our ancestors. To overcome this trouble, Mr. Greene has invented a roof bed frame, a wooden structure, 6 by 7 feet, covered with a slanting canvas roof to keep off heavy dews or rains. Side curtains of canvas, which can be spread at will, protect the enthusiast who would sleep next the tin, rain or shine. This size, 6 by 7 feet, provides for two canvas camp beds, each 6 by 3, to be stretched, with a foot-wide aisle between. The whole may be clamped to a chimney if the owner fears being blown off the roof in a high wind.

There is a group of business men, having offices in different downtown skyscrapers, who return to their office roofs to sleep. Many of these have no further equipment than rugs and pillows, and, consequently, they do not haunt the twenty-fifth floors on rainy nights. The majority of these men, too, prefer Summer to Winter for airing this their latest hobby, but a number of them threaten to continue the practice just as long as the weather and their conventional friends permit.

ROOF HABIT IN BROOKLYN

The roof habit is taking strong hold in Brooklyn, particularly on the Park Slope. From the tops of those houses there is a wonderful view of the bay, and for some years a number of the solid citizens of this region have cultivated their own roof gardens. This season, though, a number of them have gone a step further and are sleeping there as well. One of the most elaborate of these star parlors is that on the President Street residence of Mme. Alma Webster-Powell, the singer. Here is a bewildering array of rugs, hammocks, cushions, and easy chairs. After some experimental roof sleeping, Mme. Powell is about to have a canvas covering stretched over the entire housetop, to make a spacious apartment which can be used by the whole family, rain or shine.

Miss Lillian Wald, the head worker of the Nurses' Settlement in Henry Street, is another one of the subscribers to fresh-air sleeping.

"The odd part of it is," said another warm advocate of the practice, "that with the hundreds and thousands of tall buildings, where it is always cool even in the hottest weather, the great majority of New Yorkers insist on sleeping indoors, even if it's so hot they can't sleep. Think what it would mean, not only to the tenement population, but to the hundreds of thousands of families of small means, who can afford very brief vacations, and frequently none at all, if they only would abandon their prejudices and take to the roof."

Source: "Roof Sleeping Now Popular in New York," *New York Times*, July 5, 1908.

What Realism Is Leading Us To

The industrial city transformed the domestic lives of the wealthy as well. Newly rich industrialists sought to flaunt their wealth by building mansions, and after criticizing such display, more established families eventually did the same. On New York's "Millionaire's Row," the Vanderbilts, Fricks, and Carnegies competed for the most impressive homes. Designed by leading architects in European styles, these residences often included elaborate spaces for public entertaining and social gatherings, which also served as opportunities for the ostentatious display of wealth. Turning the domestic ideal inside out, the mansions of the wealthy made private life public and emphasized their ties to the marketplace. The popular humor magazine *Life* routinely made light of this distortion as in this mock wedding notice.

A fashionable wedding notice last week gave the genealogy of the bride, as well as the occupation and connections of the groom, his father's titles and degree thrown in, and closed with the announcement that so-and-so furnished the decoration.

This is what realism is leading us to. But why not carry it all the way through to its fullest extent? Thus, for instance:

Married
SMITH—JONES.—On the 20th of October, at No. 4672 Ninth Avenue (John P. Robinson, architect; Theodore Brown, builder), by the Rev. Pierre K. Goodman, author of "Side Lights of the Gospels," published by Harp-

Figure 5.5. "The Lucky Rich," from *Life*, December 31, 1896, mocks the loveless domestic lives of the wealthy, as the artist Charles Dana Gibson not so subtly suggests that conspicuous display undermines privacy and familial affection. Here the joke is on the beautiful woman who married for money and her older, rich husband—separated by the elaborate table, outnumbered by their servants, and watched even by the busts over the doorways.

ing & Brothers, 12mo, cloth $1, paper 50 cents, for sale by all respectable newsdealers, Anna Jones, daughter of Charles P. Jones, wholesale grocer, of 9276 Pearl Street, and sole agent in New York for Spile's Gurline, fifteen cents per package, and the granddaughter of Midshipman Easy, author of the *Century's* articles on "The Navy at Gettysburg,["] to Patsy J. P. Q. Jinkins of the Sandwich Islands Custom-House, and son of General Bolivar J. D. Furioso Jinkins, P.P.C., J.A.C.K., C.D. of Her Majesty's forces in Manitoba. Rebellions a speciality. Office house 6–4.

Decorations by J. Kearney, 626 Fourteenth Avenue, third son of P. Kearney, caterer, of 32 Floyd-James Street. Furnace-fire by James Higginbotham. Gas by the United Gas Trust of New York. Supper and flowers by Blunder, nephew of Lieut. Charles K. Bombastes, of the New York *Gazette*; terms $1.50 per annum, payable in advance. Conversation at Reception by the World's Entertainment Emporium, talented conversationalists and raconteurs, etc. furnished at short notice and at moderate prices.

To be sure, this would cost money, but what is money compared with the advantages accruing from the system? Perhaps the persons whose business is advertised would be willing to pay for the whole insertion, which would relieve the family of no little expense.

We do not copyright the idea.

Source: "The Marriage Notice of the Future," *Life*, November 10, 1887.

Each Room in a House Has Its Individual Uses

Reflecting the author's birth into New York City's established social elite, the novels of Edith Wharton documented the conventions and constraints of this world as well as the confusion and disruption created by the social ambitions of the newly rich. To some degree, these same themes can be found in her first published work, *The Decoration of Houses*. Here she argues for symmetry, balance, and classical design in architecture and against the excesses of Victorian decorating. Among the decorating details in the following excerpt is some sophisticated thinking about the relationship between wealth and domestic spaces. Unlike Downing and Olmstead, who depict beauty as a source of morality, Wharton highlights its connection to good taste, emphasizing that the latter could not be bought. As she notes elsewhere in the book, "Proportion is the good breeding of architecture." Filling a poorly proportioned house with overstuffed furnishings and wall hangings could in no way compensate for this failing.

Privacy would seem to be one of the first requisites of civilized life, yet it is only necessary to observe the planning and arrangement of the average house to see how little this need is recognized. Each room in a house has its individual uses: some are made to sleep in, others are for dressing, eating, study, or conversation; but whatever the uses of a room, they are seriously interfered with if it be not preserved as a small world by itself. If the drawing-room be a part of the hall and the library a part of the drawing-room, all three will be equally unfitted to serve their special purpose. The indifference to privacy which has sprung up in modern times, and which in France, for instance, has given rise to the grotesque conceit of putting sheets of plate-glass between two rooms, and of replacing doorways by openings fifteen feet wide, is of complex origin. It is probably due in part to the fact that many houses are built and decorated by people unfamiliar with the habits of those for whom they are building. It may be that architect and decorator live in a simpler manner than their clients, and are therefore ready to sacrifice a kind of comfort of which they do not feel the need to the "effects" obtainable by vast openings and extended "vistas." To the untrained observer size often appeals more than proportion and costliness than suitability. In a handsome house such an observer is attracted rather by the ornamental detail than by the underlying purpose of planning and decoration. He sees the beauty of the detail, but not its relation to the whole. He therefore regards it as elegant but useless; and his next step is to infer that there is an inherent elegance in what is useless.

Before beginning to decorate a house it is necessary to make a prolonged and careful study of its plan and elevations, both as a whole and in detail. The component parts of an undecorated room are its floor, ceiling, wall-spaces and openings. The openings consist of the doors, windows and fireplace; and of these, as has already been pointed out, the fireplace is the most important in the general scheme of decoration.

No room can be satisfactory unless its openings are properly placed and proportioned, and the decorator's task is much easier if he has also been the architect of the house he is employed to decorate; but as this seldom happens his ingenuity is frequently taxed to produce a good design upon the background of a faulty and illogical structure. Much may be done to overcome this difficulty by making slight changes in the proportions of the openings; and the skilful decorator, before applying his scheme of decoration, will do all that he can to correct the fundamental lines of the room. But the result is seldom so successful as if he had built the room, and those who employ different people to build and decorate their houses should at least try to select an architect and a decorator trained in the same school of composition, so that they may come to some understanding with regard to the general harmony of their work.

In deciding upon a scheme of decoration, it is necessary to keep in mind the relation of furniture to ornament, and of the room as a whole to other rooms in the house. As in a small house a very large room dwarfs all the others, so a room decorated in a very rich manner will make the simplicity of those about it look mean. Every house should be decorated according to a carefully graduated scale of ornamentation culminating in the most important room of the house; but this plan must be carried out with such due sense of the relation of the rooms to each other that there shall be no violent break in the continuity of treatment. If a white-and-gold drawing-room opens on a hall with a Brussels carpet and papered walls, the drawing-room will look too fine and the hall mean.

In the furnishing of each room the same rule should be as carefully observed. The simplest and most cheaply furnished room (provided the furniture be good of its kind, and the walls and carpet unobjectionable in color) will be more pleasing to the fastidious eye than one in which gilded consoles and cabinets of buhl stand side by side with cheap machine-made furniture, and delicate old marquetry tables are covered with trashy china ornaments.

It is, of course, not always possible to refurnish a room when it is redecorated. Many people must content themselves with using their old furniture, no matter how ugly and ill-assorted it may be; and it is the decorator's business to see that his background helps the furniture to look its best. It is a mistake to think that because the furniture of a room is inappropriate or ugly a good background will bring out these defects. It will, on the contrary, be a relief to the eye to escape from the bad lines of the furniture to the good lines of the walls; and should the opportunity to purchase new furniture ever come, there will be a suitable background ready to show it to the best advantage.

Most rooms contain a mixture of good, bad, and indifferent furniture. It is best to adapt the decorative treatment to the best pieces and to discard those which are in bad taste, replacing them, if necessary, by willow chairs and stained deal tables until it is possible to buy something better. When the room is to be refurnished as well as redecorated the client often makes his purchases without regard to the decoration. Besides being an injustice to the decorator, inasmuch as it makes it impossible for him to harmonize his decoration with the furniture, this generally produces a result unsatisfactory to the owner of the house. Neither decoration nor furniture, however good of its kind, can look its best unless each is chosen with reference to the other. It is therefore necessary that the decorator, before planning his treatment of a room, should be told what it is to contain. If a gilt set is put in a room the walls of which are treated in low relief and painted white, the high lights of the gilding will destroy the delicate values of the mouldings, and the walls, at a little distance, will look like flat expanses of whitewashed plaster.

When a room is to be furnished and decorated at the smallest possible cost, it must be remembered that the comfort of its occupants depends more on the nature of the furniture than of the wall-decorations or carpet. In a living-room of this kind it is best to tint the walls and put a cheerful drugget on the floor, keeping as much money as possible for the purchase of comfortable chairs and sofas and substantial tables. If little can be spent in buying furniture, willow arm-chairs with denim cushions and solid tables with stained legs and covers of denim or corduroy will be more satisfactory than the "parlor suit" turned out in thousands by the manufacturer of cheap furniture, or the pseudo-Georgian or pseudo-Empire of the dealer in "high-grade goods." Plain bookcases may be made of deal, painted or stained; and a room treated in this way, with a uniform color on the wall, and plenty of lamps and books, is sure to be comfortable and can never be vulgar.

It is to be regretted that, in this country and in England, it should be almost impossible to buy plain but well-designed and substantial furniture. Nothing can exceed the ugliness of the current designs: the bedsteads with towering head-boards fretted by the versatile jig-saw; the "bedroom suits" of "mahoganized" cherry, bird's-eye maple, or some other crude-colored wood; the tables with meaninglessly turned legs; the "Empire" chairs and consoles stuck over with ornaments of cast bronze washed in liquid gilding; and, worst of all, the supposed "Colonial" furniture, that unworthy travesty of a plain and dignified style. All this showy stuff has been produced in answer to the increasing demand for cheap "effects" in place of unobtrusive merit in material and design; but now that an appreciation of better things in architecture is becoming more general, it is to be hoped that the "artistic" furniture disfiguring so many of our shop-windows will no longer find a market. . . .

This quest of artistic novelties would be encouraging were it based on the desire for something better, rather than for something merely different. The tendency to dash from one style to another, without stopping to analyze the intrinsic qualities of any, has defeated the efforts of those who have tried to teach the true principles of furniture-designing by a return to the best models. If people will buy the stuff now offered them as Empire, Sheraton or Louis XVI, the manufacturer is not to blame for making it. It is not the maker but the purchaser who sets the standard; and there will never be any general supply of better furniture until people take time to study the subject, and find out wherein lies the radical unfitness of what now contents them.

Until this golden age arrives the householder who cannot afford to buy old pieces, or to have old models copied by a skilled cabinet-maker, had better restrict himself to the plainest of furniture, relying for the embellishment of his room upon good bookbindings and one or two old porcelain vases for his lamps. . . .

. . . It is well, as a rule, to shun the decorative schemes concocted by the writers who supply our newspapers with hints for "artistic interiors." The use of such poetic adjectives as jonquil-yellow, willow-green, shell-pink, or ashes-of-roses, gives to these descriptions of the "unique boudoir" or "ideal summer room" a charm which the reality would probably not possess. The arrangements suggested are usually cheap devices based upon the mistaken idea that defects in structure or design may be remedied by an overlaying of color or ornament. This theory often leads to the spending of much more money than would have been required to make one or two changes in the plan of the room, and the result is never satisfactory to the fastidious.

There are but two ways of dealing with a room which is fundamentally ugly: one is to accept it, and the other is courageously to correct its ugliness. Half-way remedies are a waste of money and serve rather to call attention to the defects of the room than to conceal them.

Source: Edith Wharton and Ogden Codman, *The Decoration of Houses* (New York: Scribner, 1897).

6

Dismantling the Victorian Ideal and the Future
of Domesticity

It is difficult to pinpoint the end of the nineteenth-century domestic ideal. Perhaps the best way is to consider its differences from contemporary notions. Home remains an important space and idea in American life, but twenty-first-century domesticity tends to focus on behavior and activities more than on morality and is more likely understood as a reflection of personality, social identity, and economic status. In addition to leisure, domestic activities often and visibly include work—both unpaid domestic labor and paid employment that extends beyond the home. What other differences have you noticed?

Of course, some of the nineteenth century's domestic values linger in new contradictions surrounding home and its meaning. Although more openly a repository for consumer goods, the present-day home also holds personal memories and fosters intimacy. Permeated by the market and technologies that link it to public life, it continues to serve as a private refuge. And, like Victorians, most contemporary Americans believe that owning a home can somehow stabilize public life; despite the 2008 recession and mortgage crisis, many still consider it the basis of the "American Dream." Why else would the federal government encourage homeownership by backing mortgages and legislating tax benefits?

In short, for all the unfamiliarity and inconsistency of the nineteenth-century domestic ideal, Americans continue to live with its echoes. And so the documents in this concluding chapter do not record the end of the nineteenth-century home but instead reveal various attempts to think outside of it. Together they hint at the changing importance of home as a cultural ideal at the beginning of the twentieth century and consider the disruptions posed by mass consumption, feminism, suburbanization, and a growing focus on personality and privacy. They do not draw a straight line from the past to the present but offer clues to the path, highlighting change while also suggesting home's continuity.

For example, Edward Bellamy, Helen Campbell, and Charlotte Perkins Gilman challenge the efficiency of the private home for delivering services to the family, dismissing existing arrangements as primitive and calling for the modernization of the home. Gilman and Gertrude Bustill Mossell reject the conflation of home and gender roles that constrain both women and men. Documents by Mary Abbott, Henry Wilson, and Martha Bensley Bruère rethink the goods and spaces that defined the American home, emphasizing comfort over order, informality over performance, simplicity and openness over privacy—moving closer to present-day values. And A. L. Hall describes a new role for men that reintegrates them into the life of the home on distinctively masculine terms. Finally, reformer Michael M. Davis, Jr., and the Industrial Housing Associates reconsider the home's relationship to commercial life and spaces, highlighting their interdependence and seeking to maximize the benefits of such ties.

Our Washing Is All Done at Public Laundries

At the end of the nineteenth century, an outpouring of science fiction struggled to imagine an alternative to the problems of industrialization and growing economic inequality. No utopian work was more popular than Edward Bellamy's *Looking Backward*, published in 1888. The story's protagonist, Julian West, falls asleep in 1887 and wakes in 2000 to find Boston transformed by evolutionary socialism, or what Bellamy called "Nationalism." West's guides to the future are Dr. and Mrs. Leete and their daughter Edith. In this excerpt, the Leetes answer questions about the handling of housework in the future. The emphasis is now on efficiency rather than privacy, as services are performed cooperatively in public facilities. Many women were inspired by Bellamy's example, and he, in turn, encouraged them to form cooperative laundries and kitchens of their own. To what degree have Bellamy's predictions been realized today?

"How have you disposed of the problem of domestic service? Who are willing to be domestic servants in a community where all are social equals? Our ladies found it hard enough to find such even when there was little pretence of social equality."

"It is precisely because we are all social equals whose equality nothing can compromise, and because service is honorable, in a society whose fundamental principle is that all in turn shall serve the rest, that we could easily provide a corps of domestic servants such as you never dreamed of, if we needed them," replied Dr. Leete. "But we do not need them."

"Who does your house-work, then?" I asked.

"There is none to do," said Mrs. Leete, to whom I had addressed this question. "Our washing is all done at public laundries at excessively cheap rates, and our cooking at public kitchens. The making and repairing of all we wear are done outside in public shops. Electricity, of course, takes the place of all fires and lighting. We choose houses no larger than we need, and furnish them so as to involve the minimum of trouble to keep them in order. We have no use for domestic servants."

"The fact," said Dr. Leete, "that you had in the poorer classes a boundless supply of serfs on whom you could impose all sorts of painful and disagreeable tasks, made you indifferent to devices to avoid the necessity for them. But now that we all have to do in turn whatever work is done for society, every individual in the nation has the same interest, and a personal one, in devices for lightening the burden. This fact has given a prodigious impulse to labor-saving inventions in all sorts of industry, of which the combination of the maximum of comfort and minimum of trouble in household arrangements was one of the earliest results."

"In case of special emergencies in the household," pursued Dr. Leete, "such as extensive cleaning or renovation, or sickness in the family, we can always secure assistance from the industrial force."

"But how do you recompense these assistants, since you have no money?"

"We do not pay them, of course, but the nation for them. Their services can be obtained by application at the proper bureau, and their value is pricked off the credit card of the applicant."

"What a paradise for womankind the world must be now!" I exclaimed. "In my day, even wealth and unlimited servants did not enfranchise their possessors from household cares, while the women of the merely well-to-do and poorer classes lived and died martyrs to them."

"Yes," said Mrs. Leete, "I have read something of that; enough to convince me that, badly off as the men, too, were in your day, they were more fortunate than their mothers and wives."

"The broad shoulders of the nation," said Dr. Leete, "bear now like a feather the burden that broke the backs of the women of your day. Their misery came, with all your other miseries, from that incapacity for cooperation which followed from the individualism on which your social system was founded, from your inability to perceive that you could make ten times more profit out of your fellow men by uniting with them than by contending with them. The wonder is, not that you did not live more comfortably, but that you were able to live together at all, who were all confessedly bent on making one another your servants, and securing possession of one another's goods."

Source: Edward Bellamy, *Looking Backward, 2000–1887* (Boston: Houghton Mifflin, 1888).

Keeping a Clean House Will Not Keep a Man at Home

Journalist and editor Gertrude Bustill Mossell was part of an accomplished Philadelphia African American family. She married Dr. Nathan Frances Mossell in 1893 and published *The Work of the Afro-American Woman* the following year. The volume includes essays on achievements of African American women, poems, and a few selections of domestic advice. This excerpt is taken from that last type of writing, a chapter titled "The Opposite Point of View." While Mossell nodded toward traditional domesticity by publishing the work under her married name and dedicating it to her two daughters with the prayer that "they may grow into a pure and noble womanhood," here she rejects the image of woman as the always-cheerful keeper of the hearth. Compare her advice to that of Catharine Beecher in chapter 1. How and why do they differ?

For several years, every paper or magazine that has fallen into our hands gave some such teaching as this: "The wife must always meet her husband with a smile." She must continue in the present and future married life to do a host of things for his comfort and convenience; the sure fate awaiting her failure to follow this advice being the loss of the husband's affection and the mortification of seeing it transferred to the keeping of a rival. She must stay at home, keep the house clean, prepare food properly and care for her children, or he will frequent the saloon, go out at night and spend his time unwisely at the least. These articles may be written by men or by women, but the moral is invariably pointed for the benefit of women; one rarely appearing by either sex for the benefit of men. This fact must certainly lead both men and women to suppose that women need this teaching most; now I differ from this view of the subject. In a life of some length and of close observation, having been since womanhood a part of professional life, both in teaching, preaching and otherwise, where one receives the confidences of others, I have come to the conclusion that women need these teachings least.

I have seen the inside workings of many homes; I know there are many slatterns, many gossips and poor cooks; many who are untrue to marital vows; but on the whole, according to their means, their opportunities for remaining at home, the irritating circumstances that surround them (and of our women especially), tempted by two races, they do well. After due deliberation and advisedly I repeat that they (remembering the past dreadful environment of slavery) do well. Man as often as woman gives the keynote to the home-life for the day; whether it shall be one of peace or strife. The wife may fill the house with sweet singing, have the children dressed and ready to give a joyful greeting to the father, the breakfast might be fit to tempt an epicure, and yet the whole be greeted surlily by one who considers wife and home but his rightful convenience. I may not be orthodox, but I venture to assert that keeping a clean house will not keep a man at home; to be sure it will not drive him out, but neither will it keep him in to a very large extent. And you, dear tender-hearted little darlings, that are being taught daily that it will, might as well know the truth now and not be crying your eyes out later.

Dear Willie can go out at night, yes, a little while even every night, and not be going to the bad nor failing to do his duty. Now let me tell you an open secret and look about you where you live and see if I am not right. The men that usually stay in at night are domestic in their nature, care little for the welfare or approval of the world at large, are not ambitious, are satisfied with being loved, care nothing for being honored. The men who used when single to kiss the babies, pet the cat, and fail to kick the dog where they visited are the men who remain at home most when married. A man who aspires to social pre-eminence, who is ambitious or who acquires the reputation of being a man of judgment and knowledge, useful as a public man, will be often out at night even against his own desires, on legitimate business. By becoming a member of many organizations it may become necessary for him to spend most of his evenings out, sacrificing his own will to the will of the many. Again, men after working at daily drudgery come home to their families, eat the evening meal, hear the day's doings, read the paper and then desire to meet with some masculine friends to discuss the topics of the day. The club, the church, the street corner or a chum's business place may be the meeting place. Bad men go out for evil purposes; to be sure, many men, social by nature, are tempted by the allurements of the saloon and the chance of meeting their boon companions. But these men would do the same if they had no home, or whether it was clean or not. Wives should be kind, keep house beautifully, dress beautifully if they can; but after all this is accomplished their husbands will be away from home possibly quite as much for the above-given reasons. Women must not be blamed because they are not equal to the self-sacrifice of always meeting husbands with a smile, nor the wife blamed that she does not dress after marriage as she dressed before; child-birth and nursing, the care of the sick through sleepless, nightly vigils, the exactions and irritations incident to a life whose work of head and heart never ceases, make it an impossibility to put behind them at all times all cares and smile with burdened heart and weary feet and brain.

Small means, constant sacrifice for children prevent the replenishment of a fast dwindling wardrobe. Husbands and fathers usually buy what they *need* at least[;] most mothers and wives will not even do that while children need anything. The great inducement for a woman to fulfill these commands is that she may retain her husband's love and not forfeit her place to a rival. Suppose some one should tell a man, "Now you must smile at your wife always, in her presence never appear grumpy, dress her in the latest style, and so on, or else she will transfer her affections to the keeping of another." What would be his reply? We all know. And yet women need love to live and be happy, are supposed to be most susceptible to love and flattery, and men therefore ought to fear this fate most, and the daily record teaches the fact if the magazine writers fail to do so. A good husband will do his duty even if the wife fails, as so many wives are doing to-day with bad husbands. The man who wants to lead a reckless life, will complain of his wife's bad house-keeping, extravagance, the children's noise or, if not blessed with off-spring, still complains that this fact makes home less interesting; but let me tell you, friend, it is all an excuse in nine cases out of ten. A hus-band's ill-doing is never taken as an excuse for a wife's turning bad, and why should a man be excused for doing wrong, if he has a bad wife? If he be the stronger-minded one, especially. If a husband is a true one in any sense of the word, his transference of the kiss at the door from the wife to the firstborn that runs before her to greet him will not cause even a sigh of regret.

Doing the best she can in all things will be appreciated by a true hus-band. The one remaining thought unmentioned is *temper*, the disposi-tion to scold and nag. Now no man desires a scolding, nagging wife, and no child desires such a mother; but saints are rare and I don't believe that history past or present proves that saintly women have in the past or do now *gain men's love oftenest or hold it longest*. The two women, one white, another colored, that I sorrowed with over recreant husbands, were true, loving, wives; one had just saved her small earnings toward buying the husband a birthday present and had unsuspectingly kissed good-bye the partner of his flight. The other clasped more lovingly the hand of the baby boy that most resembled him and only spoke of the facts as occasion required it in business concerning the property he had left behind; both men had found no fault with these wives, treated them kindly up to the last hour when they deserted them forever. Neither sugar nor pickles would be a good diet, but most of us could eat a greater quantity of pepper hash than of sugar after all. I believe that a woman who has a mind and will of her own will become monotonous to a less extent than one so continuously sweet and self-effacing; and I believe history proves it.

It may be humanity or masculinity's total depravity, but I believe more men tire of sweet women than even of scolds, and yet I do not desire to encourage the growth of this obnoxious creature. The desirable partner for a successful, peaceful married life is a woman of well-balanced temperament who is known among her associates as one not given to what is often called fits of temper, and yet withal possessing a mind of her own. . . .

It is not possessing a temper, but continuous outbursts of ill-temper that undermine true happiness. The home should be founded on right principles, on morality, Christian living, a due regard to heredity and environment that promise good for the future. With these taken into consideration, backed by love, or even true regard, with each having an abiding sense of duty and a desire to carry out its principles, no marriage so contracted can ever prove a failure.

Source: Mrs. N. F. (Gertrude Bustill) Mossell, "The Opposite Point of View," in *The Work of the Afro-American Woman* (Philadelphia: Geo. S. Ferguson, 1894).

The Modern Home Fails of Its Main Function

After investigating and writing about the lives of impoverished working women, Helen Stuart Campbell helped develop the field of home economics, arguing that the techniques of modern industry and management should be applied to women's domestic labor. In 1895, the economics professor Richard T. Ely invited her to deliver a series of lectures at the University of Wisconsin, and this excerpt is taken from the book that resulted. Here Campbell seeks to reverse the separation of home and work that gave rise to the Victorian domestic ideal. Housework can no longer be "pastoralized" but must be made modern like the work of men. This transformation will not only make women's domestic labor more efficient but elevate the home to the same status as the public world and better sustain familial harmony.

The household, standing nearest to the body, lowest or highest as we may choose to consider it, is thus essentially limited in many ways; rightly and nobly limited, in ways which work no more restriction than do our bodily limits. But the household economy, being in its nature part of the social organism, economy, should not be limited by the house. The cradle of industry must not seek to retain industry in its cradle, and that is precisely what our mistaken idea of household economy does to-day. It is surcharged with functional activity which does not belong there, which has long since reached a stage of development demanding far wider, deeper, and more scientific administration and execution than is possible in the private home.

There was once in the world but one place of living—the home. In it were all things done and enjoyed. It produced what it consumed, and consumed what it produced. Long ago that stage ended. There are now in the world two places of living for the larger part of civilized humanity—the home and the shop. The shop makes what the home takes. All our deepest and widest and subtlest ranges of mechanical production, bridges, ships, railroads, vast mills, founderies, stores, are all to keep in motion activities which culminate in home consumption.

The shop produces and the home consumes. In this it still stands for the primal home idea; the thought in that first beginning of home when it was but a hole in the ground to eat and sleep and hide in. All the beauty and sanctity and power of the home follow on this primal thought of security, shelter; a place in which to take food and rest, and gather strength for outside use.

It is at this point that the modern home fails of its main function, in that it persists in combining home and shop. Any form of persistent industry is foreign to the essential idea of home, the place of rest. But the man's home to-day is the woman's shop wherein she perpetually demonstrates the old song:

> "A man's work is from sun to sun.
> But a woman's work is never done."

The growth of household industry from the simple consumption of meat and fruit to all the complicated bustle of the kitchen, calls for the extension of that kitchen industry outside the home.

Let us by all means continue to eat at home. To eat together under the shelter of one's own roof is still one of the integral parts of the home idea. But there is no more need for the immediate presence of the cookshop than for the immediate presence of the butcher shop, the flour mill, and the dairy.

The preparation of food at home save in the most limited sense, as for instance the use of the chafing-dish or the making of fresh tea, does not belong to the advanced civilization of to-day. It belongs to the era when that preparation was a simple matter, easily within the pleasurable exertion of the family itself. That should be our limit still. If we wish to prepare food at home, its preparation should not require more than an hour of the time and a tiny portion of the vital force of the family. If it is otherwise, then we are expending high forces on low functions; a process as wasteful to the woman who performs it as if all our ranks of world uplifting men spent their forces in the low functions of self-defence and self-support.

We have organized our defensive function into the honorable specialization of military and civil service. We have organized our self-support into all the complex activities of farmer, grazier, fisherman, butcher, orchardist, and so on, with the manifold distribution of their supplies.

This is in the man's world. In the woman's world no organization has been allowed. Man has not forbidden it, but woman has not seen its advantages, and being conserver rather than originator, has seldom gone beyond tradition. Her world, then, in which she must live and work, remains inorganic, detached, undeveloped; a survival of past ages.

It is this underlying condition which makes one of the deeper reasons why it is so hard to "keep the boys at home." Consider the man's world as compared with the woman's. In the developed industries, the extra-domestic industries, every man has his kind of work and does it, and all kinds of work are inter-related. Friction and confusion are largely eliminated. Everyone is compelled by the nature of his position to "mind his own business," and there is room for expansion and the noble sense of mutual usefulness.

In the undeveloped domestic industries, one untrained woman tries to work at a dozen trades at once, and, if she is the mother too, at a constant sacrifice of her highest function. The growing boy as he begins to enter manhood feels this difference without understanding it; and in his scorn of home life and desire to escape from its restrictions, vaguely voices his under-lying consciousness of the lamentable division between "the home" and "the world."

The home is a most essential part of the world, not a different thing, yet our thought and modes of expression would seem to make it so. Its present separation, with all the evil consequences to both, is due to the arrested development of our household economy. Present with its bodily form; apparently moving with the age, the household carries within it conditions so primitive that the true growth of social life is retarded at every step.

The typical modern household presents both survivals and rudiments. Old and sturdy survivals; carefully maintained, flourishing rudiments, carefully cut down to the general level of this most anomalous and singular organism, half fossil and half sprout. Small wonder then that the family, over whose future speculation is incessantly at work, the family, which is the soul of the household body, is perturbed and pained, shocked, injured, at times destroyed. A large cause for the rising sea of family trouble which forms half the world's misery comes, not from the wicked world outside, but from within the sheltering walls of the home we love so well and understand so ill.

To live in two kinds of life at once; to spend one's days in the nineteenth century, and one's nights in the twelfth; to come home from the stress and press of one's fractional share in the widely differentiated activities of the world to one's full half of the un-differentiated and discordant activities of the home—this makes life harder for man than it has any right to be, than it needs to be, and so limits both his growth and his usefulness.

And for the woman to live only in one kind of life and that of a prehistoric nature; not to have any share at all in the activities of the age she lives in; to force her present-day powers to the steady performance of past-day tasks; what for her? She lives in touch with the vivid life of the modern world, yet her work carries the burdens of the past, and her growth and usefulness are not only checked but distorted. . . .

Bear in mind always that this is no protest against home duties. They are not only important, essential, but lovely and noble in their place. My work would be utterly lost if I have failed to show the magnitude and value of these functions, but it must be plain that their degree of development and method of performance are below the present grade of civilization.

This in the deeper and more scientific sense is the status of Household Economy to-day. Itself of enormous importance, its methods are so defective as to constitute a steady check on progress. For the better understanding of the subject, the course these lectures should precede and which they outline is mapped out.

By a wide study of the existing condition and its historic forerunners, we shall be able at least to know why, in all this smooth and rushing stream of progress, the household wheels still creak so noisily and turn so hard. It is as though some primeval ox-cart were brought in to connect with the railroad system, or the current of trans-continental travel left its vestibuled trains to ford some river on the way.

Source: Helen Campbell, "Organized Living," in *Household Economics: A Course of Lectures in the School of Economics of the University of Wisconsin* (New York: Putnam, 1897).

The Home Has Not Developed in Proportion to Our Other Institutions

A feminist and socialist, a lecturer and reformer, a social scientist and novelist, Charlotte Perkins Gilman was shaped by her own impoverished childhood, an unhappy marriage, the accomplishments of her famous family (including great aunts Catharine Beecher and Harriet Beecher Stowe), and the latest theories of her day. In *Women and Economics* (1898) and *The Home: Its Work and Influence* (1903), she argued that the home limited and distorted women, separating them from the world and encouraging a dangerous dependence. Such homes not only hurt women but, in keeping with Darwinian notions of her time, threatened progress of the nation and race. Instead she advocated for cooperative living and apartment hotels with public kitchens, dining rooms, and child care. In this passage from the introduction of *The Home*, Gilman explains why it is so difficult to reform the home. What do you think she means by home's "essential nature"?

The home *in its essential nature* is pure good, and in its due development is progressively good; but it must change with society's advance; and the kind of home that was wholly beneficial in one century may be largely evil in another. We must forcibly bear in mind, in any honest study of a long-accustomed environment, that our own comfort, or even happiness, in a given condition does not prove it to be good.

Comfort and happiness are very largely a matter of prolonged adjustment. We like what we are used to. When we get used to something else we like that too—and if the something else is really better, we profit by the change. To the tired farmer it is comfort to take off his coat, put up his yarn-stockinged feet on a chair, and have his wife serve him the supper she has cooked. The tired banker prefers a dressing gown or lounging jacket, slippers, a well-dressed, white-handed wife, and a neat maid or stately butler to wait on the table. The domestic Roman preferred a luxurious bath at the hands of his slaves. All these types find comfort in certain surroundings—yet the surroundings differ.

The New England farmer would not think a home comfortable that was full of slaves—even a butler he would find oppressive; the New York banker would not enjoy seeing his wife do dirty work. Ideals change—even home ideals; and whatever kind of home we have, so that we grow up in it and know no other, we learn to love. Even among homes as they now are, equally enjoyed by their inmates, there is a wide scale of difference. Why, then, is it impossible to imagine something still further varying from what we now know; yet to the children born therein as dear and deeply loved?

Again let us remember that happiness, mere physical comfort and the interchange of family affection, is not all that life is for. We may have had "a happy childhood," as far as we can recall; we may have been idolised and indulged by our parents, and have had no wish ungratified; yet even so all this is no guarantee that the beloved home has given us the best training, the best growth. Nourmahal, the Light of the Harem, no doubt enjoyed herself—but perhaps other surroundings might have done more for her mind and soul. The questions raised here touch not only upon our comfort and happiness in such homes as are happy ones, but on the formative influence of these homes; asking if our present home ideals and home conditions are really doing all for humanity that we have a right to demand. There is a difference in homes not only in races, classes, and individuals, but in periods.

The sum of the criticism in the following study is this: the home has not developed in proportion to our other institutions, and by its rudimentary condition it arrests development in other lines. Further, that the two main errors in the right adjustment of the home to our present life are these: the maintenance of primitive industries in a modern industrial community, and the confinement of women to those industries and their limited area of expression. No word is said against the real home, the true family life; but it is claimed that much we consider essential to that home and family life is not only unnecessary, but positively injurious.

The home is a beautiful ideal, but have we no others? "My Country" touches a deeper chord than even "Home, Sweet Home." A homeless man is to be pitied, but "The Man without a Country" is one of the horrors of history. The love of mother and child is beautiful; but there is a higher law than that—the love of one another.

In our great religion we are taught to love and serve all mankind. Every word and act of Christ goes to show the law of universal service. Christian love goes out to all the world; it may begin, but does not stay, at home.

The trend of all democracy is toward a wider, keener civic consciousness; a purer public service. All the great problems of our times call for the broad view, the large concept, the general action. Such gain as we have made in human life is in this larger love; in some approach to peace, safety, and world-wide inter-service; yet this so patent common good is strangely contradicted and offset by cross-currents of primitive selfishness. Our own personal lives, rich as they are to-day, broad with the consciousness of all acquainted races, deep with the consciousness of the uncovered past, strong with our universal knowledge and power; yet even so are not happy. We are confused—bewildered. Life is complicated, duties conflict, we fly and fall like tethered birds, and our new powers beat against old restrictions like ships in dock, fast moored, yet with all sail set and steam up.

It is here suggested that one cause for this irregular development of character, this contradictory social action, and this wearing unrest in life lies unsuspected in our homes; not in their undying essential factors, but in those phases of home life we should have long since peacefully outgrown. Let no one tremble in fear of losing precious things. That which is precious remains and will remain always. We do small honour to nature's laws when we imagine their fulfilment rests on this or that petty local custom of our own.

We may all have homes to love and grow in without the requirement that half of us shall never have anything else. We shall have homes of rest and peace for all, with no need for half of us to find them places of ceaseless work and care. Home and its beauty, home and its comfort, home and its refreshment to tired nerves, its inspiration to worn hearts, this is in no danger of loss or change; but the home which is so far from beautiful, so wearing to the nerves and dulling to the heart, the home life that means care and labour and disappointment, the quiet, unnoticed whirlpool that sucks down youth and beauty and enthusiasm, man's long labour and woman's longer love—this we may gladly change and safely lose. To the child who longs to grow up and be free; to the restless, rebelling boy; to the girl who marries all too hastily as a means of escape; to the man who puts his neck in the collar and pulls while life lasts to meet the unceasing demands of his little sanctuary; and to the woman—the thousands upon thousands of women, who work while life lasts to serve that sanctuary by night and day—to all these it may not be unwelcome to suggest that the home need be neither a prison, a workhouse, nor a consuming fire.

Home—with all that the sweet word means; home for each of us, in its best sense; yet shorn of its inordinate expenses, freed of its grinding labours, open to the blessed currents of progress that lead and lift us all—this we may have and keep for all time.

It is, therefore, with no iconoclastic frenzy of destruction, but as one bravely pruning a most precious tree, that this book is put forward; inquiring as to what is and what is not vital to the subject; and claiming broadly that with such and such clinging masses cut away, the real home life will be better established and more richly fruitful for good than we have ever known before.

Source: Charlotte Perkins Gilman, *The Home: Its Work and Influence* (New York: McClure, Phillips, 1903).

No Two "Homes" Can Be Alike

Mary Abbott's decorating advice is typical of her time and conveys the growing repudiation of the Victorian parlor. Less taken with the overstuffed furnishings and elaborate wall hangings of the past, middle-class Americans at the end of the nineteenth century no longer shared the belief that the right goods and furniture could shape the moral self. Instead, as Abbott explains here, domestic possessions are to conform to the individuals who use them, not the other way around. Likewise, Abbott rejects the semipublic function of the parlor as a site for entertaining and formal social life. Her "home" is entirely private and serves the comfort of its inhabitants. Recall that Edith Wharton's *The Decoration of Houses* was published just a year earlier—a reminder that changes in values and styles do not take place quickly or universally.

The French have been pitied for not possessing in their language an equivalent for the English word "home." They are really to be envied; for in English the word is distorted, perverted, and made contemptible and ridiculous. Anything that has four walls and is inhabited is a "home," in this country. It may be the abode of discord, divorce, misery, disease; it is a "lovely home," a "palatial home," a "red-brick basement home," a "four-story-high home."

The word, which is really an abstract term, and means, or ought to mean, the dwelling-place of the heart, is applied to wood, stone, laths, and plaster. "Not a home was in sight," said a woman the other day, speaking of the loneliness of a certain country district; and a newspaper commented on the action of two brothers, who married sisters and "built themselves a beautiful double-home." When they separate, change wives, or quarrel violently, as families are not unknown to do, the "double-home" will still be named by that endearing epithet; and whether for sale or to let, will remain a "home" still.

It is no doubt a mistaken idea of elegant refining of speech that prompts this use, or misuse of the most sacred of all words, if it is employed in its real sense. The same people will speak of a babe as an infant, instead of a baby; of a limb, instead of a leg; of a casket, instead of a coffin; of interment, instead of burial; of retiring, instead of going to bed; will use rising for getting up, being seated for sitting down. They use all these affected terms, thinking them more delicate than the directer words or phrases, which possibly seem abrupt.

The preposterousness of the word in the wrong place is shown, if proof were needed, in an account given the other day in the public print of a "beautiful seaside home," vacant for years on account of crime and all sorts of domestic devastation—a house that had never been a home to anybody at any time. Of course it was the structure merely to which reference was made, even although its inhabitants had infected rather than beatified it.

Home-making is an entirely separate art from house-building, even the affected speech will probably allow. The most perfect gem of the architect's skill, furnished by the best upholsterer, and adorned by decorators of exquisite taste, may be utterly barren of appropriateness to its owners—in other words, destitute of homeliness. A hut in the woods, on the other hand, may possess every attribute of a happy and a beautiful home.

"Home is not the house then; it is the furniture," says a satirist at one's elbow. If he had said it is books and pictures and an atmosphere, he would have come nearer the mark. Or even an atmosphere, without anything else. It is that only that makes a home. So let us bar out the word as a means, and consider how it may be made, as it really is, as an end; and how a house of the handsomest or ugliest may be made to conform to the uses and achieve the attributes of a home.

One of the first requisites of making a home out a house is staying in it as much as possible; living things into shape, as it were, and making them adapt themselves to look like one. The woman—for woman is the principal home-maker—who is forever out, cannot expect her visitors to feel at home where she is almost a stranger herself. The things even get stiff from misuse, chairs have to be moved round into favorite places as well as sat in to conform to the scheme of living; and books and papers and work must be more or less "left round" if the place is to be easy and lifelike. There is a difference, as every housekeeper knows, between temporary and pleasing disorder, and chronic confusion. No one wants a week-old newspaper or a last year's magazine on a sofa; but to have the morning's journal or the latest book seized and filed, or neatly arranged on a shelf, is simply discomfort.

It is encouraging that in few houses nowadays, is there an apartment so sacred that a piece of work, a book, or even a cigarette-stub may not be left for a time without derogation of its dignity. Not that a cigarette relict may be allowed to lie for three months, as did that of Amelie Rives's heroine, in any well-ordered establishment. Every house should start in with about five minutes of perfect order before breakfast, and all litter should be considered illegitimate that is more than twelve hours old. A "home" should straighten itself out, look proper and tidy, just to show it can behave itself, and that its disarrangement merely proves that it knows how to live and be comfortable. But drawing, or show-rooms, in average houses, are places where people sit stiffly up after dinner, or during "calling" hours, where there are no books, and everything is cleared up within an inch of its life. These have gone out except in stately mansions where these must be separate rooms for mere entertaining.

The living-room, library, or morning-room is considered good enough for the most distinguished guests now-a-days, and is far more comfortable than the old gold-and-brocaded over-decorated horror of yesterday.

In order to be a "home," a house, too, must have individuality. No two "homes" can be alike. The book-lover must make of the library the most prominent feature of the house; the woman who likes to sew, must do the same with her well-lighted boudoir; the musician with his sparsely-furnished music room, in which acoustics is the principal end. But even libraries, music-rooms, rooms to write and sew and talk in, are disposed and furnished according to the individual pianist's, reader's, sewer's, or tattler's taste, or they form no legitimate part of a real home. Some persons cannot live without plants and flowers about. Every room must be full of vegetation. Others object to the care or the odor or the exhaustive properties of plants; to them a houseful of odors would be simply unbearable. There are women who hate to see sheet music scattered about, who keep everything in books or folios or cabinets; other[s] again cannot get up the proper inspiration without digging in a heap for the required song or piece. To such it is absurd to say "Be tidy." It is not nature, and their rooms should look their natures.

To families in which conflicting habits and tastes occur, although such cases are not as common as might be supposed, the advice is "Do like the Boffins;" divide your room with partitions, sand one side of it and carpet the other, or let separate tastes display themselves in separated apartments. Do not force the readers to be workers, the workers to lounge idly in easy-chairs. Individual taste should govern in the furnishing of each constituent part of a real home, just as the owner's likes and dislikes should be visible in its outward and main essentials. English-women like the doors of their sitting-rooms closed. They abominate portieres and folding-doors, and openings into halls through which pryers may spy and draughts be let it; for English halls are unheated. Americans, on the other hand, prefer openings and vistas, and the whole house thrown together, room after room. One reason is, of course, the heating of the halls, and the other the attractiveness of them. Halls are often sitting-rooms, although old-fashioned mothers and fathers object to the perversion of their original function. As much may be gathered then from the open or closed condition of a living-room as by its furnishing.

The owner may be a recluse, an invalid, or an English woman. A normal American lives in the open—in a house much too hot, it is true, but hospitable in effect. The Englishman locks you into his castle if he likes you, and locks you out if he does not.

All these varieties of taste and idiosyncracy are what make national and individual homes. Questions of color, size of rooms, and other attributes governed by personal likes and dislikes will be touched upon later. Sufficient it is now to say that uniformity is the last thing on earth to be sought for in different homes, either outwardly or inwardly, just as it is in persons.

Source: Mary Abbott, "Individuality in Homes," *House Beautiful*, February 1898.

A Radical Departure from the Older Styles of Cottage

The opening decades of the twentieth century saw the rising popularity of a new housing style, the bungalow. Adopted from India, the bungalow with its open floor plan, shaded porch, and flow to the outdoors was initially associated with the climate and lifestyle of southern California. By the 1910s, it spread across the country and into urban and suburban communities. Wealthy homeowners might choose a large bungalow designed and constructed in the Arts and Crafts style, while the middle class could build from plans such as those published by Henry L. Wilson in *The Bungalow Book*. Ten dollars entitled one to the book "and a complete set of working drawings, details and specifications of any design shown." The typical modest bungalow, like those designed by Wilson, had two or three bedrooms, one bathroom, and a living room that opened to a dining room and kitchen.

In the Bungalow is the possibility of combining economy in cost with artistic beauty to an almost unlimited degree. Recognizing this fact long ago, I have for many years directed my best efforts to the perfecting of this style of building, and I take pride in exhibiting the results of my labor and study in the pages of the Bungalow Book, four large editions of which have been completely exhausted in two and a half years.

A notable feature of all my plans is the close symmetrical relation between exteriors and interiors, thus combining graceful outlines with inside convenience and comfort. I find it is a big mistake to adopt a floor plan and then endeavor to fit an exterior to it. Many architects do this, I know, but the result is never satisfactory, and a house so designed is never pleasing to the eye; in fact, it usually attracts attention only by its ugliness. Concessions must be made, and both inside and outside details must be modified to gain that atmosphere of cozy elegance which is so much admired in all of my plans, and I do not feel that my years of study and labor have been all in vain when I receive the expressions of pleasure and commendation from the thousands who have built homes from my designs.

The Bungalow is a radical departure from the older styles of cottage, not only in outward appearance but in inside arrangement. The straight, cold entrance hall and the stiff, prim, usually darkened parlor have no place in it. Entrance is usually into a large living room—the room where the family gathers, and in which the visitor feels at once the warm, homelike hospitality. Everything in this room should suggest comfort and restfulness. The open fireplace and low, broad mantel, a cozy nook or corner, or a broad window seat, are all means to the desired end. Bookcases or shelves may be fitted into convenient places, and ceiling beams add an air of homely quaintness which never grows tiresome.

Where there is room, I suggest, that by all means a den should find a place in your plan. This room need not be large, but its very name is suggestive of luxurious rest amid piles of cushions surrounded by curios and mementoes which accumulate in every family, each reminiscent of good times gone by. Many one-story Bungalows may have in the attic a den or smoking or billiard room.

The dining room should be large and well lighted, and as it will contain few articles of furniture, it may be finished somewhat elaborately, with paneled wainscoting, plate-rail, etc.

Sleeping rooms should be light and well ventilated, and decorated in rather bright, cheerful tints.

Owing to the comparative smallness of the ordinary bath room, we must strive to arrange the various fixtures in the most economical manner. To dispense with chairs, we might build a seat in some convenient corner. Aside from a medicine cabinet and a linen closet for towels, etc., very little remains to complete this room. For an inexpensive wainscot, hard wall plaster is a suitable alternative for the genuine tile. From the top of the wainscot, which is usually about four feet, a light tint for the

Figure 6.1. Modern Home No. 147 was one of over four hundred housing styles available for purchase through the Sears Modern Home mail-order catalog. The homes were for sale from 1908 to 1940, and this particular bungalow model was available from 1909 to 1917. Sears sold homes in popular styles and at several different price points. Customers picked out their home and placed their order, and Sears sent them everything they needed, from precut timber, dry wall, and nails to decorative glass and plate rails. Mass-production of materials kept prices down. As shown in the catalog copy, Sears also encouraged would-be homeowners to invest in the latest technologies in heating and plumbing, although this particular house relies on gas lighting. Note that the catalog also lists communities in which this particular home had already been built.

walls and ceiling, together with white enameled woodwork, is suggestive of purity and cleanliness, and is very pleasing. Where one can afford decorations, a continuous design of a water scene with lilies and swan thrown in at intervals adds richness to the room.

I am inclined to believe that every housewife who plans a house commences with the kitchen, and I am still more inclined to believe that she is right. It is a most important room, and should be made as cheerful and convenient as possible. Saving of steps means conservation of energy and health, and consequently promotes the general welfare of the family. Where it is possible, the sink should be in the center of the long drain-board, so that the soiled dishes can be placed at one end and when washed laid on the other. The space underneath the drain-board may be utilized for kitchen utensils. In the modern kitchen much attention is given to the proper distribution of the various cupboards, flour bins, spice receptacles and the many little contrivances which appeal to women. Here, too, the hard wall wainscot, well painted, or better still enameled, is valuable from the standpoint of sanitation, as it washes easily and does not absorb dust. White enameled wood work, although more expensive than the natural finish or paint, makes an ideal finish for the kitchen.

Source: Henry L. Wilson, *The Bungalow Book* (Chicago: Henry L. Wilson, 1910).

Our Need To-Day Is for Labor-Saving Devices

The last decades of the nineteenth century saw a decline in the demand for servants as well as in the numbers of women willing to take on the job. These trends were driven by demographic changes as well as new employment opportunities for women. The loss of servants both reflected and inspired new domestic arrangements. (Certainly Henry Wilson's bungalows were designed to minimize the toll of domestic labor.) As noted in this excerpt, labor-saving devices often filled the void created when servants left. For Martha Bensley Bruère, new technologies in the home were evidence of progress. Elsewhere in the article, she writes, "All the flutteration to put hand sewing, and home baking, and preserving and the making of Christmas mince-meat on a plane of what might be called moral elegance is just a bracing back against tomorrow." Ironically, the historian Ruth Schwartz Cowan has shown that new technologies ultimately increased women's domestic labor, raising standards and reinforcing expectations that women could manage their homes alone.

The middle-class servant is obsolescent, being in the reprehensible act of vanishing into her home on the one hand, and into the factory on the other. It may look as though I were confusing the problem of home administration with the servant problem; but how one shall administer one's home depends largely upon what tools one has, and the servant is a tool, the vanishing of which leaves us in a lingering emergency. To be sure, people do not realize she is a tool. "The scarcity of good servant girls is breaking up homes of America," writes a despairing gentleman from Pennsylvania, as though the servant girl were corn or meat, water or air. I suppose there was a time when primitive man cried out that stone axes were vanishing, and how could civilization go on without them! But civilization wasn't parasitic upon the stone ax, any more than home is parasitic upon the cook. The need was for a new tool to take the place of the old one—a bow and arrows in place of the ax—as our need to-day is for labor-saving devices in place of the cook.

A man with three thousand a year writes:

"We used to have a woman come in by the day. When she stopped coming, we just purchased a vacuum cleaner for $120, which the women folks now prefer to outside help. . . . We have also a motor-operated washing-machine, two electric sad-irons, and one gas iron."

The wife of a New England physician, with an income ranging between three and four thousand dollars a year, says:

"In the last tear I have kept no maid, having discharged my last one after nearly six years of service, and have enjoyed the year more than any previous one. I never hesitate to spend money on any labor-saving device. I use a gas range, a fireless cooker, have an excellent vacuum cleaner, and an adequate supply of all kitchen utensils and conveniences. My household expenses have been cut down about five hundred dollars a year, and I know of no easier way of saving that amount than by being free from the care and annoyance of a maid. I am surprised to find how small our total for food has been this last year."

"Our house," writes a man with an income of $5,000 a year, "is arranged all on one floor, and all unnecessary rooms and partitions eliminated. Our efforts are directed towards keeping down the accumulation of 'things,' so that we will not be crowded, and dusting and cleaning will be simplified. Electric current costs us twelve cents per kw. hour, and is used rather freely—in fuel, only in the flat-iron and a small heater for the dinning-room table; for power in the vacuum cleaner and washer and wringer; and for light. For light and power we do not find the electric current expensive, but for heating it is very much so. It is not possible to figure how much we save in using electrical energy. Without translating this saving into dollars and cents, we are content to know that there is a saving of labor, which, were we deprived of help, would not make us fare so badly."

A well-to-do minister writes:

Figure 6.2. The "Little Servants in the House" series of advertisements appeared in New York newspapers such as the *Evening Post*, the *New York Times*, the *New York Tribune*, and the *Yonkers Statesman* in 1915 and 1916. Electric companies were eager to encourage the adoption of electric appliances by depicting them as replacements for servants. In this ad, a seemingly aristocratic woman performs her own domestic labor with an electric iron, sewing machine, chafing dish, and vacuum cleaner. The appliances have freed her from servants or perhaps have given her a sense of elevated social status as her routine work has been transformed by this new technology. Eager to sell electricity, the New York Edison Company offered demonstrations of appliances at its Home Economics Bureau and in its showrooms. The Yonkers Electric Light and Power Company also advertised a deferred payment plan. This particular advertisement appeared in the *Evening Post* on December 18, 1915, and the *New York Times* on December 20, 1915.

"With reference to labor-saving appliances, the vacuum carpet cleaner cost $135. It costs about two cents an hour for electricity. Eight cents a week will give the house of two halls and nine rooms a thorough sweeping. The electric washer and wringer is sold on the guarantee that it will do the washing for a family of six persons in one hour and half, at three cents for electricity. We bought the machine on that guarantee, and find that it will do the work in the given time at the given cost. Our gas iron cost three dollars and a half, and does not consume any more gas than an ordinary lighting jet. We use about fifteen barrels of water per week in the house. The hot-air pump will pump that amount of water in a hundred minutes, using as much gas as five or six open gas jets would consume in that time. The engine cost one hundred dollars. In five years I have spent only fifty-five cents on repairs, and that was for new leather valves. The electric heat regulator, which controls the flow of natural gas into the furnace, cost twenty-eight dollars, and is operated by dry batteries which need to be replaced every year at a cost of fifty cents for two. You will notice that the wages of an ordinary maid who is willing to do any kind of work about the house would, in a year and a half, amount to more than the cost and operation of all my labor-saving appliances."

None of these families have supplanted servants with labor-saving devices to save money, but because they think them better tools with which to run their homes.

Source: Martha Bensley Bruère, "The New Home-Making," *Outlook*, March 16, 1912, 591–595.

A Workshop at Home May Be Made a Means of Pleasant and Profitable Recreation

A. L. Hall's short description of his home workshop captures the confluence of several trends reincorporating middle-class men into the life of the home at the turn of the century. At a time when industrialization and managerial capitalism offered men less control over their professional lives, home handiwork provided a sense of mastery. Suburbanization and the new bungalow style provided an ideal setting. Here men's craftsmanship is reimagined as masculine leisure in service of the home. Significantly, these domestic contributions are distinguished from those of women, as Hall highlights his financial investment in tools and equipment as well as the economic worth of his projects. The regendering of domestic space is suggested in the transformation of old sewing-machine parts into a workbench and a saw table. The result is a new domestic setting in which men and boys can pursue recreation that is fun, valuable, and manly.

To have a workshop in one's home, well supplied with tools, where simple pieces of furniture can be made on the lines of one's own choosing, is to have a source of unlimited pleasure always at hand. I have such a shop, where I spend many hours, and find in it no little satisfaction.

When we moved into our present home, a house of moderate size, the rear room on the second floor was given to me for a den, and was furnished according to the usually accepted idea of what a man's sanctum should contain to soothe his weary nerves.

I had, also, the usual tools which are to be found about almost any commuter's or suburban residence—a couple of saws, a hammer, a plane or two, and a square. These were kept in a kitchen closet, and had as neighbors the pots and pans, and other large and necessary culinary utensils. I suspect that my wife begrudged the room which they occupied. Anyway, one evening she suggested that the den be turned into a workshop for my benefit.

The suggestion was acted upon at once, and inside of two hours the room had been stripped of its comfortable furnishings, and the old bench from the cellar and the few tools I owned substituted.

The giving up of the den for a workshop may seem to some to have been a hardship, but such was not the case. My business permits me to spend only the weekend at home. When I had the den, I would occupy it only long enough to attend to my mail, the balance of the time being spent with the family in the general living-room, so that the den was really used for only an hour or two each week.

The old bench which was moved up from the cellar was not good enough for the new shop, so I made a better one by using the iron legs of a sewing-machine and a two-inch plank two feet wide and seven feet long. To this a wooden vise, such as is used by carpenters, was attached. This is really a cheap bench, as the iron legs cost me only fifty cents. It is as rigid and strong as if the frame were of wood, and is heavy enough for any strain that I probably shall ever subject it to. It was not necessary, however, to use so wide a plank; one twelve inches wide and two inches thick, for the front of the bench, would have been sufficient. The balance of the top might have been made of inch stuff, the top being brought flush with the two-inch plank by putting small blocks under it.

The next piece of furniture for the shop was a saw-table. No good shop should be without a circular saw, as it saves a great deal of time, besides lightening the work. Here, again, an old sewing-machine base was used. I bought a heavy combination pulley and fly-wheel to take the place of the one already on the machine. The top I also made new from oak. It is three feet square, and is hinged, so that it can be raised to any height, enabling me to make grooves in the lumber to any required depth. Any one who knows how hard it is to push a carpenter's plow will readily understand what a saver of strength this device is. . . .

The only other large pieces of machinery in the room are a combined lathe and scroll-saw, and a grindstone. The grindstone is a wonder. It is mounted on an iron frame and on ball-bearings. On one end is a seat in which I can sit, revolving the stone by means of a pair of pedals, as though I were riding a bicycle. I wish my father had had one of them when I was a boy, so that the hired man could have turned his own stone, when grinding scythes and mowing-machine cutter-bars, for it would have saved me from hours of back-breaking drudgery. . . .

I have now invested in the shop something like $175. However, this sum was not expended all at one time, for I have bought the different tools as I needed them. I have even made a few articles, such as plane-stocks and chisel handles.

This stock of tools has enabled me to make many little repairs about the house, whereby we have saved carpenters' bills, but the chief uses to which it has been put has been building furniture, such as chairs and tables. The morris-chair . . . is one of my own productions; even the cushions are home-made. I have not had patterns to go by in any of my work; I had my idea of about what the result should be, and have worked to that end. In many cases the pieces have been designed to fit particular needs. For instance, there is a desk in the house which is too high to work at comfortably when one is sitting in an ordinary chair; so I made a chair with a seat high enough. To afford comfort, the back is made very straight to give support from behind. If such a chair had been bought at the store, hours would undoubtedly have been consumed in finding it, and then the chances are that it would not have matched the desk.

I believe that a workshop in the home, particularly if one has growing boys, is an essential part of the household equipment. One need not necessarily devote a room to it, for a small house in the back yard, or a corner in the cellar, if the latter is dry, can be used equally well. In fact, in most houses there are no spare rooms.

I know one cellar workshop that was light and dry, and which furnished an untold amount of interest to a couple of growing boys. In that shop they built, when still small, toy boats for sailing in the sink; and later, as they grew older, they made real boats out of packing-cases, cheese-boxes, and canvas. This shop kept them off the streets altogether. A workshop at home may be made a means of pleasant and profitable recreation, both for father and son.

From persons who do not know just how to draw plans for furniture, various firms have published what are called mill-plans. They include all kinds of furniture such as tables, chairs, desks and smaller pieces in the so-called mission and craftsman designs.

In making this furniture, the work at home can be simplified somewhat by having the lumber sawn out into suitable sizes, at the mill where purchased, the charge for which will be only nominal.

Source: A. L. Hall, "My Workshop at Home," *Suburban Life*, November 1908, 256.

Most of the Normal Tendencies of Life Must Find New Forms

Michael M. Davis, Jr., gathered the information for the study excerpted here in 1910, while serving as the secretary of the Committee of Recreation and Amusements of the New York Child Welfare Committee. Throughout, he emphasizes the necessity of leisure—including the importance or commercial entertainments—and concludes that for too many city dwellers home is inadequate for recreation. While noting that all public recreation is not equally wholesome, Davis (and like-minded reformers) recognizes that leisure activities are not likely to return exclusively to the home. Instead they must be understood as a public concern, subject to government regulation. Looking back to the nineteenth-century ideal of home, Davis acknowledges the rise of the

street as a site of social life and escape, and rather than rejecting this transformation, he hopes to regulate it.

Home, sweet Home! To the well-to-do novel-reader and to our Colonial forefathers "home" meant a house big enough for a family of five, or seventeen, to sleep and eat, work and play in. All the natural activities of life centered themselves about the home, and most could express themselves within its physical limits. Consequently, home was the spiritual center of life, and, particularly for the children and the adolescents, formed most of its circumference as well.

How the city changes all this! The home shrinks to a nest of boxes tucked four stories in the air, or the half of a duplex house huddled upon its neighbors. There is space to sleep and eat, but not to live. The habitation becomes a sleeping box and eating den—too often no more. Specialized industry, the basis of the modern city, makes it possible for large numbers of people to live and support themselves within a restricted area. This crowding of population creates a human pressure under which most of the normal tendencies of life must find new forms or at least new modes of manifestation. This is a result of the mere fact that the physical limits of space fall so far beneath the minimum human demand for self-expression.

When each of ten thousand girls could learn to dance in her own home society might have little concern with the matter; but when no more than ten of those ten thousand are able to learn to dance elsewhere than in academies commercially established and run for profit, the quality of these academies becomes a matter with which the state that cares for its citizens has every need to concern itself. When five hundred boys may vent their energies upon five square miles of hill, wood and greensward around their town we may leave their doings to their parents; when those five hundred must play upon a street a quarter-mile long, crowded with traffic, shops and saloons, the city should, and *must*, have something to say about the conditions that shall exist on that street. The individual parent is helpless before a condition which may mean the physical and moral destruction of his child.

In a word, recreation within the modern city has become a matter of public concern; *laissez faire*, in recreation as in industry, can no longer be the policy of the state.

The natural divisions of the Recreation side of life are three: The spontaneous, the communally organized, and the commercially organized. In the large city most of the spontaneous recreation activities must seek some facilities through which to manifest themselves, and these facilities, we observe, must as a rule be provided by the city government, by philanthropic benevolence or by commercial enterprise. The men's lodge must have its meeting place in saloon or public hall; the boy's gang must use the street, park or playground; the social circle must go to the settlement or to the recreation center. A hundred activities which in the Fifth Avenue home find their *loci* in parlor, study, den and garden, must among the mass of people be somewhere outside the limits of the home. *Where* outside, is a matter of vital importance to the public welfare.

Thus the spontaneous effort for recreation is thwarted or nullified unless conscious communal or institutional effort steps in. Here the settlements have led the way; public institutions have followed. Now, all settlements, Young Men's and Young Women's Christian Associations, and a large proportion of churches, recognize the public demand, and do the larger part of their social and educational work through the offer to their clientele of opportunities for recreation. The municipality, recognizing recreation traditionally in the establishment of parks, first faced the modern problem in relation to the school system; and, in an urgent and militant form, in connection with the playground movement.

In devoting public funds to indoor and outdoor playgrounds, parks, lectures, libraries, museums, recreation centers, vacation schools, music, and popular festivals, civic leaders recognize that the municipality is not only offering its people something of positive value, but is also counteracting influences which are generally detrimental, and against which only the power of the municipality can effectively work. The recreation policy of the modern city, even to the slight extent thus far developed, is twofold: it offers recreation opportunities, and it counteracts certain opportunities already offered. Reformers and legislators are beginning to see that this counteractive effect can best be gained through counter-*attraction* rather than through the old blue-law policy of repression. Yet, as we shall see, certain types of repressive laws are important factors in a recreation policy.

Commercially Organized Recreations

Picture children that we know—hungry-eyed youngsters with abounding surplus energies, seeking passionately to touch, enjoy and understand this world of wonders. From the home, the logical and the actual beginning, stretches a series of stages, linked with a chain whose logic is life. Yearly the circles of activity widen: the tot plays beside the family stoop, the little boy's range is his block, the older urchin scours the district, the young man travels about the city.

In a crowded city there is human pressure upon the street hardly less great than that within the home; offshoots from the street arise to meet this pressure,—the candy shop for the children, the ice cream and soda parlor, the moving-picture show, the vaudeville, the dance hall, the saloon. To these places people pay to go, partly to seek positive pleasure, partly because to remain within the straits of the home or the moil of the street means positive pain or discomfort. Out of the twofold impulse,—towards the pleasant and away from the unpleasant,—commercial enterprise builds the gaudy structure of profit-paying recreation.

Source: Michael M. Davis, Jr., introduction to *The Exploitation of Pleasure: A Study of Commercial Recreations in New York City* (New York: Russell Sage Foundation, 1911).

Proper Housing Is an Essential to the Employer

While Bellamy, Campbell, and Gilman imagined that cooperatives might improve domestic life through shared household labor, the Industrial Housing Associates offered another version of domestic cooperation. At a time of marked labor unrest, they provided employers and communities with the tools to make workers "content." Their language partially echoes that of reformers such as Riis, emphasizing good housing as a community concern. But whereas Riis feared that landlords' drive for profits would always fuel the slums, the Industrial Home Associates made the opposite case. Considering the impact of good housing on the worker and his employer in purely economic terms, they conclude that it is a good investment for the latter. This argument reflected a growing appreciation of workers as potential consumers and

the belief that homeownership was both carrot and stick—incentivizing hard work and discouraging labor unrest.

What sort of home does your workman come from in the morning? What does he look forward to when his day of toil is over?

The answer concerns the employer and the whole community, for it determines in large measure the worker's degree of contentment, his efficiency, and his attachment to the community interests.

The Problem

"Yes, we need houses, but how are we going to get them?" A business man was speaking. And dozens of business men in dozens of communities are asking the same question.

This query is the reason for the Industrial Housing Associates and this folder. If you need houses, we can help you get them. . . .

The Value of Good Housing

Do you realize what poor housing means to the individual, to the employers of your city, and to your community as a whole?

Man's chief interest is in his home. If it is unhealthy and uncomfortable, neither he nor his family will be happy or effective as citizens. And discontent is a serious breeder of trouble.

Good workers never come from poor houses. It is now becoming generally recognized that adequate and proper housing is an essential to the employer who would have an efficient working force. Happy workers invariably mean bigger profits, while unhappy workers are never a good investment.

A community exists for the people in it, not the reverse. It cannot be sound, prosperous, and progressive if a large number of its people are housed under conditions which menace their health and happiness, and which consequently make them uninterested and spiritless as workers and citizens. Go personally to the district where the rank and file of your workers live. Find out just what their living conditions are and decide for yourself whether or not these are such that good workers and good citi-

Figure 6.3. The title page of the Industrial Housing Associates' *Good Homes Make Contented Workers* (1919) holds out the promise of bungalow-style living to the working class and encourages employers to see their employees as potential homeowners.

zens can be expected to accept them. If not, you have a responsibility to better conditions.

To the trained observer the housing conditions in any community are an accurate guide to its spirit and development. All students of the subject agree that *whatever* the cost of establishing and maintaining good housing, it is always less than the loss bound to result from bad housing. More[o]ver, money wisely used to provide better housing is not an expenditure, but an extremely good investment. Therefore, good housing pays from every standpoint.

Source: Industrial Housing Associates, *Good Homes Make Contented Workers* (Philadelphia: Biddle, 1919).

Chapter 1: The Emergence of the Nineteenth-Century Domestic Ideal

There is a significant body of secondary-source literature on the ideal of home, Victorian notions of domesticity, and the emergence of separate spheres. See Barbara Welter's groundbreaking "The Cult of True Womanhood, 1820–1860," *American Quarterly* 18, no. 2 (Summer 1966): 151–175; Nancy Cott, *The Bonds of Womanhood: "Woman's Sphere" in New England, 1780–1835* (Yale University Press, 1977); Gwendolyn Wright, *Building the Dream: A Social History of Housing in America* (MIT Press, 1983); Jeanne Boydston, *Home and Work: Housework, Wages, and the Ideology of Labor in the Early Republic* (Oxford University Press, 1990); and Louise L. Stevenson, *The Victorian Homefront: American Thought and Culture, 1860–1880* (Twayne, 1991). On domestic spaces and material culture as a reflection of changing values, consult Richard Bushman, *The Refinement of America: Persons, Houses, Cities* (Vintage, 1992). See also Clifford E. Clark, Jr., "Domestic Architecture as an Index to Social History: The Romantic Revival and the Cult of Domesticity in America, 1840–1870," *Journal of Interdisciplinary History* 7, no. 1 (Summer 1976): 33–56; Clark, *The American Family Home, 1800–1960* (University of North Carolina Press, 1986); Katherine Grier, *Culture and Comfort: People, Parlors, and Upholstery* (Strong Museum, 1988); Kenneth Ames, *Death in the Dining Room and Other Tales of Victorian Culture* (Temple University Press, 1995); and Jack Larkin, *Where We Lived: Discovering the Places We Once Called Home; the American Home from 1775 to 1840* (Taunton, 2006).

On the relationship between middle-class status and new understandings of domestic life, see Mary Ryan, *Cradle of the Middle Class: The Family in Oneida County, New York, 1790–1865* (Cambridge University Press, 1981); and Stuart M. Blumin, *The Emergence of the Middle Class: Social Experience in the American City, 1760–1900* (Cambridge University Press, 1989). Karen Halttunen's *Confidence Men and Painted Women: A Study of Middle-Class Culture in America, 1830–1870* (Yale

University Press, 1982) offers insight into the perceived and real dangers that young men and women encountered when they ventured beyond the home, and Kenneth Jackson's *Crabgrass Frontier: The Suburbanization of the United States* (Oxford University Press, 1985) captures the idyllic landscape of the early nineteenth-century home as envisioned by Andrew Jackson Downing.

Finally, Jane P. Tompkins's *Sensational Designs: The Cultural Work of American Fiction, 1790–1860* (Oxford University Press, 1985) and Sarah Leavitt's *From Catharine Beecher to Martha Stewart: A Cultural History of Domestic Advice* (University of North Carolina Press, 2002) provide two different treatments of the relationship between domesticity and women's writing. The former considers women's fiction, including Warner's *Wide, Wide World*, and the latter offers a thoughtful reading of prescriptive literature regarding the home. See also Sarah Wilson's "Melville and the Architecture of Antebellum Masculinity," *American Literature* 76, no. 1 (March 2004): 59–87, for an interpretation of the male literary response to the new domestic ideal.

Chapter 2: The Persistence of Domestic Labor

For histories of women's unpaid domestic labor, see Susan Strasser, *Never Done: A History of American Housework* (Holt, 1986); Glenna Matthews, *"Just a Housewife": The Rise and Fall of Domesticity in America* (Oxford University Press, 1989); and Suellen Hoy, *Chasing Dirt: The American Pursuit of Cleanliness* (Oxford University Press, 1995). Christine Stansell's *City of Women: Sex and Class in New York, 1789–1860* (University of Illinois Press, 1987) depicts domesticity among the working poor and critiques the efforts of middle-class benevolent reformers, including home visiting. Her account also enumerates the types of relief work that charities offered poor women in the early nineteenth century. For more on moral reformers and their values, see Paul Boyer, *Urban Masses and Moral Order in America, 1820–1920* (Harvard University Press, 1978); Michael B. Katz, *In the Shadow of the Poorhouse: A Social History of Welfare in America* (Basic Books, 1986); Lori D. Ginzberg, *Women and the Work of Benevolence: Morality, Politics, and Class in the Nineteenth-Century United States* (Yale University Press, 1992); and Anne M. Boylan, *The Origins of Women's Activism: New York and Boston,*

1797–1840 (University of North Carolina Press, 2002). The last two works pay special attention to the relationship between domesticity and moral reform.

Domestic service and boarding highlighted the play between the market and domestic settings. For the most inclusive overview and analysis of the nineteenth-century American boardinghouse, see Wendy Gamber, *The Boarding House in Nineteenth-Century America* (Johns Hopkins University Press, 2007). Thomas Dublin's *Women at Work: The Transformation of Work and Community in Lowell, Massachusetts, 1826–1860* (Columbia University Press, 1981) describes the Lowell boardinghouse experience, and Howard P. Chudacoff's *The Age of the Bachelor: Creating an American Subculture* (Princeton University Press, 1999) depicts the living arrangements of single men in the city. David Katzman's *Seven Days a Week: Women and Domestic Service in Industrializing America* (Oxford University Press, 1978) and Faye E. Dudden's *Serving Women: Household Service in Nineteenth-Century America* (Wesleyan University Press, 1985) offer accounts of women's employment in domestic service. For a different take on the marketplace's penetration of domestic life and space, see Ellen Gruber Garvey, *The Adman in the Parlor: Magazines and the Gendering of Consumer Culture, 1880s–1910s* (Oxford University Press, 1996).

For more on the housing arrangements of slaves and the ideology of slaveholders, see James O. Breeden, ed., *Advice among Masters: The Ideal in Slave Management in the Old South* (Greenwood, 1980); John Michael Vlach, "'Snug Li'l House with Flue and Oven': Nineteenth-Century Reforms in Plantation Slave Housing," in *Gender, Class, and Shelter: Perspectives in Vernacular Architecture*, ed. Elizabeth C. Cromley and Carter L. Hudgins (University of Tennessee Press, 1995); and Clifton Ellis and Rebecca Ginsburg, eds., *Cabin, Quarter, Plantation: Architecture and Landscapes of North American Slavery* (Yale University Press, 2010).

Chapter 3: Home, Civilization, and Citizenship

There are many studies exploring the mobilization of domestic ideals in the service of political causes. Relevant examples include Paula Baker, "The Domestication of Politics: Women and American Political Society, 1780–1920," *American Historical Review* 89, no. 3 (June 1984): 620–647;

and Barbara Leslie Epstein, *The Politics of Domesticity: Women, Evangelism, and Temperance in Nineteenth-Century America* (Wesleyan University Press, 1986). On the blending of antislavery fervor and domesticity in *Uncle Tom's Cabin,* useful insights can be found in Mary Kelley, *Private Woman, Public Stage: Literary Domesticity in Nineteenth-Century America* (Oxford University Press, 1984); Gillian Brown, "Getting in the Kitchen with Dinah: Domestic Politics in *Uncle Tom's Cabin,*" *American Quarterly* 36, no. 4 (Autumn 1984): 503–523; and Jane P. Tompkins, *Sensational Designs: The Cultural Work of American Fiction, 1790–1860* (Oxford University Press, 1985).

On African American women's use of domesticity and the "politics of respectability," see Evelyn Brooks Higginbotham, *Righteous Discontent: The Women's Movement in the Black Baptist Church, 1880–1920* (Harvard University Press, 1994). For more on Ida B. Wells, see Paula Giddings, *When and Where I Enter: The Impact of Black Women on Race and Sex in America* (William Morrow, 1984); Giddings, *Ida: A Sword among Lions; Ida B. Wells and the Campaign against Lynching* (HarperCollins, 2008); Patricia A. Schechter, *Ida B. Wells-Barnett and American Reform, 1880–1930* (University of North Carolina Press, 2001); and Mia Bay, *To Tell the Truth Freely: The Life of Ida B. Wells* (Hill and Wang, 2009). On W. E. B. Du Bois's photographic exhibit, consult Shawn Michelle Smith, *Photography on the Color Line: W. E. B. Du Bois, Race, and Visual Culture* (Duke University Press, 2004). See also Laura Wexler's *Tender Violence: Domestic Visions in an Age of U.S. Imperialism* (University of North Carolina Press, 2000) on photographic depictions of African American life and domesticity. Wexler's *Tender Violence* also considers the work of race and domesticity at Hampton Institute.

For two wonderful studies of Native American life and domestic ideology, see Peggy Pascoe, *Relations of Rescue: The Search for Female Moral Authority in the American West, 1874–1939* (Oxford University Press, 1990); and Jane E. Simonsen, *Making Home Work: Domesticity and Native American Assimilation in the American West, 1860–1919* (University of North Carolina Press, 2006). There are several fine works exploring the laws governing marriage and women's earnings, including Amy Dru Stanley, *From Bondage to Contract: Wage Labor, Marriage, and the Market in the Age of Slave Emancipation* (Cambridge University Press, 1998); Nancy Cott, *Public Vows: A History of Marriage and the Nation* (Harvard

University Press, 2000). See also Sara L. Zeigler, "Wifely Duties: Marriage, Labor, and the Common Law in Nineteenth-Century America," *Social Science History* 20, no. 1 (Spring 1996): 63–96. Finally, on women's paid employment, domesticity, and the labor movement, see Jeanne Boydston, *Home and Work: Housework, Wages, and the Ideology of Labor in the Early Republic* (Oxford University Press, 1990); and Eileen Boris, *Home to Work: Motherhood and the Politics of Industrial Homework in the United States* (Cambridge University Press 1994).

Chapter 4: The American Home on the Move in the Age of Expansion

Although the history of American expansion has usually focused on manly exploits, a growing body of scholarship considers the place of women and domesticity. On the significance of domestic settings and values on the American frontier, see Angel Kwolek-Folland, "The Elegant Dugout: Domesticity and Moveable Culture in the United States, 1870–1900," *American Studies* 25, no. 2 (Fall 1984): 21–37; and Andrea O. Radke, "Refining Rural Spaces: Women and Vernacular Gentility in the Great Plains, 1880–1920," *Great Plains Quarterly* 24, no. 4 (Fall 2004): 227–248. Railroads and the movement of domesticity across the continent are discussed in Amy G. Richter, *Home on the Rails: Women, the Railroad, and the Rise of Public Domesticity* (University of North Carolina Press, 2005).

On the uses of domestic ideals in the context of overseas expansion, see the work of Amy Kaplan, especially "Manifest Domesticity," *American Literature* 70, no. 3 (September 1998): 581–605; and "Romancing the Empire: The Embodiment of American Masculinity in the Popular Historical Novel of the 1890s," *American Literary History* 2, no. 4 (Winter 1990): 659–690. Consult also Vicente L. Rafael, "Colonial Domesticity: White Women and United States Rule in the Philippines," *American Literature* 67, no. 4 (December 1995): 639–666; and Laura Wexler, *Tender Violence: Domestic Visions in an Age of U.S Imperialism* (University of North Carolina Press, 2000).

As depicted in Robert W. Rydell's *All the World's a Fair: Visions of Empire at American International Expositions, 1876–1916* (University of Chicago Press, 1984), world's fairs educated Americans about their place in the global order and propagated the values of U.S. imperialism. Likewise, Kristin Hoganson's *Consumers' Imperium: the Global Production of American Domesticity, 1865–1920* (University of North Carolina Press, 2007) recasts the home as a site in which women encountered and interpreted global expansion through the consumption of goods. Hoganson's analysis suggests a rereading of the rich scholarship on immigrant women, consumption, and domesticity. See, for example, Lizabeth Cohen, "Embellishing a Life of Labor: An Interpretation of the Material Culture of American Working-Class Homes, 1885–1915," *Journal of American Culture* 3, no. 4 (Winter 1980): 752–775; Elizabeth Ewen, *Immigrant Women in the Land of Dollars: Life and Culture on the Lower East Side 1890–1925* (Monthly Review Press, 1985); and Magdalena Zaborowska, *How We Found America: Reading Gender through East European Immigrant Narratives* (University of North Carolina Press, 1995).

Chapter 5: At Home in the Late Nineteenth-Century City

The history of multifamily dwellings in New York City is told in Elizabeth Blackmar, *Manhattan for Rent, 1785–1850* (Cornell University Press, 1989); and Elizabeth Collins Cromley, *Alone Together: A History of New York's Early Apartments* (Cornell University Press, 1990). For a sense of life in New York City tenements, consult Andrew Dolkart, *Biography of a Tenement House in New York City: An Architectural History of 97 Orchard Street* (Center for American Places, 2006). See also the chapter on Jacob Riis in Betsy Klimasmith's wonderful *At Home in the City: Urban Domesticity in American Literature and Culture, 1850–1930* (University of New Hampshire Press, 2005). Several studies offer insight into the nineteenth-century hotel, including Carolyn Brucken, "In the Public Eye: Women and the American Luxury Hotel," *Winterthur Portfolio* 31, no. 4 (Winter 1996): 203–220; Catherine Cocks, *Doing the Town: The Rise of Urban Tourism in the United States* (University of California Press, 2001); and Andrew Sandoval-Strausz, *Hotel: An American History* (Yale University Press, 2007). For a taste of elite New York and domestic arrangements, consult Maureen E. Montgomery, *Displaying Women: Spectacles of Leisure in Edith Wharton's New York* (Routledge, 1998).

Urban life posed both challenges and opportunities for single women. On single women as historical actors and a social problem, see Kathy

Peiss, *Cheap Amusements: Working Women and Leisure in Turn-of-the-Century New York* (Temple University Press, 1986); and Joanne Meyerowitz, *Women Adrift: Independent Wage Earners in Chicago, 1880–1930* (University of Chicago Press, 1988). On reformers' use of domesticity to create literal and ideological space for their work as well as for respectable working-class women, see Sarah Deutsch, *Women and the City: Gender, Space, and Power in Boston, 1870–1940* (Oxford University Press, 2000); Daphne Spain, *How Women Saved the City* (University of Minnesota Press, 2001); and Sharon E. Wood, *The Freedom of the Streets: Work, Citizenship, and Sexuality in a Gilded Age City* (University of North Carolina Press, 2005).

On the public domesticity of Hull-House, see the editors' introduction to *Jane Addams and the Practice of Democracy*, ed. Marilyn Fischer, Carol Nackenoff, Wendy Chmielewski (University of Illinois Press, 2009); and Kathryn Kish Sklar's *Florence Kelley and the Nation's Work: The Rise of Women's Political Culture, 1830–1900* (Yale University Press, 1997). Finally, on the domestic qualities of urban parks and other public spaces, see Thomas Bender, *Toward an Urban Vision: Baltimore* (Johns Hopkins University Press, 1975); Mary Ryan, *Women in Public: Between Banners and Ballots, 1825–1880* (Johns Hopkins University Press, 1990); and Roy Rosenzweig and Elizabeth Blackmar, *The Park and the People: A History of Central Park* (Cornell University Press, 1992).

Chapter 6: Dismantling the Victorian Ideal and the Future of Domesticity

On utopian and feminist challenges to the nineteenth-century domestic ideal, there is no better source than Dolores Hayden, *The Grand Domestic Revolution: A History of Feminist Designs for American Homes, Neighborhoods, and Cities* (MIT Press, 1981). Gwendolyn Wright's *Moralism and the Model Home: Domestic Architecture and Cultural Conflict in Chicago, 1873–1913* (University of Chicago Press, 1980) also provides important insights on reform and domestic architecture at the end of the nineteenth century. Other studies chart the changing appearance of domestic interiors, especially the waning popularity of the parlor and the growing appeal of the open floor plan. See, for example, Karen Halttunen, "From Parlor to Living Room: Domestic Space, Interior

Decoration, and the Culture of Personality," in *Consuming Visions: Accumulation and Display of Goods in America: 1880–1920*, ed. Simon J. Bronner (Henry Francis du Pont Winterthur Museum, 1989); Katherine Grier, "The Decline of the Memory Palace: The Parlor after 1890," in *American Home Life, 1880–1930: A Social History of Spaces and Services*, ed. Jessica H. Foy and Thomas J. Schlereth (University of Tennessee Press, 1992); and Candace M. Volz, "The Modern Look of the Early Twentieth-Century House: A Mirror of Changing Lifestyles," also in Foy and Schlereth, *American Home Life*.

On the modernization of women's domestic work (unpaid and paid) and labor-saving devices at the turn of the twentieth century, refer to Ruth Schwartz Cowan, *More Work for Mother: The Ironies of Household Technology from the Open Hearth to the Microwave* (Basic Books, 1983); and Daniel E. Sutherland, "Modernizing Domestic Service," in Foy and Schlereth, *American Home Life*. For additional information on home economics as a field and its impact on the home, consult Laura Shapiro, *Perfection Salad: Women and Cooking at the Turn of the Century* (Farrar, Straus and Giroux, 1986); and Carolyn M. Goldstein, *Creating Consumers: Home Economists in Twentieth-Century America* (University of North Carolina Press, 2012). Finally, for two important considerations of the place of men in the home and their relationship to domestic spaces and values, see Margaret Marsh, "Suburban Men and Masculine Domesticity, 1870–1915," *American Quarterly* 40, no. 2 (June 1988): 165–186; and Steven M. Gelber, "Do-It-Yourself: Constructing, Repairing, and Maintaining Domestic Masculinity," *American Quarterly* 49, no. 1 (March 1997): 66–112.

INDEX

ABOUT THE AUTHOR

Amy G. Richter is Associate Professor of History at Clark University, where she teaches U.S. women's, urban, and cultural history. She is the author of *Home on the Rails: Women, the Railroad, and the Rise of Public Domesticity* (2005).